Hard Questions for Democracy

The recent financial and economic crisis has forced governments and people from around the globe to ask some hard questions about how democracy has evolved. Some of these are old questions; others are new. Is democracy really the most desirable form of government? How democratic is policy-making during the financial and economic crisis? Why do vote-seeking parties in modern democracies actually make voters miserable? Can women's under-representation in politics be explained because of voter bias? Why are some citizens still excluded from voting in their country? And can terrorist organizations that promote violence one day, really become democratic the next?

This represents the first book of its kind to ask and answer a broad range of hard questions that need to be addressed in times of both flux and calls for democratic change throughout the world. It does so by bringing together leading social scientists and rising stars from around the globe. Interdisciplinary in its analysis, it is essential reading for students of comparative and international politics, political philosophy, gender studies and economics.

The book's website can be found at: www.democracyquestions.com and it was originally published as a special issue of *Irish Political Studies*.

Raj Chari is Associate Professor in Political Science at Trinity College Dublin.

Hard Questions for Democracy

Edited by
Raj Chari

Routledge
Taylor & Francis Group

LONDON AND NEW YORK

First published 2013 by Routledge

2 Park Square, Milton Park, Abingdon, Oxon OX14 4RN
711 Third Avenue, New York, NY 10017, USA

Routledge is an imprint of the Taylor & Francis Group, an informa business

First issued in paperback 2017

British Library Cataloguing in Publication Data
A catalogue record for this book is available from the British Library

ISBN13: 978-0-415-52305-9 (hbk)
ISBN13: 978-1-138-10988-9 (pbk)

Typeset in Times New Roman
by Taylor & Francis Books

Publisher's Note
The publisher would like to make readers aware that the chapters in this book may be referred to as articles as they are identical to the articles published in the special issue. The publisher accepts responsibility for any inconsistencies that may have arisen in the course of preparing this volume for print.

Contents

Introducing Hard Questions for Democracy

RAJ CHARI
Trinity College Dublin, Ireland

In December 2008, Girvin and Murphy edited a significant issue of *Irish Political Studies* in which contributors analysed continuity, crisis and change in Ireland, focusing on developments during the 1960s, 1970s and 1980s. In many ways, this issue builds on their insights, but in the context of a very changed Ireland. The country – indeed, the world – now finds itself questioning many aspects of democratic development in the second decade of the 2000s given the recent financial and economic crisis.

In fact the *raison d'être* of this issue is based on the recent global crisis, the effects of which have been deeply felt, especially in small states in world markets: the crisis has caused students of Irish and comparative politics to ask some hard questions about how democracy has evolved. Some of these are old questions with new answers; others are new questions with both old and new answers. The underlying theme of *Hard Questions for Democracy* is whether democracy as it was originally conceived in Ireland and the world can live up to people's expectations in modern times. That is, can democracy function *democratically* in the twenty-first century?

With this in mind, the objectives of this issue are to address hard questions about the theoretical, institutional, policy, partisan, participatory and conflictive aspects of democracy that are so relevant today.

The issue is subdivided into five main thematic sections, where each paper in each section addresses specific hard questions. The first section is 'democracy and legitimacy', where Hyland starts by exploring the roots of democratic legitimacy and questions if democracy is really the most desirable form of government. Mackie then ponders what the values of democratic proceduralism are.

The second section considers 'democracy and the markets', focusing on institutions and policymakers. In the first of two 'back-to-back' papers, Bernhagen and Chari ask which theoretical explanations from the political science literature are useful in understanding why the global financial and economic crisis that started in 2007 occurred. Chari and Bernhagen then evaluate which of these theoretical explanations are of more value in understanding, more specifically, the crisis starting in 2008 in Ireland.

The third section focuses on 'democracy, political parties and voters', offering five papers. First, Laver asks why vote-seeking parties may make voters miserable. Brandenburg then reflects on what factors give politics such a bad name. Humphreys questions how much of a constraint compactness places on would-be gerrymanderers. McElroy and Marsh then consider whether or not women's under-representation in Irish politics can be explained by voter bias, or be understood in the recruitment practices of parties and supply-side issues. Gallagher closes by asking whether referendums weaken parties and constitute a threat to liberal democracies such as Ireland.

The fourth section highlights issues related to 'democracy and participation'. Situating the Irish case in comparative perspective, Honohan contemplates whether or not Irish emigrants should have votes. Sudulich then asks whether or not the Internet promotes increased political participation in Ireland.

The final section examines 'democracy, violence and conflict'. McKeogh questions whether or not citizens of a democracy can be considered 'just targets' for terrorists. Focusing on the Irish Republican movement, O'Boyle finishes by asking how those who have been politically violent ultimately become democrats.

In addressing significant hard questions, leading academics and rising stars from around the globe are brought together, many of whom have been students or colleagues of Eddie Hyland, whose 'hard questions' during seminars and presentations have always proved to be the toughest to answer. In this tradition, the work presented here is envisaged to provide social scientists with both a basis for reflection and a foundation to pursue novel work.

Acknowledgements

Chari thanks the editors of *Irish Political Studies*, Eoin O'Malley and Richard Grayson, for their guidance and belief in this project since its inception. A significant debt of gratitude is particularly owed to Eoin for ensuring the smooth running of the review process. Advice from Michael Laver and the PSAI President, Gary Murphy, was also invaluable in the formative stage of this project. Patrick Bernhagen was instrumental in organizing the two sessions in the Political Studies Association Annual Conference in Edinburgh (March–April 2010) where several of these papers were presented previously. All authors are indebted to the two anonymous reviewers who offered excellent constructive comments and to Shelley Barry and her team at Taylor and Francis for their stellar work in the production of this issue.

Democracy and Moral Autonomy

JAMES L. HYLAND
Trinity College Dublin, Ireland

ABSTRACT   *The focus of this paper is on the justificatory basis of democracy. The paper operates on two levels, theoretical and historical. On the theoretical level the author claims that many of the arguments put forward to justify democracy, such as that formulated by Dahl in 'Democracy and its Critics' based on his two principles of equality, although not without merit, suffer certain crucial weaknesses and do not, in fact, get at the real basis of the belief in the unique legitimacy of democracy. He goes on to argue that this legitimacy is grounded not simply in the positive egalitarian consequences expected from democracy, but rather is to be found in the moral autonomy of the human being. Further, he claims, this moral autonomy is itself rooted in what the author calls the Cartesian autonomy of reason. On the historical level he claims that, while Descartes was himself extremely conservative with regard to orthodox Christian belief and traditional structures of political authority, many self-styled followers of Descartes saw the autonomy of reason as implying a radical rejection of all 'external' authority, first in respect of religious belief, but also, then, with respect to the secular authority. The result was that within what Jonathan Israel refers to as the 'Radical Enlightenment', there developed as early as the mid-seventeenth century a tradition of liberal and democratic radicalism, based explicitly on the Cartesian autonomy of reason and what was referred to as the 'freedom to philosophise'. The author illustrates this with a brief account of the Dutch radical thinker Franciscus Van den Enden. He argues that if we posit moral autonomy as the basis of democratic legitimacy, this privileges one particular conception of democracy, namely deliberative democracy, as its paradigmatic form. Throughout the whole argument he gives a central role to the autonomy of reason as, in particular, it began to sweep across Europe with the influence of Cartesianism. It is possible that there are older egalitarian roots to modern democratic ideology or that democratic authority is grounded on democracy's epistemic properties. The author looks at these claims towards the end of the paper and concludes that the autonomy of the moral agent as based itself on the autonomy of human reason is the most plausible basis of the unique legitimacy of democracy.*

Introduction: Dahl's Two Principles of Equality

One common form of justificatory argument in favour of democracy is what I call the egalitarian instrumental argument. The arguments in question are instrumental in that they take having a share in political power as an instrumental good; for example, a share in political power can enable people to protect and promote either their own interests or the interests of others that they might be concerned with. As arguments specifically for *democracy*, i.e. a collective decision-making procedure in which everybody affected by decisions has an equal effective right to participate in the making of those decisions, the arguments necessarily depend on a normative egalitarian premise. After all, from the perspective of power as an instrumental good, the most favourable distribution of power for any individual is a dictatorship in which that individual has a monopoly of power. Only if we assume that everyone has an equal right to the protection and promotion of interests would it follow that power as an instrumental good ought to be distributed equally; and this is exactly the structure of the basic argument for democracy that Dahl uses in his *Democracy and its Critics* (1989: 83–97).

He begins by stating what he calls his 'Equal Intrinsic Worth' principle. On the assumption, to put it negatively, that no one person's well-being is more important than any other person's well-being, we arrive at the 'equal consideration' thesis, namely that, specifically in the process of arriving at collectively binding decisions, each person's interest should be given the same consideration as every other person's interest. Dahl is well aware that the Equal Intrinsic Worth principle is not in itself sufficient to justify democracy as the best form of government. From the instrumentalist point of view a form of government is good if it results in egalitarian interest consideration. But could not a benevolent dictatorship produce just these consequences? A wise and virtuous ruler might rule impartially with the equal well-being of all citizens in mind.

There are two factors involved in determining whether appropriate and adequate consideration is given to a person's well-being in the exercise of political power, knowledge and motivation. With regard to motivation, the argument in favour of democracy is almost completely decisive. It is near to being true by definition that a person has an interest in his/her own interest satisfaction, and, hence, if I have a share in political power I can be relied upon to be motivated to protect and promote my interests and the interests of others that I might be particularly concerned about. On the other hand, if someone has power over me, I have no guarantee that they will use that power to protect and promote my interests; and Dahl argues plausibly that human history is testimony to the fact that minorities with a monopoly of political power tend to use that power to pursue their own interest satisfaction at the expense of the interests of those over whom they rule.

From the point of view of cognitive capacity, the argument in favour of democracy is less clear-cut. Granted that if I have a share in political power I can be relied on to use that power to promote the interests about which I am concerned; but surely having such a share in power is only an instrumental good if I am more likely than not to understand those interests and how they are likely to be affected by specific political decisions. Dahl quite explicitly recognises this, and hence introduces what he refers to as his 'Strong Equality' principle. This is not a normative principle at all; rather, it is an alleged substantive factual truth that most normal adult human beings *do* have the cognitive capacity to understand what is and what is not in their interest and to judge potential political decisions from this perspective.[1]

With the Strong Equality principle in place we are in a position to articulate the instrumental egalitarian argument for democracy. From the Equal Intrinsic Worth principle it is argued that, specifically with respect to the political decisions, everyone's interests ought to be given equal consideration. The most direct way to ensure this is to give everyone whose interests are likely to be affected by political decisions an equal effective right to participate in the making of such decisions, provided they satisfy the Strong Equality principle. It can be concluded that democracy, with, it should be added, a highly inclusive franchise, is clearly the best form of government. Put another way, a share in political power is an instrumental *basic good* and from an egalitarian perspective such basic goods ought to be distributed equally. An equal distribution of political power is, fundamentally, what is meant by democracy. So democracy is the 'egalitarianly' best form of government.

As I said in my introduction, the argument is obviously not without merit; but it does suffer from certain weaknesses. The weaknesses stem from the fact that the argument makes the desirability and legitimacy of democracy contingent on the truth of the Strong Equality principle. I would have two interrelated concerns here. First, the Strong Equality principle is nowhere near to being obviously true. Even if it is assumed that people do understand their basic interests in, say, having sufficient food, clothing, housing, employment, health, etc. might it not be the case that there are other really important components of human well-being that many people may not initially appreciate? Even more damagingly, given that people understand where their immediate interests lie, will people generally understand how those interests are likely to be affected by complex economic, social welfare, educational, foreign policy, etc. political decisions?

Of more fundamental concern, I think, is the sheer fact of the contingency of the justification. I do not have, here, a logically conclusive, knock-down argument, but consider the following situation. Suppose we encountered a race of superior beings. Not only was their technology and science far in advance of our own, but we rapidly came to the conclusion that they were wholly benevolent and seemed to have some kind of extrasensory perception on the basis of which they could unerringly divine our deepest desires and interests. In addition to which they could infallibly construct a set of social policies that always resulted in the maximum positive interest satisfaction for all of us in a completely egalitarian way. Do we really believe that these superior capacities would necessarily imply that these beings had the right to rule us? Instinctively, I think, we would answer this question in the negative. Why we would so answer is what I intend to explore in the next section.

Moral Autonomy

Dahl himself is not, I think, wholly satisfied with the instrumental egalitarian argument. In *Democracy and its Critics* he introduces a very different form of argument that goes some way towards the conclusion that I argue for. Dahl's second type of argument is based on the notion of autonomy and its place in our conception of a worthwhile human life (Dahl, 1989: 97–105). Although he does not spend a great deal of time explaining what he means by autonomy, it is clear from what he says that he is referring to what I shall call *de facto* autonomy. A person's *de facto* autonomy consists of their actual ability to think and decide for themselves and, in addition, to be in a situation where they can implement their decisions. When a person's life is so lived we say that they are in charge of their life, responsible for their decisions. Dahl makes the valid point that being so responsible for our lives is thought to be a central part of what it is to live as an adult, mature human being. He goes on to argue that no political system other than democracy offers the multiplicity of channels for the exercise and development of such autonomy.

These constitute a set of important considerations, though in the manner in which Dahl formulates them there is a crucial weakness. In analysing *de facto* autonomy we need to identify first what I call literal individual autonomy. This consists of, in line with the above definition, the situation in which an individual person can think and decide for her/himself and successfully implement those decisions. Does democracy as such directly maximise such autonomy? The answer, I think, is no. In a *liberal* democratic regime, where the scope of central decision-making is limited, individuals have the negative freedom that puts a wide range of possible choices under their own, individual control; but this is down to the liberal restriction on government authority, not to its democratic character. What democracy as such guarantees is the right and opportunity to participate in the exercise of what we could call collective autonomy; but as a supposedly independent argument for the value of democracy this suffers the defect of being almost completely tautological. Democracy is said to be a valuable form of government because it guarantees equal rights and opportunities of participation in the exercise of collective authority; but a system of government that guarantees such equal rights and opportunities is what we mean by democracy. So democracy is the best form of government because it is the most democratic![2] We need to dig a little more deeply.

My argument is that to appreciate fully even the value of *de facto* autonomy in either sense of the term we need to turn our attention to the moral autonomy mentioned in the title of the paper. In the rest of this section I shall explain what I mean by moral autonomy, explore its implications for democracy and trace what I believe are the roots of moral autonomy in the Cartesian autonomy of reason.

The moral autonomy of individuals consists of what we can call their 'moral status', what they can be obliged by. It is conceptually and empirically independent of *de facto* autonomy in any of its meanings and dimensions. A person who was, as a matter of fact, a slave, or so under the domination of another as to be completely subject to that other's manipulation, would still have what I call moral autonomy. Positively, it means that both in terms of what is required of me by my fundamental values and even what I should do, simply from a pragmatic perspective, in the pursuit of my interests and my goals can only be legitimately determined by myself. It was perhaps most famously formulated by the nineteenth century American writer Henry David Thoreau in his essay *On the Duty of Civil Disobedience*, where he says that the only thing that I can be bound by is that which I believe to be my duty (Thoreau, 2008). Thoreau asserted this in an explicitly political context, namely his refusal to pay poll tax to the government, which he believed was pursuing totally illegitimate policies – imperialism and the extension of slavery to the 'New Territories'. As such Thoreau was emphasising the negative aspect of moral autonomy, namely that there is no external agency that has the fundamental right to bind an individual morally. It is this moral autonomy, I claim, that is the fundamental basis of our positive evaluation of *de facto* autonomy in both dimensions.

De facto autonomy, it is true, has a definitive pragmatic consequentialist value, namely the protection and promotion of interests, as discussed previously. On a much more fundamental level, however, it is the only situation that conforms to acceptance of the moral autonomy of the individual. Let us apply this specifically to democracy. We assume that living in the community with others will require specific decisions that are collectively binding on all members of the community. The claim of the moral autonomy thesis with respect to democracy is that there is no agency outside the group of citizens (or minority within the group) that has the right legitimately to require obedience to its will; the only form of authority compatible with that moral autonomy is one in which all share equally in the determination of the decisions by which all will be bound.

Although I do not believe that a conclusive foundational proof of the moral autonomy thesis is possible, I think its roots can be traced to a more fundamental autonomy, what I have been calling the Cartesian autonomy of reason. All students of philosophy know the name of Descartes and his '*cogito, ergo sum*'; and although he is duly credited with identifying in the modern era the necessity for the provision of a foundational base for provable knowledge of the world, there is a tendency to see his positive contribution thereto as problematic, to say the least, and, perhaps, wrongheaded in a fashion that would make his philosophy outdated and of merely antiquarian interest. In the first place, the foundation for human knowledge as constructed by Descartes moves directly from certainty of the '*cogito*' to the existence of God as a guarantor of the reliability of our cognitive capacities; a distinctly 'unmodern' basis for scientific truth (Descartes, 1968). Second, Descartes' actual knowledge construction method was wholly 'rationalist' in the sense that he believed that substantive knowledge could be achieved *a priori* through deduction from simple ideas and first principles, as in geometry, a deductive rationalism that was soon to be discarded by a robust empiricism that insisted that substantive knowledge of the world had to be mediated by perceptual experience. There is, however, an aspect of Descartes' method that is still of enduring relevance, and this is the basis of what I am calling the autonomy of reason.

Descartes begins his attempt to provide the foundations of human knowledge by engaging in what he calls 'methodic doubt', and it was this that had, and was seen to have, really radical implications. The straightforward assumption behind Descartes' method of doubt was that no belief, no matter how venerable the authority is that asserts it, no matter how universal its current acceptance, can be accepted unless, here and now, I can prove it to the satisfaction of my own reason. As

Diderot was to put it so trenchantly 100 years later in an article in his great Encyclopaedia: using 'Eclecticism' as a euphemism for critical reason, he defined a practitioner of critical reasoning as:

> a philosopher, who trampling underfoot, prejudice, tradition, venerability, universal assent, authority – in a word everything that overawes the crowd – dares to think for himself, to ascend to the clearest general principles, to examine them, to discuss them, *to admit nothing save on the testimony of his own reason and experience*. (Taylor, 1989: 323, emphasis added)

This was the idea that was eventually to set Europe on fire. Initially it was used to challenge the authority of Aristotelianism in the universities (Israel, 2001). Soon it was challenging the right of ecclesiastical 'authority'. It was extended, in the hands of radical thinkers such as Spinoza, to questioning the authority of the Prophets and of the Bible itself. Finally, it was used to reject the so-called 'right' of secular authorities first to dictate to people what they could think and say and, then, finally the right of such authorities to rule over people's lives. Where no external 'authority' could possibly have the right to dictate what was true and false, what was right and wrong, what was to be done and not to be done, the only legitimate structure of political power was one in which that power was vested in people themselves.

I have been arguing that, both theoretically and historically, one of the central pillars of the claim that only inclusive democracy could be considered a legitimate form of political power can be found in the autonomy of Cartesian reason and its associated moral autonomy. It could be suggested that rooting democratic legitimacy in this exclusively secular perspective overlooks what might be a completely independent basis of support for democracy in the modern world to be found in the radical Christian religious egalitarian movements that arose periodically throughout the Middle Ages. While it is true that many of these radical Christian movements espoused very egalitarian doctrines, leading their members to reject the unequal social, economic and authoritarian structures of their contemporary societies, it would, I contend, be a serious mistake to link them theoretically with the underpinning of the modern democratic ideology, despite the fact that there is a historical connection between, for example, the contemporary Amish communities (well known for their spirit of equality) and the early modern Anabaptists. I argue this for three main reasons.

First, even when a genuinely universalist egalitarianism was present, it was grounded in a quite specific interpretation of the Christian world view, in which the coming Utopia was seen as an explicit part of God's plan for the world. The relevant beliefs almost universally took the form of the acceptance of a plethora of myths and symbols (Cohn, 1993).

Second, although many of these movements were universalistically egalitarian in principle, many were also fiercely sectarian and exclusionary in practice. The heavenly paradise of equality 'embraced a kingdom of righteousness that was fiercely intolerant of all who failed to respond to the rigors and delights of the Anabaptist

Valhalla' (Williams, 1992: 554). This exclusionary mentality could, as in the case of the Münster Anabaptists, be so extreme as to justify the expropriation, exile and even execution of those – the wicked – who rejected their specific world view (Williams, 1992: 564 – see specifically Ch. 13.3, 'Restitution and vengeance'). Indeed, this was not just pious rhetoric but led to actual widespread exile and execution.

The third point bears more directly on the issue of democratic self-government. The egalitarian traditions we are dealing with were concerned almost exclusively with simple economic equality and communism of goods. There was a complete absence of reflection on the appropriate structures of political power. Cohn refers in the subtitle of his book to 'mystical anarchists' and when the issue of freedom and authority is raised it is in the form of individual freedom, often of a radical anti-nomianist nature, rejecting all moral constraints (see Cohn on 'The brethren of the free spirit', especially Ch. 9, pp. 163–186). In fact, in practice many of these movements, in particular the Münster Anabaptist movements, were fiercely oppressive in two related ways.

First, when the movements were not anti-nomian they often did reject much of traditional morality, particularly sexual morality (Cohn, 1993: 220). However, as was specifically the case with the Münster Anabaptists, a strictly authoritarian alternative was decreed. An example would be the moral code of Jan of Leiden (sometimes called John Beukels or John Bockelson), who was for a time a leader of the Anabaptists in Münster. Decreeing compulsory polygamy, he also made 'blasphemy, seditious language, scolding one's parents, disobeying one's master in a household, adultery, lewd conduct, backbiting, spreading scandal and complaining' sins punishable by death (Williams, 1992: 567). In fact, Jan personally executed one of his wives for complaining of his rule and trampled all over her body in public (Williams, 1992: 581–582).

The second type of authoritarianism was authoritarianism in the actual structure of power. The above-mentioned Jan of Leiden became the self-declared leader of the Anabaptists of Münster. He dissolved the city council, declaring it to have been only 'chosen by men' (Williams, 1992: 567) and shortly after had himself anointed king, first of Münster and then of the whole world. Both in practice and even in theory, this monarchic power was wielded in an extremely oppressive manner, leading to a continuous series of imprisonments and executions of the most brutal kind (Williams, 1992: 554ff). Even though the New Jerusalem was envisaged as a kingdom of peace (after the vengeance wrought on the wicked was finally complete), it was still envisaged as a kingdom.

My conclusion is that, despite the egalitarian critique of actual structures of inequality, poverty and exploitation, it is difficult to see these movements as having much to do with democracy in the modern sense of the word. For that, we need to return to the idea of the freedom of critical reason.

Of course, for most thinkers in the seventeenth century the radical implications of the freedom of critical reason (the freedom to philosophise, as it was called) were merely elaborated theoretically. However, even as early as the late 1600s there were exceptions, one of whom was Franciscus Van den Enden.

Franciscus Van den Enden

Van den Enden was born, probably in Amsterdam, in 1602 (Israel, 2001: 175–184). His family were Catholic and, in fact, he himself joined the Jesuits. While with the Jesuits he studied philosophy and eventually became a devotee of Cartesianism. As his thinking in philosophical and religious matters became more radical, he left the Jesuits. Thereafter, he maintained a precarious existence as a teacher of Latin and it is thought that he first introduced Spinoza to Cartesianism. By the 1660s he was well known in Amsterdam as an outspoken philosophical atheist and radical egalitarian; he cooperated with Peter Cornelius Plockhoy in designing an egalitarian 'cooperative' Utopia, which the latter actually founded in Delaware. Van den Enden himself became involved in a political conspiracy that would lead to his death. In 1665 he published his *Free Political Institutions* (Enden, 1665) and persuaded a group of disaffected French noblemen to back his ideas. Led by Gilles de Hamel, this group conspired to incite an insurrection in Normandy, to free Normandy from French rule and to declare it a democratic republic. Van den Enden continued in the conspiracy after he had left Amsterdam, under pressure from the city authorities, and opened a Latin school in Paris. Unfortunately, the conspiracy was revealed to the French authorities by one of Van den Enden's pupils. He and his co-conspirators were arrested and taken to the Bastille, where Van den Enden was interrogated and tortured. While the nobility involved in the conspiracy were beheaded, Van den Enden, as a commoner, was, as Israel puts it, 'escorted to the gallows and unceremoniously hanged' in the inner courtyard of the Bastille (Israel, 2001: 184) in September 1674, a martyr to democratic republicanism, but also to the freedom of critical reason.

I am not arguing, of course, that the spread of the idea of critical reason in the seventeenth century was the direct cause of the waves of democratisation that were to transform the modern world. I am arguing, though, that the relationship between the idea of critical reason, moral autonomy and democracy is not just a theoretical relationship. In Descartes' own time the radical implications of the autonomy of reason were plain to see and the inferences challenging so-called 'authorities' were explicitly made and, sometimes, as in the case of Van den Enden, acted on. A final point: if the basis of our belief in the legitimacy of democracy really is the autonomy of reason, and the ideal to be striven for is, as Rousseau puts it in *Émile*, that a person be 'governed only by the authority of his own reason' (Damrosch, 2005: 334), then it follows, I would argue, that the ideal form of democracy is one that has rational persuasion as its core, an ideal such as that adopted by deliberative democrats.

Moral Autonomy and Epistemic Democracy

As mentioned already, there is another very distinctive type of justificatory argument in favour of democracy, based on its 'epistemic' qualities, in particular on the claim that democratic decision-making has a good chance of arriving at good (perhaps, even, 'correct') decisions. It might be thought that such arguments would have little bearing on the moral autonomy argument. If it is true that democratic decisions are more likely than not to be good decisions, then this would simply be an added bonus for democracy; it is the only form of decision-making that conforms to the moral autonomy of a reasoning agent and is likely to produce good decisions. Matters, however, are not that simple; one version of the epistemic argument threatens such a direct conflict with the moral autonomy argument that a short discussion is warranted.

I distinguish two versions of the epistemic argument, which I call the 'traditional' version and the 'epistemic procedural' version ('epistemic proceduralism' is the name given to this approach by its foremost contemporary defender, David Estlund). The traditional version goes back as far as Aristotle's *Politics*. Not a great lover of democracy, Aristotle did admit that the pooled experience of the many, who individually might not have great wisdom, could conceivably outstrip the competence of the individually wiser few. Famously, the argument was given a formalisation in Condorcet's 'jury theorem', which states that if a randomly selected voter has just a slightly better than evens chance of making the correct decision, then, as the group of voters increases, the probability of the majority decision being the correct decision rapidly approaches certain; a group of only 10,000 has a probability over 99 per cent of being right. Whatever the validity of these arguments, they do not seem to confront the moral autonomy argument in a negative way. They simply provide, if anything, additional reasons to value democracy.[3]

The case is otherwise with David Estlund's 'epistemic proceduralism' (Estlund, 2008); the basic reason for this is that Estlund claims that a decision-making procedure can have, in principle, authority over someone based on its epistemic characteristics, even if it is not a democratic procedure and even if someone has not given consent. In practice, Estlund believes that all non-democratic decision procedures fail the test of justifiable authority structures, namely that an authority structure should be acceptable to all reasonable perspectives. Still, priority seems to be being given to the positive epistemic characteristics of a procedure rather than to the autonomy of the moral agent. Estlund's argument is somewhat complex, but when it is broken down into its three essential parts it can be shown, I would claim, to challenge fundamentally the moral autonomy perspective, but, in fact, to have a close alignment with it.

The first part of Estlund's argument attempts to establish that a person might be morally subject to an authority even if that person has not consented to the authority in question. I shall formulate the argument in personal terms. If I am under a general moral obligation to contribute to an urgent task, and if my acceptance of an authority is necessary for the achievement of that task, then I am obliged to accept the authority. When Estlund (2008: 136–158) is arguing explicitly for this position he speaks in terms of there being an obligation to contribute to an urgent task that actually requires the acceptance of an authority; but all these things are open to reasonable doubt. It is only, I would claim, when I accept that there is an obligation to contribute and when I accept that an authority is required. On a fundamental level, this institutes the moral autonomy of the agent as the basis for moral authority of an agency.

The second part of Estlund's argument is an attempt to show that, even if it is objectively true that some non-democratic form of authority would be objectively better at guiding our collective attempts to address the urgent task facing us, no putative non-democratic authority can meet the fundamental conditions of justifiable authority. Even if some minority group is wiser that the rest of us, the contention that some particular group is the one in question is always open to objection from some reasonable perspectives. The basic reason is that 'no invidious comparison among citizens with respect to their normative political wisdom can pass the appropriate general acceptability criterion ...' (Estlund, 2008: 36). As Estlund accepts the 'no invidious comparison' thesis on normative matters, he claims that given that 'there is widespread disagreement about what justice requires ... No citizen is required to defer to the expertise or authority of any other' (2008: 98). In a nutshell, Estlund's anti-epistocracy (rule by the wise) comes down to the thesis that there are numerous qualified, reasonable perspectives that can legitimately question any putative non-democratic authority. This, I would argue, is fundamentally identical to the moral autonomy perspective.

The third part of Estlund's argument is not directly relevant, either positively or negatively, to the moral autonomy thesis. In my analysis, this part of the argument attempts to show that democracy can meet one crucial condition of authority. Even if it is accepted that (because of the obligation to contribute to the solution of an urgent task that requires an accepted authority) we are obliged to accept some authority structure, surely there are conditions on the claim of any particular suggested authority. The whole of Estlund's argument (2008: 159–183) is based on the assumption that a putative authority that was provably hopeless at making decisions (i.e. was pretty sure to be worse than random at avoiding really awful decisions) could hardly command any authority at all. This is why Estlund has to make the very modest epistemic claim for democracy that it is likely to be better than random in avoiding such awful outcomes. Without expanding on the suggestion, I would say that rejecting the right of any minority or external agency to command, the choice is between anarchism and democracy and we could begin to argue for democracy only if we could show that the results were likely to be better than ungoverned anarchistic interrelationships.

But that is another question.

Notes

1. There are arguments for democratic legitimacy that focus specifically on democracy's alleged positive epistemic characteristics. For a discussion of how these relate to the moral autonomy argument, see the final section of this paper.
2. I am not dismissing the argument as totally pointless. On the one hand it focuses attention on the idea of participating in the exercise of collective autonomy and the role of this in our conception of a worthwhile human life. On the other hand, Dahl might be alluding to the possibility that participation in the exercise of collective autonomy might have the beneficial consequences of enhancing our actual capacity for autonomy in all spheres of life.
3. For a discussion of these arguments, see the chapter in Estlund (2008: 104–105) on the Condorcet jury theorem.

References

Cohn, N. (1993) *The Pursuit of the Millennium: Revolutionary Millenarians and Mystical Anarchists of the Middle Ages* (London: Pimlico).

Dahl, R. A. (1989) *Democracy and its Critics* (New Haven: Yale University Press).

Damrosch, L. (2005) *Jean-Jacques Rousseau: Restless Genius* (New York: Mariner Books).

Descartes, R. (1968) *Discourse on Method and the Meditations*, translated by F. E. Sutcliffe (Harmondsworth: Penguin).

Enden, F., Van den (1665) *Vrije Politijke Stellingen* (Amsterdam: Wereldbibliotheek, 1992).

Estlund, D. M. (2008) *Democratic Authority: A Philosophical Framework* (Princeton, NJ: Princeton University Press).

Israel, J. (2001) *Radical Enlightenment: Philosophy and the Making of Modernity, 1650–1750* (Oxford: Oxford University Press).

Taylor, C. (1989) *Sources of the Self* (Cambridge: Cambridge University Press).

Thoreau, H. D. (1965) *Walden: Or, Life in the Woods, and On the Duty of Civil Disobedience* (New York: Harper & Row).

Williams, G. H. (1992) *The Radical Reformation* (Kirksville, MO: Sixteenth Century Journal Publishers).

The Values of Democratic Proceduralism

GERRY MACKIE

University of California, San Diego, USA

ABSTRACT   *A standard justification of democratic voting is that it is a fair procedure, providing for the equal treatment of voters. Democratic theorist David Estlund challenges the adequacy of that justification: flipping a coin between alternatives is also a fair procedure, but no one would propose substituting random draw for voting. Estlund provides several arguments that fair proceduralism is an untenable view, and this article counters those arguments. He concludes that what distinguishes democratic voting from random choice is its better epistemic value in approximating a standard of justice independent of the procedure. The author replies that a less controversial distinction between voting and coin flip is that voting tends to select what is thought best by the most people.*

Introduction

Do you think that modern political democracy, the collective authorization of laws by voting (Estlund, 2008: 66), is valuable just because it is a fair procedure? For many years now, David Estlund has posed the coin-flip challenge to such *fair proceduralism* (FP; I shall label Estlund's own views as *epistemic proceduralism*, or EP, and will often use those labels in the remainder of the paper).

> Why not understand democracy as a way of giving every (adult) person an equal chance to influence the outcome of the decision? ... That way we would not need to make any claims about the decision tending to be good or right or true ... so far it looks like democracy is one fair procedure, and choosing between two proposals by flipping a coin is another one ... If the value of democracy is its fairness, this random procedure should be just as good. Of course, this is impossible to accept. There is something about democracy other than its fairness that contributes to our sense that it can justify authority and legal coercion. (Estlund, 2008: 6)

15

The something other than fairness is, for Estlund's EP, the epistemic value of the procedure in yielding outcomes that approximate a standard of justice independent of the decision procedure. This epistemic value distinguishes democratic voting from equally random choice among alternatives. The fair proceduralist's flight from substance, by contrast, drives her all the way to the untenable procedure of equal random choice among possible alternatives not sensitive to participants' preferences or judgments (aims, in short). Why? Reference to the aims of voters is a procedure-independent standard, according to EP; thus, a procedure would not be *intrinsically* fair if it responded to voters' aims. I counter that such reference to aims *is* an intrinsic procedural value, pertaining to the fair handling of inputs to the procedure. Moreover, I say, both fair democratic voting and fair coin flip are sensitive to participants' aims; the latter because it is not drawn over all alternatives, but over a smaller number of alternatives by prior decision already judged to be among the best. If I am correct, then EP's account of FP's untenable flight from substance does not go through. Finally, I conclude that something less demanding than approximation of an independent standard of justice distinguishes democratic voting from random choice: voting selects what is thought best by the most people. At the outset of the paper, I shall review a few proceduralist theories, so we have a better idea about what motivates them, and provide an unconventional exposition of the May theorem about majority voting, the conditions of which inform some of EP's arguments and my responses to them.

Estlund's *Democratic Authority* is deservedly recognized as one of the leading philosophical treatments of the idea of democracy. It is a rich volume full of good arguments, and my queries about one strand of its arguments manifest respect for its importance.

Why Proceduralism?

A strong source of the emphasis on procedural value in democratic theory is horror at the doctrines and massive atrocities of Bolshevism, Fascism and National Socialism, the twentieth century autocracies. Hans Kelsen (1955), a literal refugee from one of those '*true* democracies', argued that all governments are *for* the people, or say they are, but only democracy is *by* the people. Democracy is essentially government by the people, in his view. If a government is evaluated according to whether it is for the people, on the basis of aiming at some objectively ascertainable common good, then that allows an autocrat to rule for the people in the name of that common good. Kelsen is a relativist, and says that democracy is the form of government that best realizes political relativism. There is no objective common good, only subjective value judgments grounded in wishes and fears (those individual value judgments are not uniform and hence there is no common will, either). The autocrat's claim to know the common good is in fact a controversial subjective value judgment. The results of universal, free, equal and secret suffrage, and of the majority votes of democratic legislatures, however, are objectively ascertainable fact, he says. Democracy is justifiable only if there is no objective common good; because there is not, then democracy 'is justifiable to enforce a social order against reluctant individuals only if this order is in harmony with the greatest possible number of equal individuals, that is to say, with the will of the majority' (Kelsen, 1955: 39). The reader will probably notice that it would be difficult for a subjectivist relativism to justify the last claim. What if my wishes and fears recommend my way only, and I hold the wishes and fears of the majority in contempt?

It is a short step from values relativism to values nihilism. From about 1950 to 2000, Schumpeter's definition of democracy ruled in American political science and beyond (Schumpeter, 1942: 250–283). Democracy is only a procedure, he argued, and only the most minimal procedure at that: the competitive election of leaders, and nothing else. American political scientists adopted *descriptive* and minimalist proceduralism because in comparative regime research it is clear and easy to measure whether or not a country's leader is appointed by competitive election. Unfortunately, a descriptive definition suitable in a limited era for a limited purpose was promiscuously generalized to an all-purpose and even lamely *justificatory* definition of democracy. Schumpeterian proceduralism collapsed when comparative regime theorists found around the beginning of this century that about a fourth to a third of the regimes satisfying the 'electoralist' definition are in fact pseudodemocracies lacking the institutions and values otherwise associated with modern democracies, and that such pseudodemocracies were proliferating in response to incentives flowing from acceptance of the merely electoralist definition by international institutions (Mackie, 2010).

Dahl, the dean of twentieth century democratic theorists, once summarized his approach as 'procedural democracy' (Dahl, 2006). Dahl wants to discern the criteria necessary and sufficient for democratic procedure in a human association whose members need to reach binding decisions. Among other requirements, the decision process includes at least two stages: setting the agenda and deciding outcomes. The criteria are, first, that members should have adequate and equal opportunity for effective participation. Second, equal opportunity to express a choice at the decisive stage of collective decisions, a choice counted equal in weight to the choice expressed by any other citizen. Third, each member should have equal and adequate opportunity to discover and validate her choice on the matter to be decided. Fourth, members must have final control of the agenda, to decide how and whether matters are to be placed on the agenda of the association. These criteria will be more or less imperfectly realized. Although he once termed his doctrine procedural democracy, later it is clear that for him democracy has strong substantive as well as procedural values. Democracy, he says, is an imperfect procedure, or a quasi-pure procedure, in Rawls's terminology (Dahl, 1989: 163–175).

Arrow's social choice theory seeks to identify social welfare, but social welfare is a function, a mathematical function, aggregating each individual's preference orderings over all social states. An individual's orderings can reflect mere tastes for direct consumption, or also values including social and moral considerations; but all such tastes or values enter only through individual orderings, processed by aggregation, into an overall measure of social welfare. There are no values independent of individual orderings over social states aggregated by a social welfare function. This shows up in the so-called Pareto condition of his famous impossibility theorem: if every individual ranks x over y, then the social choice should rank x over y. At first glance, condition P seems unassailable, but consider that it excludes all values that are independent of the content of individual preferences. Everyone could favor Sharia law, but if they do not it has no independent value, nor would any bill of rights, nor Rousseau's general will, nor counterfactual criteria of fully informed and publicly motivated preferences, nor any theory of objective welfare. Arrow explicitly dismisses the notion that 'there exists an objective social good defined independently of individual desires' (Arrow, 1963: 22) as Platonic realism.

Riker (1982) radicalizes Arrow. Riker mistakenly concludes from various results of social choice theory that democratic voting is arbitrary and meaningless.[1] There is no knowable connection between citizens' votes and the outcome of an election: 'we do not and cannot know what the people want' (Riker, 1982: 238); superficially, democratic voting is formally responsive to the voter, but a full formal and empirical investigation shows that it is not. Democracy is nothing more than 'an intermittent, sometimes random, even perverse, popular veto' (Riker, 1982: 244). Riker believes that his 'liberal' interpretation of voting and its random veto promotes liberty because it accidentally removes tyrants. He also emphasizes that his liberal interpretation promotes equality: each citizen has an equal chance to veto officials (Riker, 1982: 246).

The May Theorem on Majority Rule over Two Alternatives

The May theorem will be central to our discussion.[2] Here is an unconventional introduction to the theorem. Social choice theory explores the logical properties of rules for aggregating more than one list of relations among variables into a single list of relations among variables. A variety of assumptions is made, and from each set of them a variety of implications is deduced. The assumptions explored by social choice theory are not overwhelmingly compelling in the way that, say, Euclid's first four axioms of geometry are. One does not know what to say to someone who denies that a line is the shortest distance between two points, but it is quite easy to find real counterexamples to typical social-choice assumptions.

Social choice theory does not take us up to a Platonic realm of truth, but rather forms logically consistent demonstrations that can imperfectly model the earthly realities of collective choice by humans. For example, the May theorem is routinely offered as some kind of higher truth about the nature of democracy, despite Beitz's (1989: 60) warning 20 years ago that it 'does not reproduce any problem that arises in commonplace reflection about political morality; indeed by abstracting from contextual considerations ... it deflects attention from factors that ordinarily play an important, and sometimes a determining ... role.' I shall illustrate.

May's theorem says that four independent assumptions together uniquely identify majority rule over two alternatives: *decisiveness* (an alternative wins, loses or ties), equivalent to *universality*; *anonymity*, in that if voters trade names the result is unchanged (that is, it treats all voters equally); *neutrality*, in that if alternatives trade names the result is unchanged (it does not privilege any alternatives); and *positive responsiveness*, that is, all else being equal, if a voter changes their vote to favor an otherwise winning option it remains a winning one, *and* if a voter changes their vote to favor an otherwise tied option it becomes a winning one. The decisiveness condition, which counts ties as decisive, has little to do with the practical need for a choice, not a tie. Anonymity would block delegation of decisions from the citizens to the legislative assembly, or from the assembly to its leadership and committees, or to executive and judicial authorities, but that violation does not imply that ideal representative democracy fails to accept each citizen's vote at equal value. The idea of equal basic rights, a sphere of decisions reserved to the individual, also violates anonymity, but no one should be concerned that it does. Constitutional entrenchments violate the condition that a voting rule be neutral between alternatives, but that violation is good for democracy, not bad for it. The neutrality condition also says that a vote by two rich to tax one poor is no different from a vote by two poor to tax one rich.

Much is made of the fact that simple majority rule, given two alternatives, is uniquely identified by the four assumptions. One of Riker's (1982: 60) arguments, often repeated in subsequent literature, is that democracy is arbitrary and meaningless because May's theorem and its venerable assumptions are limited to votes over two alternatives, but politics is always about many alternatives. The four assumptions are written, however, in terms of the two-alternative case. Utterly unobjectionable generalizations of the four assumptions to the many-alternative case are consistent with the Borda and Black voting rules (Tideman, 1986). Several commonly discussed democratic voting rules that can handle more than two alternatives satisfy decisiveness, anonymity, neutrality and *non-negative responsiveness*, that is, all else being equal, if a voter changes their vote to favor an otherwise winning option it remains a winning one, and if a voter changes their vote to favor an otherwise tied option it *remains tied or* becomes a winning one. Nor is it necessarily a worry for a voting rule, such as plurality runoff or single transferable vote, not to satisfy non-negative responsiveness as a *logical* possibility. The proper question should be: Is the voting rule *generally* responsive in *empirical* settings (yes, for each), and what are its other *empirical* advantages and disadvantages, compared with the *empirical* advantages and disadvantages of some alternative voting rule?

Epistemic Proceduralism versus Fair Proceduralism

Estlund (2008: 60) says that a popular account of the legitimacy and authority of democratically enacted laws is that voting is a fair procedure, 'everyone had an equal role in determining the outcome'; call it *fair proceduralism*. Estlund's epistemic proceduralism pursues the fair proceduralist, draining him of the substance he abhors, until he is driven into an indefensible corner. Epistemic proceduralism first marks out a procedure-independent substantive fairness. Next, consider what Rawls calls *pure procedural justice* (which EP for its own purposes calls retrospective fairness): a pure procedure defines the justice of each of its outcomes. Any outcome of a lottery, voluntarily entered into and honestly played, would be fair in terms of the lottery, for example. Further, for Rawls, *perfect procedural justice* always yields an outcome just by some substantive procedure-independent standard, and *imperfect procedural justice* approximately yields outcomes just by that independent standard (called prospective fairness by EP). Finally, according to EP, there is intrinsic procedural fairness, neither retrospective nor prospective. The given procedure is intrinsically fair, neither looking backward to a parent procedure that begat it, nor looking forward to the substantively fair outcomes it tends to beget. The idea is that anyone who claims to value democracy only as a fair procedure, say, only because it provides for an equal vote for each person, is driven to the thin and occasional fairness of intrinsic proceduralism.

A possible problem for such an intrinsic proceduralist is that democratic voting rules should be responsive, that is, they should respond in the right way to votes cast. May's theorem requires positive responsiveness, but, as we have seen, a strong tendency to positive responsiveness could suffice in the weighing up of empirical advantages and disadvantages of a voting rule. A voting rule could be anonymous, that is, treat each voter equally, but be negatively responsive. A democratic voting rule, however, should not be negatively responsive. For example, it should not add up what the majority wants and then always choose the opposite. May's positive responsiveness condition is a formal and narrow implementation of a broader idea, that a collective decision procedure should be sensitive to the aims of those participating in it. Estlund's EP generalizes the idea of responsiveness and calls it 'aggregativity': a collective decision procedure is aggregative if and only if there exists a possible change in individual preferences that would result in a different collective preference. Epistemic proceduralism continues that an intrinsic proceduralist could not count aggregativity as part of procedural fairness. Aggregativity, and hence positive responsiveness, are procedure-independent standards, and not intrinsic to the voting procedure, according to EP. An equal random choice of outcome from among possible alternatives, though, is completely insensitive to individuals' preferences and hence is not aggregative, Estlund continues, and thus is available to the intrinsic proceduralist. He argues that consistent application of procedural fairness must reduce to equal treatment of alternatives, and have nothing to do with equal treatment of voters. I shall argue the contrary, that responsiveness *is* intrinsic to voting procedure, and that random choice *is* aggregative.

Epistemic proceduralism acknowledges that social choice theory considers responsiveness a procedural matter (Estlund, 2008: 74). Epistemic proceduralism goes on to claim, if I understand it correctly, that social choice theory models actual procedures and thus serves as the procedure-independent standard for their evaluation. Thus, general responsiveness of any kind would be substantive and not procedural; as I understand it, because the ideal standard of positive responsiveness could be poorly or perversely approximated in actual practice (e.g. voters could be mistaken, votes could be mistakenly or fraudulently counted, and the like). It seems to me, the EP argument here implies that, when it comes to actual procedures, there can be no proceduralists. Those commonly considered to be proceduralists in democratic theory would not be counted as such. This collapses a useful and real distinction.

Brettschneider (2005: 424), for example, distinguishes pure outcomes theorists who understand democratic procedures as solely instrumental from pure procedures theorists who 'locate the standard of legitimacy for the outcomes of a process entirely in the fact that they were produced by democratic procedures'. If EP's construal of social choice theory were correct, then we would need a new pair of terms for theories of actual collective decision procedures: one for the procedure-independent correctness of aspects of the actual procedure, and one for the procedure-independent correctness of the actual procedure's substantive outcomes. The contrast between procedural values and substantive values would recur.

Social choice theory defines a variety of conditions, shows that one or more functions is consistent or inconsistent with one or more conditions, and can show more ambitiously that an already given function is uniquely consistent with a set of conditions, as in May's theorem (or that no function is consistent with a set of conditions, as in Arrow's theorem).[3] The given procedure here is simple majority rule over two alternatives. The procedure happens to satisfy the formal properties of decisiveness, anonymity, neutrality and positive responsiveness. Each is a property *of the procedure*. It would no longer be the same procedure if it lacked one of the properties. The given procedure has the procedural value of always yielding an outcome, the different procedural value of equality among voters, the different procedural value of equality among alternatives and the different procedural value of positively responding to inputs (to repeat, each of the properties is logically independent of the other). Permissible inputs are defined as individual preference or indifference over alternatives x and y, and permissible outputs as group preference or indifference over the same two alternatives.

Epistemic proceduralism correctly identifies an error made by some democratic theorists: the idea that the procedural value of equality among voters is the *only* value of voting. But EP, I propose, makes a similar error. We might attribute potential value to a democratic procedure because it counts citizens' votes equally, and we might also attribute potential value to the procedure because it is properly responsive to citizens' votes. There are two questions: whether or not a value of a collective decision procedure is procedural or substantive, and if procedural whether or not it should be called 'fair'. For equal citizens to have equal votes is a procedural value, and it might have to do with fairness, in the sense of equal treatment of the parties. For the procedure to be positively responsive to all citizens' votes is a procedural value, and it might have to do with fairness, not in the sense of equal treatment of the parties, but in the sense that the procedure responds to citizens' judgments as they expect it should. The once fair proceduralist could concede that equal votes are fair but that positive responsiveness is right in some other way, and become a more defensible proceduralist: call her now a 'fair-and-right proceduralist'.

Positive response to inputs is a common background assumption. Consider the following analogy. The four of us share a dinner that costs $120 and agree that equal division would be a fair procedure. Three of us put in $30, but one of us balks. To be procedurally fair, he says, equal division must make no reference to the total restaurant bill; rather, it must randomly assign a dollar amount from the set of all rational numbers, positive and negative, as the object of equal division. The first three diners could respond to the fourth that, given the *input* of the restaurant bill, it must be a *part* of a fair procedure that each diner's equal contribution respond positively to the input. Whether the *output* of each paying $30 is fair by standards independent of the procedure of equal and positive contribution – desert, need, equity – is indeed a separate question, they could acknowledge.

For EP, the input is a substantive matter, independent of the procedure. Consider, however, that voting is, among other things, a mathematical function. A full description of a function defines the set of permissible inputs (or domain), the rule of correspondence and the set of the permissible outputs (or codomain). Change the domain, or change the codomain, and it is no longer the same function. The domain of May's simple majority decision is citizen votes of preference or indifference over alternatives x and y. Change the domain to the set of alternatives$\{x, y\}$, and it is no longer the same function. With no votes as inputs, there is no aggregation of votes; equality of votes and positive responsiveness to votes become inapplicable conditions. To manufacture gunpowder, take saltpeter, charcoal, sulfur and other inputs, and process them in proper quantity, sequence and conditions. The materials exist prior to the procedure, but they become inputs to the procedure, which must handle them properly, for example mixing the inputs in the proper proportion. Neither the materials *as inputs* nor their right *handling* is independent of the manufacturing procedure.

May defines a *general decision function*, that the group decision prefers or is indifferent to x over y, or prefers or is indifferent to y over x, and the group decision is some function of all relevant individuals' preference and indifference relations over x and y. Then, May's set of four independent necessary and sufficient conditions uniquely constrain the general decision function to be simple majority rule. One condition of May's theorem is that 'each individual be treated the same as far as his influence on the outcome is concerned' (1952: 681), and he says that this would usually be called an equality condition. His formal definition requires that the group decision function be a symmetric function of its inputs, and he mentions that it could be called an anonymity condition, because it says roughly that you could permute the names of the preference holders without changing the outcome. I speculate that the anonymity label stuck because it successfully dodged mid-twentieth-century squeamishness about values claims such as the equality of voters; but equality of voters and its meanings are what the condition is about, not anonymity and its meanings.[4] Estlund (2008: 78) defines anonymity thus: 'A rule is anonymous if and only if no difference is made in the collective ordering if the identity of the owner of the preference ranking is change'. He says that a condition such as May's is sensitive to preferences, but not to preference-holders. It remains a mixture of non-anonymity and anonymity, and thus Estlund (2008: 80) objects that it is not fully anonymous: 'A procedure is fully anonymous if and only if it is blind to personal features; its results would not be different if any features of the relevant people were changed'. The consistent fair proceduralist, says EP, must embrace full anonymity, and hence would only be able to justify coin flip.

The full anonymity ascribed by EP to FP is no longer about votes, equal or unequal, or about positive responsiveness, as aspects of the procedure. Full anonymity rejects not only simple majority vote over two alternatives (in this illustration), but also *any* general decision function. All that is left is what May called neutrality (equality among alternatives). A fully anonymous procedure chooses with equal chance among possible alternatives a, b, c, ... x, y, z, aa, bb, ... , even though the humans in the illustration express preferences only over alternatives x and y. However, if EP is correct that general positive responsiveness (more broadly, aggregativity) is not a procedural value of actual voting because it refers to a procedure-independent standard of procedural correctness, then for the same reason anonymity (equality) is not a procedural value of actual voting. More dramatically, neutrality could not be a procedural value of actual voting, because an ideal standard of neutrality could be poorly or perversely approximated in actual practice (e.g. someone neglected to include many of the possible alternatives). Fair proceduralism would not be able to advocate any actual decision procedure. But let us set this objection aside, and return to EP's main account of FP's purported flight from substance.

Estlund says that someone might object that full anonymity is not about fairness at all, but if that were right, 'we should never think of a coin flip, *which gives no regard to preferences at all*, as a fair way to resolve a dispute, and yet we often do' (Estlund, 2008: 80, emphasis added). Are disputes that are actually and fairly resolved by coin flip about 'possible decisions' (Estlund, 2008: 82), however, or are they about a narrow range of decisions valued by the individuals involved in the flip? If the latter, then the coin flip would violate full anonymity, and FP would not be able to advocate even the thin alternative of equal draw among possible alternatives. In response to Thomas Christiano (2009), who first raised this objection, Estlund (2009) proposed that alternatives mentioned in the newspaper as supported by some or opposed by others could be arbitrarily selected.[5] I say that this still violates the full anonymity condition though, because, if the alternatives supported or opposed by individuals involved were to change, then they would not appear in the newspaper, and hence the results of the procedure would change.

Epistemic proceduralism goes astray, I think, because it does not explicitly conceptualize agenda formation. In Arrow's social choice theory individuals have preference orderings over all conceivable social states; whatever the formalization, the general idea is that that there is a set of possible alternatives, that some subset of those alternatives comes under consideration by a procedure, and that the procedure selects one or more of the alternatives under consideration. The problem of agenda formation came to the attention of political scientists after Dahl's landmark *Who Governs* (1961), which found that of alternatives under consideration by the city government of New Haven, Connecticut, no one economic group had special sway. Later critics hypothesized and showed that a special interest could almost undetectably keep an alternative entirely off the political agenda, as US Steel kept the issue of air pollution off the agenda of Gary, Indiana city government, in the 1950s (Bachrach & Baratz, 1962).

Dahl's later work was sensitive to agenda formation as a problem in democratic theory. His 'procedural democracy' emphasizes that the decision process has two stages: setting the agenda and deciding the outcome. Also, one of Dahl's four necessary and sufficient conditions of democratic procedure is that members must be able to decide how and whether matters are to be placed on the agenda of the association. The claim that agenda formation is essential to understanding democratic procedure is not idiosyncratic. Social choice theorist Nicolaus Tideman (2006: 17, emphasis added) defines voting as follows:

> A collective decision is made by voting if and only if, *on the basis of a previous collective decision, a set of possible options is identified for consideration*, the members of the collectivity report one or more aspects of their evaluations of the outcomes, and an outcome is selected on the basis of a mathematical function of these reports.

The previous collective decision could be a democratic one, as explicitly required by Dahl, or a non-democratic one. Tideman (2006: 16, emphasis added) defines making a decision by a random process as follows:

> A collective decision is made by random process if and only if, *on the basis of a previous collective decision, a set of possible options is identified for consideration*, and the outcome is selected from among these on the basis of the outcome of a random process.

Epistemic proceduralism's claim that we consider as fair an equal random choice among possible alternatives is a descriptive generalization. It is not clear to me that the descriptive claim that the choice be among possible alternatives is correct. Generally, it seems to me, a prior collective decision selects a set of more favored options that would be randomly chosen from. Often a lottery is used when there is no good argument for choosing one alternative over another within the top set. The US military conscription lottery of 1969 chose among all US residents born between 1944 and 1950, not all American males, not all humans, not all possible social states. Coin flips are used in politics, and are sometimes mandated by statute as a way of breaking a tie vote. The coin flip is between the tied vote-getters at the top, however, not among all alternatives voted on, and not among all possible alternatives. Peter Stone (2007: 278), a student of the subject, suggests that the circumstances of a just lottery are: '1) two or more individuals have equally strong claims to a good; 2) the claim of each of these individuals is stronger than the claim of anyone else with an outstanding claim; and 3) there is not enough of the good to satisfy the claims of all of these individuals with equally and maximally strong claims'.

If a lifeboat is capable of holding only four but five are aboard, and if no better argument prevailed, a lottery might be held to select one person for sacrifice. There is no sense of fairness or of anonymity that demands that the random draw be among all possible combinations of the five individuals in the lifeboat (not include, for example, choosing Messrs Alpha, Bravo and Charlie together for sacrifice when only one need go, and not include choosing no one), or that it be among all possible alternatives in the world, whatever that means. There is a prior consensus that the exclusive alternatives are A goes, B goes, C goes, D goes or E goes. Each of the five prefers a sacrifice of any one of the five to a sacrifice of any combinations of more than one of the five.[6] Epistemic proceduralism holds that random draw does not violate the full anonymity condition, but notice in the lifeboat example that for the random draw to choose only among one of the five would, contrary to EP, violate the condition. To check, suppose that each of the five now most prefers a draw of any combination of four out of the five to be sacrificed. Now the draw would be among all those combinations, and the outcome would change. Thus, I submit, coin flip in practice does not satisfy the full anonymity condition.

Estlund might say (as suggested by his informal comments on a previous draft) that, *after* agenda formation, equal random choice among items on the agenda is not aim-sensitive (aggregative). I think Estlund's claim would be that we generally consider as fair an equal random choice among alternatives on a final agenda. However, I claim that random equal draw among alternatives on an agenda would be considered fair *only* by reference to fair treatment of participants in a previous decision to form the agenda, and thus would be aggregative. Although it might be considered fair for two people to agree to flipping a coin to allocate between them an indivisible good owed them, it would not be considered fair for one of them to flip a coin to decide whether or not she murders the other one.

If democracy were only about equal influence over the outcome, then there would be no difference between democratic voting and equal draw among possible alternatives, but democratic voting is better than equal draw. Estlund says that the logic of such fair proceduralism drives it to intrinsic proceduralism (IP). The logic of IP, he says, is that an intrinsically valued procedure cannot be responsive to the preference rankings of citizens (cannot be aggregative); to so respond would appeal to a substantive matter independent of the procedure. The intrinsic proceduralist must endorse full anonymity, and is left only with equal draw among possible alternatives. I counter, on the one hand, that sensitivity to the aims of participants *is* intrinsic to democratic voting procedure, and, on the other hand, that in practice equal draw among possible alternatives *is* sensitive to aims of participants and thus violates the full anonymity condition. I am not convinced that Estlund's account of the fair proceduralist's necessary flight from substance is correct. Another argument I understand to imply that no actual procedure has any procedural values. I observe that this would abolish the real and useful distinction between procedural values and outcome values.

Centrality Value and Epistemic Value of Democratic Decision

Whether or not we label any of the proposed values of democratic voting as procedural or substantive, each is still a value requiring explication and evaluation. Even if the equal vote were the only procedural value of democratic voting, and all other proposed values of voting are better called substantive, we would still need to investigate and compare all proposed values, procedural and substantive. If I am correct that decisiveness, anonymity, neutrality and responsiveness are examples of procedural values, some of which might fairly handle inputs, I would still need to enquire as to whether there is a procedure-independent value of fairness to the outputs.

Democratic voting possesses one striking outcome value; it tends to select what is thought best for the collective, or what is most wanted for the collective, by the most people.[7] What is thought best or is most wanted by the most people need not be true, right or wise. We hope that majority decision is true, right or wise, or more soberly that it tends to be, compared with feasible alternative institutions, but for the moment I want to isolate one value, that the decision be one thought best by the most people.

It is well known that, under standard conditions, if alternatives are along a single dimension, then pairwise majority voting will select the alternative favored by the median voter, and if alternatives are along several dimensions then strategic pairwise voting will tend to select alternatives in the center of the multidimensional issue space. All practiced or seriously proposed democratic voting rules share the tendency to centrality – surely that is a major reason why they are used or proposed. Return to the single-dimension case for illustration, and suppose there are 21 alternatives. We know that the median alternative will be selected by pairwise majority voting. The value of centrality is that no other alternative is thought best by more people. When random choice is actually used in democratic politics, it is usually to select among tied central alternatives, and it makes sense in that context. It would not make sense to choose randomly among the 21 alternatives: there is only a $1/21$ chance of choosing the alternative thought best by the most people, and, worse, a $2/21$ chance of choosing one or the other of the most extreme alternatives, thought best by the fewest people.

Suppose that people tend to be biased towards their own judgment of what is best for all, or towards their own advantage in a compromise of wants. Democratic voting tends to cancel out those particularistic biases in favor of more general alternatives. Assume there are three voters, P, Q and R, and four alternatives, all for P, all for Q, all for R, and equal accommodation among P, Q and R. PQR need not be equal division of a pie, but could be something like Kolakowski's conservative-liberal-socialism (that our institutions respect the best value from each doctrine that is tolerable by all three doctrines). The three voters rank the options as shown in Table 1.

PQR, the more general alternative, is no one's first-ranked alternative, yet it wins by pairwise majority voting or by Borda count, each an imperfect but attractive implementation of the idea of finding the alternative thought best by the most.

What does the example show? First, that thinking of democracy in terms of plurality voting, which pays attention only to voters' first-ranked alternatives, can be misleading. In this example, P, Q and R would be tied in a plurality vote, and PQR would never be considered. Second, that a democratic voting rule tends to select the alternative judged best by the most people, and that choice tends to be more general. Third, suppose we allow unequal voting: P gets five votes, Q gets one and R gets one. Alternative 'All for P' would win, not the alternative judged best by most people, not the more general choice. Fourth, suppose we draw randomly one of the three voters to decide. Then, one of P, Q or R would be selected, one of the more partial

Table 1. Preferences of voters P, Q, R, over alternatives P, Q, R, PQR

	P	Q	R
All for P	1st	4th	3rd
PQR	2nd	2nd	2nd
All for Q	3rd	1st	4th
All for R	4th	3rd	1st

alternatives and not the more general alternative. Fifth, suppose we draw randomly over the four alternatives. There is a 3/4 chance that one of the more partial alternatives would be selected, rather than the more general alternative.

Estlund (2008: 6) says that 'there is something about democracy other than its fairness' that contributes to our sense that it can justify coercion. The example shows that a strong reason that democratic vote is better than random choice is that democratic vote tends to pick the alternative judged best by the most people, and in comparison random choice does not. There is something to be said for this (even if it were not enough for a full justification of democracy). A modern-day Kelsen could argue that democracy is justifiable because its commands are 'in harmony with the greatest possible number of equal individuals', but that random choice is unjustifiable because its commands would not be. Recall the historical phenomena that made people like Kelsen hostile to the notion that the idea of a procedure-independent standard helps us to understand and to justify democracy. It could be that a substantive Kelsenian claim is less controversial and more justifiable than EP's substantive claim that democratic voting is justified (among other reasons) because it is better than random in its tendency to produce *outcomes* that are correct by independent standards (Estlund, 2008: 98). I do not say so, but merely state the possibility.

Conclusion

I do not disagree that much with the outlines of EP. I have examined only one strand of its arguments, concerning the limits of fair procedure. It seems to me that these arguments are more complex, more risky and more controversial than they need to be. The clear and easy way to slay the claim that democracy is wholly justified by the ideal of equal influence over the outcome, and Estlund (2005: 208) has done it elsewhere, is to confront her with the problem of a procedure with the properties of equal influence and negative responsiveness. Jonathan Swift was the first to propose negative responsive governance. A professor at his fictional Grand Academy of Lagado recommended, 'That every senator in the great council of a nation, after he had delivered his opinion, and argued in the defence of it, should be obliged to give his vote directly contrary; because if that were done, the result would infallibly terminate in the good of the public' (Swift, 1826: 51). Values-allergic political scientists sometimes tell me that democracy is only about the procedural equality of citizens, and I reply, fine, you will not mind then if we add up their votes and do the opposite of what they deem best. When they say they would mind, I then ask, why should we do what the citizens think best? Finally, I ask them, is it possible to be mistaken about what is best?

Acknowledgements

The author thanks Eddie Hyland for a long conversation about democracy in Dublin, and more importantly for his accomplishments in democratic theory. The author thanks Corey Brettschneider and Thomas Christiano for thoughtful comments and David Estlund for patient and thorough comments on two drafts, correcting many confusions and errors.

Notes

1. Riker's views are rebutted in Mackie (2003).
2. Democracy is much more than majority vote over two alternatives. This sketch concentrates on that for simplicity of exposition. A fuller argument would have to incorporate a more general account of voting, public deliberation, delegation including representation, constitutionalism and other features of modern political democracy.
3. The consistency of various conditions with a given voting procedure does not exhaust the meaning of that procedure, because the procedure behaves differently with different patterns of inputs, actual humans in actual votes may act in ways not contemplated by the formal model, and so on.
4. May (1952: 681) calls it the equality condition, says it has to do with equal influence of individuals on the outcome, and says that his 'simple majority decision' is meant to be the same as Arrow's 'method of majority decision'. Arrow's (1963: 46) definition of the method of majority decision does not refer to symmetric inputs but instead refers directly to counting the number of individual humans voting for each alternative.
5. Estlund's (2009) replies to Christiano are implicitly addressed at various points herein; to rehearse explicitly those arguments and my responses to them is not possible within the available space.
6. Each of the five has preferences not only over their most favored alternatives, but also over their less-favored and least-favored alternatives. The idea of preference is not limited to top-ranked preference.
7. It is a mistake to consider plurality voting, which considers only each voter's top-ranked alternative, the exemplary democratic voting rule. Voting rules that aggregate all of each voter's rankings allow us to talk about an alternative that, although not top-ranked by any, is most wanted by all, as will be shown in the upcoming example.

References

Arrow, K. (1963) *Social Choice and Individual Values* (New Haven, CT: Yale University Press).
Bachrach, P. & Baratz, M. S. (1962) Two faces of power, *American Political Science Review*, 56, pp. 947–952.
Beitz, C. (1989) *Democratic Equality* (Princeton, NJ: Princeton University Press).
Brettschneider, C. (2005) Balancing procedures and outcomes within democratic theory, *Political Studies*, 53(2), pp. 423–441.
Christiano, T. (2009) Debate: Estlund on democratic authority, *Journal of Political Philosophy*, 17(2), pp. 228–240.
Dahl, R. (1961) *Who Governs* (New Haven, CT: Yale University Press).
Dahl, R. (1989) *Democracy and its Critics* (New Haven, CT: Yale University Press).

Dahl, R. (2006) Procedural democracy, in: R. Goodin & P. Pettit (Eds) *Contemporary Political Philosophy: An Anthology*, pp. 107–125 (Oxford: Blackwell).

Estlund, D. (2005) Democratic theory, in: F. Jackson & M. Smith (Eds) *The Oxford Handbook of Contemporary Philosophy* (Oxford: Oxford University Press).

Estlund, D. (2008) *Democratic Authority: A Philosophical Framework* (Princeton, NJ: Princeton University Press).

Estlund, D. (2009) Debate: on Christiano's The Constitution of Equality, *Journal of Political Philosophy*, 17(2), pp. 241–252.

Kelsen, H. (1955) Foundations of democracy, *Ethics*, 66(1), pp. 1–101.

Mackie, G. (2003) *Democracy Defended* (Cambridge: Cambridge University Press).

Mackie, G. (2010) Schumpeter's leadership democracy, *Political Theory*, 37(1), pp. 128–153.

May, K. O. (1952) A set of independent necessary and sufficient conditions for simple majority decision, *Econometrica*, 20(4), pp. 680–684.

Riker, W. (1982) *Liberalism against Populism* (Long Grove, IL: Waveland Press).

Schumpeter, J. A. (1942) *Capitalism, Socialism, and Democracy* (New York: Harper and Brothers).

Stone, P. (2007) Why lotteries are just, *Journal of Political Philosophy*, 15(3), pp. 276–295.

Swift, J. (1826) *Gulliver's Travels* (London: Jones and Co.).

Tideman, N. (1986) A majority-rule characterization with multiple extensions, *Social Choice and Welfare*, 3(1), pp. 17–30.

Tideman, N. (2006) *Collective Decisions and Voting: The Potential for Public Choice* (Farnham: Ashgate Publishing).

Financial and Economic Crisis: Theoretical Explanations of the Global Sunset

PATRICK BERNHAGEN* & RAJ CHARI**
*University of Aberdeen, Scotland; **Trinity College Dublin, Ireland

ABSTRACT *The authors identify and examine the most promising political science theories for explaining the financial and economic crisis that started in 2007. Surveying the literature on lobbying, elite integration, ideological hegemony, structural state dependence and varieties of capitalism, they review the potential contributions of these different theoretical perspectives to our understanding of the causes of the current crisis specifically, and of the factors driving policymaking and macroeconomic management decisions more generally. They conclude by arguing that these different theories are not mutually exclusive while highlighting the utility of approaches focusing on elite integration, lobbying and structural dominance for making sense of the crisis in Ireland and elsewhere.*

Introduction

In capitalist systems, markets and private property provide the building blocks of economic activity. A major task for policymakers is to contain moral hazard by regulating markets in such a way as to prevent 'prodigals and projectors' (Smith, 1776: 128) from destabilising the system through over-speculation. Over the course of the past quarter century or so, governments of all advanced capitalist democracies have failed spectacularly in this task, which eventually led to the financial and economic crisis of 2007 onward. How can these failures be explained? Although attempts to make sense of the crisis and its causes have been made by economists, current affairs commentators and journalists, political scientists have to date not utilised the explanatory tools of their discipline to contribute to our understanding of the crisis. In this article, the most promising approaches are identified and reviewed.

A first approach identified in our survey of the literature focuses on lobbying by financial actors aimed at coaxing governments into enacting inadequate regulation or removing useful rules. Second, theories of elite integration emphasise how policy-makers, regulators and the regulated form common perspectives on economic policy and financial market regulation. Rooted in a neo-liberal ideology of unfettered markets and deregulation, these perspectives have led policymakers around the world to rely unduly on the ability of markets to correct themselves. A third approach points to the role of mass preferences in Western democracies, highlighting how voters have consistently returned parties to office whose policies promised homeownership and infinite increases in personal wealth and consumption for ever larger sections of society. Fourth, theories of structural state dependence focus on the ability of thriving financial markets to provide tax revenues, employment and electoral support for governments in mature capitalist democracies. Fifth, institutionalist theories suggest that the crisis has been generated primarily in the context of liberal market economies and that it has affected these economies more severely than coordinated market economies.

Our aim is to identify the potential contributions of these different theoretical approaches to our understanding of the causes of, and political response to, the current crisis specifically, and of the factors driving policymaking and macroeconomic management decisions more generally. The article thereby contributes to the theoretical debates surrounding political scientists' efforts to examine developments in different political systems generally as well as to analyse the financial and economic crisis of 2007 onward more specifically. In doing so, the article also prepares the theoretical ground for an empirical case study in this issue by Chari and Bernhagen, which will investigate the crisis in Ireland in the light of the theoretical approaches reviewed here.

Economic crises have many causes, and not all of them may be amenable to political control. Important factors that contributed to the 2007 onward crisis but can barely be addressed by political measures include international structural developments such as China's increasing role in the world economy as a producer and capital exporter. However, for those factors that can be manipulated by political decision-making, we have to ask why policymakers in liberal democracies acted the way they did. As this question is about political actors and their decisions, we can expect political scientists to have a lot to offer. Yet, when looking for explanations in the political science literature we find that there are very few. Further, where political scientists have attempted to make sense of the causes of the crisis, they have done so without reaching very deeply into their discipline's conceptual and analytical toolbox. Instead, they have joined economists, historians, journalists and other experts on their respective turf. Often, these analyses are of very high quality and certainly do not need to hide behind the contributions from other academic disciplines and public commentary.[1] Yet, they also tend to confine themselves to accounts of *how* the crisis unfolded rather than explanations for *why* it did. Even the best treatments by political scientists to date interpret the crisis more in the light of the political economy literature than explain it with the use of political science theories (e.g. Gamble, 2009). Rather than investigating the crisis with the aid of the discipline's diverse repertoire of nomothetic explanations, idiographic, anecdotal and historical storytelling prevails. Cogent political science should transcend *ad hoc* interpretation and offer theoretically grounded explanations with sufficient leverage to account for, and understand better, the causes and effects of significant events such as the 2007 onward financial and economic crisis. With this in mind, the article concentrates on examining and evaluating the main theoretical strands in the discipline that might contribute to this task.

To clarify just what it is that we ask political scientists to explain, we start by summarising the main aspects and implications of the crisis as they are known to date. We then examine five theoretical explanations found in standard political science literature and evaluate them with a view to gaining a better understanding of how policymakers paved the way for the crisis to unfold. In the concluding section, we discuss the relationships between the most relevant approaches.

In a Nutshell: The Financial and Economic Crisis of 2007 Onward

A plethora of chronological accounts of the crisis exist; we therefore provide only the minimum necessary summary.[2] While opinions diverge as to whether the problem was caused by too little or by ineffective regulation, it is uncontentious that the political context and regulatory framework in which financial markets operate constitute the conditions under which the crisis developed. Over the past quarter of a century, an effective redistribution of income and wealth from the bottom to the top has taken place in the developed industrialised countries, creating a massive concentration of financial assets in the hands of a relatively small group of individuals, firms, and institutional investors such as pension funds and insurance companies (Huffschmid, 2007; OECD, 2008). In their search for higher returns to these assets, private investors have increasingly turned to 'alternative investments', such as private equity, hedge funds and real estate investment trusts. Bankers and traders were ingenious at creating new financial instruments – most famously the collateralised debt obligation that eventually led to an inextricable pooling of 'prime' and 'sub-prime' mortgages and the creation of vast amounts of fictional assets.

These developments have taken place against the backdrop of the replacement of the Bretton Woods system with a global financial system of floating currencies, which greatly facilitated international trading in securitised debt. They necessitated adjustments to the regulatory framework to enable regulators to monitor activities accurately, detect destabilising developments on time, and intervene if necessary. These adjustments were not made. Instead, many of the safeguards against large-scale financial crises put in place earlier, such as the US Glass-Steagall Act from the 1930s, which prohibited a bank holding company from owning non-bank financial institutions, thereby lending force to minimum base capital requirements, were scrapped. Instead, different jurisdictions competed with one another to offer the least intrusive regulation on financial institutions in order to attract the business of the big international banks. Light-touch regulation was embraced, albeit to different extents, by policymakers in all countries and of all mainstream partisan affinity. Rather than containing moral hazard, these regimes encouraged bankers and consumers alike to take bad risks and join effective Ponzi schemes of unprecedented scale.

This deterioration of the regulatory environment relative to the increasing size and complexity of financial markets allowed asset bubbles to grow to enormous proportions. In spring 2007, defaults in the sub-prime housing market in the USA exposed the level of bad debt carried by overextended financial institutions and triggered a shock to collective confidence in the world's financial systems (Gamble, 2009). The ensuing financial crisis led to numerous bank failures and government rescues, the most dramatic of these in Ireland, the UK and the USA. Reduced liquidity, sector price inflations (mainly in food and energy) and the general slowdown of the US economy meant that the crisis could spread to the 'real economy' by the autumn of 2008. Other large, Western economies contracted as well, and countries with large financial exposure entered recession. Responses by central banks around the world included aggressive cutting of interest rates, creating additional money electronically and using this to buy government bonds and assets from financial institutions ('quantitative easing'). It was hoped that the resulting rises in liquidity, asset relief funds and nationalisations would aid economic recovery. While these hopes have met with different success in different countries, public efforts to abate the crisis put unprecedented strains on public finances everywhere and have reinforced ongoing shifts of financial burden and risk from elites to non-elites (Hacker, 2008).

Explaining Political Decision-making

Lobbying

Many commentators have blamed aggressive lobbying for the inadequate regulation of financial markets that contributed to the crisis. For example, Luce (2009) describes how the top 25 US originators of sub-prime mortgages spent almost $370m throughout the 1990s on lobbying and campaign donations in Washington. These actors were mostly controlled by the largest US banks, including Citigroup, Goldman Sachs, Wells Fargo, JP Morgan and Bank of America (*ibid.*) In order to lobby policymakers with the aim of obtaining desired regulation or preferential taxation, financial interests first have to gain access to these political decision-makers (Truman, 1951; Schlozman & Tierney, 1986: 104; Baumgartner *et al.*, 2009). Economic elites find it easier to gain access to politicians than other groups. They are better resourced and have smaller collective action problems (Olson, 1965). Corporations and trade associations have a systematic advantage in politics because they are 'institutional groups', and as such able to sustain a more permanent presence in the policymaking process (Salisbury, 1984). Furthermore, in the case of many public goods sought by business actors, the costs of provision are less than their benefits accruing to single players. In these instances, business is a 'privileged group' (Olson, 1965: 49–50). Accordingly, financial firms will become politically active to secure a public or collective good when a firm is sufficiently large, or the industry sufficiently small, that the firm gets 'such a large fraction of the total benefit that they find it worthwhile to see the collective good is provided, even if they have to pay the entire cost' (Olson, 1965: 46). The heavy lobbying by Citicorp to have the remaining provisions of the Glass-Steagall Act removed through the Gramm-Leach-Bliley Act of 1999 is an example of public goods provision by a single actor – albeit of a public good that has eventually led to much larger public bads.

Left-leaning policymakers in particular have traditionally been accessible for non-business interests, such as trade union representatives or, indeed, ordinary citizens. Moreover, for the US case, Chin *et al.* (2000) found that politicians of any partisan affiliation value ordinary constituents' interests no less than business and money givers. According to a Washington staffer they interviewed, '[i]nterest groups may use PAC status to get a foot in the door, but constituents generally find that door open when they call' (quoted in Chin *et al.*, 2000: 545). In countries such as Ireland, the USA or the UK, this limits any bias in favour of business lobbyists – at least as far as the representation of interests to parliamentarians is concerned; but few citizens can hope to have the kind of access to senior civil servants or other executive or regulatory staff that is frequently enjoyed by business interests.

Enjoying preferential access to policymakers is one thing, but translating these opportunities into political influence may be quite another. While conceding that business has superior political resources such as money, organisation and status, pluralists have long argued that the existence of these resources does not imply that they are effectively employed or actually make a difference to political outcomes (Wilson, 1981: 37). Elected politicians may talk to just about anybody in their constituency and listen to their concerns, but that does not tell us much about how they weigh the information they receive. Here, much depends on the reputation of the lobbyist and on the importance they can claim for the information they provide to policymakers (Austen-Smith, 1993; Bernhagen, 2007).

Determining the influence of lobbyists is complicated by the difficulties of identifying when influence has occurred and when there is really only parallelism of purpose and action between lobbyists and government officials (Salisbury, 1975; Dowding, 1996). As Baron (2006: 629) pointed out, '[a]ny theory of lobbying is difficult to test directly because the support (other than campaign contributions) provided to individual legislators is not reported'. It may not be surprising, then, that empirical studies of the effects of interest group activities on political outcomes have produced inconsistent and non-robust findings. In particular, researchers have found little evidence of legislative and regulatory outcomes being affected by overt political pressure from organised interests or by the resources injected into a lobbying campaign (Smith, 2000: 115–141; Roscoe & Jenkins, 2005). Given that in most countries party and campaign contributions are legally restricted to the equivalent of a few thousand euros at a time, while larger sums that may change hands illegally are difficult to trace, this is perhaps not very surprising.

Another reason for the many weak and contradictory findings in studies on the policy effects of interest group activity is the implicit, unrealistic assumption that voters would condone sell-outs by incumbent politicians to organised interests (Denzau & Munger, 1986; Morton & Cameron, 1992). This qualification applies *a fortiori* to big business and financial interests and echoes Truman's earlier claim that the efficacy of pressure politics by interest groups is ultimately circumscribed and constrained by largely unorganised interests that are so widely held in society that they are 'taken for granted' (Truman, 1951: 512).

The idea of small, efficient groups hijacking the policy process at the expense of latent groups therefore has to rely on some degree of voter ignorance. Political incumbents have to be able to fool systematically a majority of voters by favouring special interests while keeping the costs imposed on the majority below some awareness threshold (Becker, 1983: 391–394). In the case of financial market regulation, this is arguably not difficult to achieve. First, because information gathering is costly, voter rationality implies incentives for the electorate to be ill-informed (Downs, 1957). Second, the potential costs from risky financial strategies and permissive regulation are widely dispersed across a large number of potential victims. Third, any costs are likely to be incurred at an unknown point of time in the future. Finally, there may not be any costs, at least as perceived by all the relevant actors, as the possibility of something going wrong is just that – a possibility, and one of unknown probability at that.

Agency Capture, Elite Networks and Epistemic Communities

According to Stigler's theory of regulation, policies are 'acquired' by industry and designed and operated primarily for industry's benefit (Stigler, 1975: 114). Known as the theory of regulatory or agency capture, this approach portrays business interests as seeking beneficial regulation from governments (i.e. subsidies, control over market entry and price-fixing arrangements) as well as trying to avert policies that impose costs. While Stigler expressed little doubt that business can generally expect to get what it wants, the notion that entire industries can influence the formulation and implementation of policies intended to regulate their behaviour assumes that firms in the same sector hold largely similar views on public policy. As Dahl put it over a decade earlier, '[t]he actual *political effectiveness* of a group is a function of its potential for control *and* its potential for unity' (Dahl, 1958: 465, original emphasis). While the interests and preferences of firms often diverge across different sectors, they can be expected to be relatively aligned within the financial sector.

Even a coherent and tightly organised business community might not be able to influence public policy if countervailing interests can mobilise as well (Galbraith, 1954) and economic elites are somewhat distinct from political elites. However, the personal involvement with business and its leaders of politicians such as Silvio Berlusconi, Mary Harney or Gerhard Schröder, or appointments of business leaders to ministerial posts like that of the former boss of HSBC, Stephen Green, to UK Minister of State for Trade and Investment, remind us that personal and family unions between political and business empires are a regular occurrence in Western democracies. The leaders of industry and finance share many social, professional, educational and recreational experiences with politicians and leading civil servants. This has been the subject of social science enquiry since the elite theories of Hunter (1953) and Mills (1956). In the USA, elite preparatory schools have traditionally played an important role in the formation and maintenance of the American upper class – a process of elite integration that is continued in the Ivy League universities (Cookson & Persell, 1984). In the UK, similar functions are performed by 'public' schools and the 'Oxbridge colleges', while in France the Ecole Nationale d'Administration is a cadre production facility that few aspiring politicians, civil servants or business people can afford to bypass (Miliband, 1969: 55–67).

For the US case, Moore (1979) has demonstrated the existence of largely unfragmented elites in different political, economic and social institutions. The structure of the networks indicates that a strong potential for unity among elites exists, and that almost all of the individuals involved have a high potential for political influence as a result of their incumbency in high-level positions. However, rather than building on common privilege from birth or upbringing, membership in elite networks often derives from the issue-related interests shared by the members of the network (Moore, 1979). This echoes the earlier political science literature on policy communities, which argued that economic elites develop professional relationships with ministerial civil servants or parliamentary committees, forming 'islands of functional power', 'policy subsystems' or 'iron triangles' (Maass, 1951; Redford, 1969; Sayre & Kaufman, 1965).

Richardson and Jordan's (1979) analysis of elite integration in British 'policy communities' also highlights the role of clusters of special interests and policymakers within a given policy area. These communities can be quite institutionalised and effectively exclude other groups from the policy process. In a similar vein, 'policy network analysis' views the political involvement of business primarily as the developing and maintaining of close relationships with policymakers and other actors with common stakes in a policy area (Marsh & Rhodes, 1992). Common to these theories is the notion that '[t]he existence of a policy network, or more particularly a policy community, constrains the policy agenda and shapes the policy outcomes' (Rhodes & Marsh, 1992: 197). Policy change takes place if and when the relevant policy community agrees it is necessary and a consensus exists on the direction of change (Knoke et al., 1996; Richardson, 2000: 1006).

These functional, rather than social, ties between economic and political elites are reinforced by the politics of the 'revolving door' (Salisbury et al., 1989). Firms find it attractive to hire former senior civil servants, regulators and cabinet ministers for their technical expertise and social connections. Once in their new private sector positions, the former policymakers use their connections and influence to further their new employers' political interests as well as using their factual expertise to advise them on government relations and regulatory matters. Tony Blair's move from heading successive UK governments pursuing the light-touch approach to financial market regulation to JP Morgan – one of the prime beneficiaries of such policy – is perhaps the most high-profile example of revolving-door politics linking political and financial elites. In recent years, the appointment of business leaders to senior government positions has lost much of its negative image, a development that is reflected in the strategy of the Conservative–Liberal Democrat government in the UK of recruiting the bosses of the country's largest corporations as non-executive directors in numerous Whitehall departments in an effort to 'cut public spending and reform public services' (*The Guardian*, 16 December 2010).

Passage in the opposite direction also occurs. Many former top bankers personally run the agencies charged with regulating their industry, illustrating how financial market regulation has been marked by extreme levels of agency capture. The current Chief Executive Officer of the UK's Financial Services Authority, Hector Sants, is a former Head of European Equities at Warburg Dillon Read and former First Vice-President of UBS Securities. The chairman of the same agency, Adair Turner, is a former director of McKinsey & Co., a management consulting firm with a strong role in finance and investment. A former Director-General of the Confederation of British Industry (CBI), Turner also worked as Vice-Chairman of Merrill Lynch Europe. His predecessor, Callum McCarthy, who headed the agency throughout the run-up to the financial and economic crisis, had previously been Director of Corporate Finance at investment bank Kleinwort Benson, as well as Managing Director and Deputy Head of Corporate Finance of Barclays' investment banking arm, BZW, and subsequently CEO of Barclays Bank group operations in Japan and North America. Finally, some travel the revolving door full circle, such as the aforementioned Stephen Green, who was a civil servant at the UK's Ministry of Overseas Development before embarking on a business and banking career with McKinsey & Co., Inc. and HSBC and eventually returning to the state apparatus as Minister of State for Trade.

An important dimension of policy communities is the development of common perspectives. This is the substance of 'epistemic communities', defined by Haas (1992: 27) as 'channels through which new ideas circulate from societies to governments as well as from country to country'. As networks of experts or groups with an authoritative claim to policy-relevant knowledge within their domain of expertise, epistemic communities shape conceptions of the public interest by defining cause-and-effect relationships and predicting the chain of events that might follow either from failure to take action or from enacting a particular policy. Their members hold a common set of causal beliefs that in turn produce normative commitments. Through framing of alternatives and implications of possible actions, epistemic communities effectively shape policy.[3]

As the recent UK experience illustrates, when bankers become regulators or when policymakers become bankers, they do not simply promote the interests of the institutions that paid their incomes in the past (Turner) or future (Blair). Above all, they participate in the development and cultivation of common understandings and knowledge about how the economic and financial world works and what policies are best suited for a smooth and successful performance of the economy. These ideas are generated, refined and reinforced in epistemic communities comprising banks, policymakers, regulators and academics. The epistemic community of finance cultivated a perspective on financial markets and their regulation that prohibited its members from spotting the danger to the financial system until it was too late. This perspective is part of a neo-liberal ideology of unfettered markets and deregulation that has shaped political discourse and action in Western democracies since the 1970s. It has led policymakers around the world to rely unduly on the supposed ability of markets to correct themselves, perhaps with the aid of occasional monetary adjustments by central banks. It is worth noting, as Casey (2011) does, that neo-liberal economic thinking does not recommend *per se* an excessive reliance on financial market growth. Instead, neo-liberal doctrine became gradually modified to incorporate an ideology of financialisation: the idea of financial activity becoming an, if not the most, important driver of economic growth in mature capitalism. This included the belief that credit derivatives brought more stability to financial markets. The hegemonic grip of this ideology was such that even the left-of-centre governments that were in charge of many West European and North American countries throughout much of the 1990s subscribed to it and steered their economies towards the – then distant – abyss.

Mass Beliefs

The theoretical approaches surveyed so far are elite-centred. They imply that the beliefs shared by members of elite policy communities or the policy effects of lobbying are distinct from, or may run counter to, the preferences of a majority of citizens. However, it is possible that economic elites and the masses of citizens largely agree on how the economic and housing needs of private households are best served. The commodity fetishism underlying the belief that annual increases in house *prices* of 20 per cent or more reflect similar increases in the *value* of these houses was widely shared, and its validity in the eyes of mortgage lenders and homebuyers alike seemed to have been confirmed by experience of almost a decade. Furthermore, citizens throughout the Western world have lent strong electoral support to political parties campaigning on 'pro-market', neo-liberal programmes and promoting the increasing financialisation of citizens and societies (Martin, 2002). And while the fallout of the crisis led to a certain amount of blame being put on policymakers by the public, public opinion as well as voter behaviour in the USA and UK continue to favour neo-liberal agendas of 'small government' and 'deregulation' even after the dramatic failures of the policies that are traded under these banners (Wilson, 2011).

Economic ideas are powerful political tools that can be used by actors to shape policy. This is done most effectively by defining how the economy works, what is wrong with it and what would improve it. Blyth (2002) has shown how economic ideas played a critical role in effecting the profound changes in the economic order in major capitalist countries in the 1930s and 1970s, respectively. However, even if these ideas and the policies they justified benefited business actors more than any other group, in any political system in which citizens wield control over government such ideas would have to be shared by large sections of the population in order to be effective. This raises the question of how economic elites are supposed to utilise economic ideas for their political ends.

One route would involve spreading ideas of favourable content throughout society in order to ensure popular acquiescence, if not approval, with one's political agenda. Indeed, the mass media are often said to be easily accessible and sympathetic to the business message (Miliband, 1969: 227–238; Mitchell, 1997: 50–51). Recent British polls found a good deal of scepticism towards business leaders, with 25 per cent of respondents to a 2010 Ipsos MORI poll stating they do not 'generally trust them to tell the truth' (Skinner *et al.*, 2010: 12). Still, business leaders fare a good deal better than politicians, for whom only 13 per cent of respondents expressed such trust.

Page *et al.* (1987) have shown that it is possible to influence public policy preferences if the position of those doing the influencing is backed up by expert opinion or framed as being in the public interest. The required expertise and scientific support for business-friendly messages are regularly provided by right-leaning think tanks such as the Heritage Foundation and the American Enterprise Institute in the USA, or the Centre for Policy Studies and the Adam Smith Institute in the UK (Smith, 2000: 189–96) as well as by economists in universities and business schools around the world. Thus, the prerequisites are there for financial interests to influence citizens' preferences and public opinion in such a way that will seldom be vitally challenged in politics. In this sense, financial institutions are politically powerful to the extent that they enjoy ideological hegemony and prevent people from conceptualising challenges to their interests (Wilson, 2006: 35).

The notion of a dominance of elite interests in the formation of public opinion was famously theorised by Lukes (2005), who argues that the social and political world is characterised foremost by latent conflicts of *interests* rather than by open conflicts of *preferences*. A latent conflict will not erupt into an open clash of wills as long as people's preferences diverge from their interests. What prevents them from realising this and bringing their preferences in line with their interests is 'third-dimensional power', i.e. the ability of some actors to manipulate intentionally other actors' beliefs and preferences (Lukes, 2005: 27). Hyland (1995) has identified two flaws in this argument. First, the necessity of giving a coherent account of a person's objective interests independent from subjective preferences inevitably has to employ a normative theory of human nature, which will not be open to straightforward proof and disproof (Hyland, 1995: 203).[4] Second, any defensible theory of human nature will inevitably be based on human experience (*ibid.*). According to the concept of third-dimensional power, however, human experience is itself distorted, because it is exposed to the working of third-dimensional power in the form of 'the control of information, through the mass media and through the process of socialisation' (Lukes, 2005: 27). This leads to circularity of the argument: 'If we base our theory of human nature on distorted experience we will be unable to detect third-dimensional power; but we will only be able to determine which experiences and forms of consciousness are the products of distortion after we have formulated a defensible theory of human nature' (Hyland, 1995: 203).

This is not to say that elites are inactive with respect to beliefs and desires held by others. Indeed, attempts at ideological indoctrination have always been part of political discourse in a broader sense, and most probably always will be. Moreover, the growth of advertising and marketing suggests that attempts to influence people's wants and needs are not in vain. However, such instances of indoctrination are as much the ideology of the elites as they shape the beliefs of the masses (Elster, 1983: 116). To the extent that indoctrination takes place, it can be successful only because the elites themselves believe it (Elster, 1983: 117). Attempts purposively to produce mental states in other persons are bound to fail unless there is little doubt on the part of the recipient that the propagated beliefs are genuinely shared by the sender (Elster, 1983: 66–71).[5] As argued in the previous section, beliefs favouring light-touch regulation of financial institutions and the financialisation of households have been very much shared by economic and political elites alike. Moreover, these beliefs are not without certain grounding in reality. This is because in capitalist democracies, the fortunes of citizens and policymakers alike are linked to the fortunes of capital, including financial capital. We turn to this in the next section.

Structural Dependence of the State on (Financial) Capital

Macroeconomic performance is of overarching importance both for the welfare of citizens and for the popularity and electoral success of politicians. Since Key's (1966) study, *The Responsible Electorate*, popularity functions have assumed a reward–punishment model of political popularity and electoral success: if economic conditions are good the electorate will reward incumbents, whereas it will punish them if the economy is less than satisfactory (Lewis-Beck & Stegmaier, 2000; Duch & Stevenson, 2008; van der Brug *et al.*, 2007). Policymakers anticipate the effects of economic voting in their policy decisions and strategic behaviour (Kiewiet, 2000). As a special case of Friedrich's (1963) 'law of anticipated reactions', economic voting is the mechanism through which the structural dominance of business unfolds. As portrayed by Przeworski and Wallerstein, structural dependence means that

> [t]he effective capacity of any government to attain whatever are its goals is circumscribed by the public power of capital ... Capitalists do not even have to organise and act collectively: it suffices that they blindly pursue narrow, private self-interest to sharply restrict the options of all governments. (Przeworski & Wallerstein, 1988: 12)

Far from being an exclusive claim of structural Marxist theories of the state in capitalist society, this notion is also a central tenet of neoclassical political economy (e.g. Becker, 1983). The social and political implications are considerable: because their political survival depends on a healthy economy guaranteeing adequate state revenues and political support, and major investment decisions affecting economic performance are usually private, governments in capitalist democracies cannot risk proposing policies that are disliked by the owners of capital (Lindblom, 1977: 170–188).

Far from being restricted to (re-)distributive policies, structural dependence theory predicts constraints on all policies that could adversely affect businesses' revenue prospects, including regulatory policies. Four decades ago, Peltzman (1973) showed how safety and efficacy regulation on drugs can backfire by thwarting innovation and research on new and improved drugs. Elaborating this problem in the context of risk regulation, Sunstein (1998: 235–236) has highlighted how the aggregate outcomes of decentralised responses to political decision-making can have unintended consequences that render public policies inefficient, reverse their intended effects, or even avert their very formulation in the first place should policymakers anticipate such adverse reactions.

The dependence of governments on revenues from business activities is perhaps nowhere better illustrated than in the context of successive New Labour governments in the UK throughout the late 1990 and first decade of the new millennium. The Labour government's 'tax-and-spend' policies (e.g. on health and education) were financed in no small part by tax and foreign currency earnings from a thriving City. According to Gamble (2009), the reason why so many countries were prepared to abandon or forgo tighter regulation of financial market activities was that the growth of the financial services sector was a key engine of the growth that was experienced in the 1990s. By not pursuing more stringent regulation of market activities, policymakers and regulators were effectively acting in the interest of financial capital, but without the latter's participation. This lies in some contrast to the elite integration approach discussed above: policymakers and regulators may have acted in the interest of private actors even though they did not need to make any effort to 'capture' regulatory agencies.

The structural explanation of business political privilege is a powerful theoretical argument, but it has a number of problems. First, if the structural power thesis holds, we should rarely witness policy change over time that overrides business complaints regarding the detrimental effects of a policy. However, instances of business failing in the policy struggle are frequently observed. They are more likely when external events such as scandals or crises create an environment that is conducive for policymakers to embark on a 'fit' of heroic policymaking (Mitchell, 1997: 10). In these situations, policymakers are able to override temporarily the business confidence factor. In their responses to the financial and economic crisis, governments around the world have made (more or less concerted) efforts to prescribe insurance funds against bank failures and higher liquidity ratios despite the opposition of the financial sector.

Second, the theory's implication that it does not matter for political outcomes 'who the state managers are' (Przeworski & Wallerstein, 1988: 12) does not stand up to empirical evidence either. Whereas some authors detect a process of convergence of party platforms (Caul & Gray, 2000), others have found that the partisan composition of government continues to have noticeable effects on tax policies (Quinn & Shapiro, 1991), government spending (Garrett, 1998) and fiscal and monetary policies more generally (Cusack, 2001). The notion that parties matter is also shared by business representatives. Business leaders overwhelmingly believe that Social Democratic or Labour governments are bad for business; whereas right-leaning parties are expected to do a better job in that regard (Grant, 1993: 137–138). Business leaders in the UK still support the Conservative Party more than Labour in election campaigns, even though this support is often pegged to specific policies, such as the debate about national insurance contributions in spring 2010 (*The Guardian*, 1 April 2010). Nevertheless, in the area of financial regulation we find rather few differences between the major centre-left and centre-right parties within a country.

Institutions: Varieties of Capitalism

Whatever differences in the promises, commitments and actual policies different political parties may pursue in the area of financial market regulation, any such differences within one country tend to be small compared with differences between countries. 'Modellers of capitalism', to use Moran's phrase (2009: 9), have offered insights on important differences between liberal market economies (LMEs) such as Britian, coordinated market economies (CMEs) such as Germany and state-led or state-enhanced economies such as France (Hall & Soskice, 2001; Schmidt, 2003). Distinguishing these varieties of capitalism might explain the relative resilience with which coordinated market economies such as Germany are handling the financial and economic crisis compared with the more liberally organised economies of the Anglo-Saxon world. Indeed, the landmark events and processes that have characterised the crisis, as well as the political decisions facilitating these processes, have mostly occurred in the LMEs of the USA and the UK. Partly, this has to do with the sheer size of the US economy and the importance of the City of London as a financial marketplace. By comparison, French and German banks have traditionally tended to be domestically, even regionally, oriented (Hardie & Howarth, 2010).

There are three weaknesses in the varieties of capitalism approach to understanding the crisis. First, while British bank financialisation still exceeds the levels found in Germany and France overall, authors have noted a convergence in the German and French financial systems over the past decade towards the British system, potentially undermining distinctive national varieties of financial capitalism (Hardie & Howarth, 2010). This convergence concerns primarily the 'financialisation' of bank operations with regard to both assets and liabilities. Indeed, many German banks, including Hypo Real Estate, Dresdner Bank, Deutsche Bank, WestLB and SachsenLB, were deeply implicated in imprudent behaviour over many years.

A second weakness is that there are a variety of democracies – beyond the UK, USA and Germany – that do not confirm a clear trend or fit neatly into the classification scheme. For example, Canada, which is classified as an LME by Hall and Soskice (2001: 19), survived the crisis almost unscathed, faring better than all CMEs. Iceland, classified as a CME by Hall and Soskice (2001: 20), was one of the hardest hit in the world; and Spain, which is classified as neither an LME nor a CME by Hall and Soskice (2000: 20), saw a wave of local 'cajas', particularly in Andalusia, get badly damaged during the crisis. Nevertheless, giants such as Banco Santander and Banco Bilbao Vizcaya Argentaria have since consolidated their position as world leaders in the banking sector (*El País*, 6 August 2009).

Third, as Wilson (2011) points out, the measures taken in the USA by the administrations of George W. Bush and Barak Obama – whole or part nationalisation of large banks, insurance companies and automobile producers – were scarcely compatible with the varieties of capitalism school's assertion of a dominance of liberal economic beliefs and practices in that country.

Perhaps the biggest insight to be gained from emphasising distinct forms of capitalism is in the context of collective efforts of improving the regulation of international finance with the aim of avoiding similar crises in the future. As Kalinowski (2011) points out, financialised economies such as the UK or USA tend to favour internationally coordinated fiscal stimulus packages but are sceptical towards international currency coordination and the regulation of financial flows. By contrast, export-oriented countries such as Germany and the big East Asian economies prefer tighter regulation of financial actors and markets and an international currency regime but are reluctant to increase government spending or reduce their dependence on exports. With such divergence of interests it is difficult to see how tangible progress can be made in designing regulatory frameworks for more stable and sustainable financial markets.

Discussion

Do the five explanatory strands outlined above help us understand how the world got into the mess it is in at present? Is any one of these theories better suited than the others for explaining the regulatory inadequacies, or does it require more than one to make sense of what happened and help to prevent a repeat of the drama in the future? It is important to recognise that these different theoretical lenses do not necessarily describe or emphasise different elements of political-economic systems. For example, although the market may not be quite as rigid a prison as Lindblom (1982) portrayed it, the pervasive problem of structural state dependence is frequently invoked by lobbyists in their political strategies. Asymmetric information about the likely consequences of policy underlies a lobbyist's ability to persuade policymakers of policies preferred by the lobbyist. This factor is likely to have played a major role in lobbying for laxer regulation of financial markets and services: had policymakers had a better understanding of the likely consequences of a 'light-touch' regulatory regime, independently of the information they were given by lobbyists, they may have decided to act differently. This suggests that direct, resource-based pressure may not be necessary in order for regulators to act in the interests of financial institutions, but persuasive arguments are. Being part of 'epistemic communities' shared with financial capitalists reduces further the chance that policymakers acquire independent information on the likely effects of different regulatory measures.

Re-regulating financial markets in the wake of the crisis may not be easy to accomplish. Furthermore, there are big question marks concerning the political will of policymakers around the world (Kalinowski, 2011). In the short term, legal restrictions on financial speculation would be an effective means of preventing the build-up of the next bubble. There are indeed indications that governments around the world are getting serious about strengthening the regulation, supervision and risk management of the financial sector with the aid of new capital, leverage and liquidity standards such as those proposed in the Basel III standards. In the long term, a comprehensive strategy to reduce the influence of the financial sector in economy and society is required to ensure that, once established, the necessary level and quality of regulation can be sustained.

A sound understanding of the political-economic dynamics that prevented the creation of adequate regulation in the past is needed if lessons are to be learned from recent and current experience. Political scientists have the means to aid in this explanatory endeavour. In this article we have sought to start the process by discussing the contextual determinants of the political decisions and non-decisions that were 'needed' for the crisis to unfold the way it did in the light of standard political science theories. We hope that the comparison of theoretical frameworks offered here may aid others in their efforts to analyse the political causes of financial and economic crises with the use of the rich theoretical machinery political science has to offer.

Acknowledgements

This paper was previously presented at the University of Glasgow's Department of Politics Seminar on 15 March 2010 and the 60th Political Studies Association Annual Conference, 29 March–1 April 2010, Edinburgh, UK. The authors thank the participants at these events as well as Richard Rose and Benigno Valdés for inspiring conversations on ideas for this paper.

Notes

1. See, for example, the contributions to a recent symposium in *Political Studies Review*, 8(1).
2. Readers are referred to the thorough accounts of the financial and economic crisis by Cable (2009), Gamble (2009) and Peston (2008). Bibliographies on the crisis have been compiled by the *Review of International Political Economy*, 16(5), 743–745, and the European University Institute (Bibliography of the Global Financial/Economic Crisis and its Aftermath, available at: http://www. eui.eu/Documents/Research/Library/ResearchGuides/Economics/PDFs/GlobalCrisisBibliography Webed.pdf).
3. A similar argument is developed by Hall (1993).
4. Lukes is aware of this problem and admits that different conceptions of interests are based on different moral and political positions (Lukes, 2005: 37). Far from solving the problem of objective interests, however, this illustrates the 'epistemological relativism' of the concept of third-dimensional power (Hyland, 1995: 203).
5. Analogously, we expect that, exceptions notwithstanding, advertisers and marketers generally believe that the products they try to sell are worth buying.

References

Austen-Smith, D. (1993) Information and influence: lobbying for agendas and votes, *American Journal of Political Science*, 37(3), pp. 799–833.

Baron, D. P. (2006) Competitive lobbying and supermajorities in a majority-rule institution, *Scandinavian Journal of Economics*, 108(4), pp. 607–642.

Baumgartner, F. R., Berry, J. M., Hojnacki, M., Kimball, D. C. & Leech, B. L. (2009) *Lobbying and Policy Change: Who Wins, Who Loses, and Why* (Chicago: University of Chicago Press).

Becker, G. S. (1983) A theory of competition among pressure groups for political influence, *Quarterly Journal of Economics*, 98(3), pp. 371–400.

Bernhagen, P. (2007) *The Political Power of Business: Structure and Information in Public Policymaking* (London and New York: Routledge).

Blyth, M. (2002) *Great Transformations: Economic Ideas and Institutional Change in the Twentieth Century* (Cambridge: Cambridge University Press).

Cable, V. (2009) *The Storm* (London: Atlantic Books).

Casey, T. (Ed.) (2011) Capitalism, crisis, and a zombie named TINA, in: *Legacy of the Crash: How the Financial Crisis Changed America and Britain* (Basingstoke and New York: Palgrave Macmillan).

Caul, M. L. & Gray, M. M. (2000) From platform declarations to policy outcomes: changing party profiles and partisan influence over policy, in: R. J. Dalton & M. P. Wattenberg (Eds) *Parties without Partisans: Political Change in Advanced Industrial Democracies* (Oxford: Oxford University Press).

Chin, M. L., Bond, J. R. & Geva, N. (2000) A foot in the door: an experimental study of PAC and constituency effects on access, *Journal of Politics*, 62(2), pp. 534–549.

Cookson, P. W., Jr & Persell, C. H. (1984) *Preparing for Power: Americas Elite Boarding Schools* (New York: Basic Books).

Cusack, T. R. (2001) Partisanship in the setting and coordination of fiscal and monetary policies, *European Journal of Political Research*, 40, pp. 93–115.

Dahl, R. A. (1958) A critique of the ruling elite model, *American Political Science Review*, 52(2), pp. 463–469.

Denzau, A. T. & Munger, M. C. (1986) Legislators and interest groups: how unorganized interests get represented, *American Political Science Review*, 80(1), pp. 89–106.

Dowding, K. (1996) *Power* (Buckingham: Open University Press).

Downs, A. (1957) *An Economic Theory of Democracy* (New York: Harper).

Duch, R. M. & Stevenson, R. T. (2008) *The Economic Vote: How Political and Economic Institutions Condition Election Results* (Cambridge: Cambridge University Press).

Elster, J. (1983) *Sour Grapes* (Cambridge: Cambridge University Press).

Friedrich, C. J. (1963) *Man and His Government: An Empirical Theory of Politics* (New York: McGraw-Hill).

Galbraith, J. K. (1954) Countervailing power, *American Economic Review*, 44(1), pp. 1–6.

Gamble, A. (2009) *The Spectre at the Feast: Capitalist Crisis and the Politics of Recession* (Basingstoke: Palgrave Macmillan).

Garrett, G. (1998) *Partisan Politics in the Global Economy* (Cambridge: Cambridge University Press).

Grant, W. (1993) *Business and Politics in Britain*, 2nd ed. (London: Macmillan).

Haas, P. M. (1992) Introduction: epistemic communities and international policy, *International Organization*, 46(1), pp. 1–35.

Hacker, J. (2008) *The Great Risk Shift: The New Economic Insecurity and the Decline of the American Dream* (New York: Oxford University Press).

Hall, P. A. (1993) Policy paradigms, social learning, and the state: the case of economic policymaking in Britain, *Comparative Politics*, 25(3), pp. 275–296.

Hall, P. A. & Soskice, D. (Eds) (2001) *Varieties of Capitalism: The Institutional Foundations of Comparative Advantage* (Oxford: Oxford University Press).

Hardie, I. & Howarth, D. (2010) Die Krise but not La Crise? The financial crisis and the transformation of German and French banking systems, *Journal of Common Market Studies*, 47(5), pp. 1017–1039.

Huffschmid, J. (2007) Hedge funds and private equity: beneficial or dangerous? Paper presented at the conference *The Political Economy of Financial Markets, of the Netherlands Organisation for Research in Business Economics and Management*, 16 November, Utrecht.

Hunter, F. (1953) *Community Power Structure: A Study of Decision Makers* (Chapel Hill: University of North Carolina Press).

Hyland, J. L. (1995) *Democratic Theory: The Philosophical Foundations* (Manchester: Manchester University Press).

Kalinowski, T. (2011) Regulating International Finance and the Evolving Imbalance of Capitalisms since the 1970s, *MPIfG Discussion Paper 11/10* (Cologne: Max Planck Institute for the Study of Societies).

Key, V. O. (1966) *The Responsible Electorate: Rationality in Presidential Voting, 1936–1960* (Cambridge, MA: Belknap Press).

Kiewiet, D. R. (2000) Economic retrospective voting incentives for policymaking, *Electoral Studies*, 19(2), pp. 427–444.

Knoke, D., Pappi, F. U., Broadbent, J. & Tsujinaka, Y. (1996) *Comparing Policy Networks* (Cambridge: Cambridge University Press).

Lewis-Beck, M. S. & Stegmaier, M. (2000) Economic determinants of electoral outcomes, *Annual Review of Political Science*, 3, pp. 183–219.

Lindblom, C. E. (1977) *Politics and Markets: The World's Political-Economic Systems* (New York: Basic Books).

Lindblom, C. E. (1982) The market as prison, *Journal of Politics*, 44(4), pp. 323–336.

Luce, E. (2009) Subprime lobbyists in $370m battle, *Financial Times*, 6 May, available at: http://www.ft.com/home/us

Lukes, S. (2005) *Power: A Radical View*, 2nd ed. (London: Macmillan).

Maass, A. (1951) *Muddy Waters: The Army Engineers and the Nation's Rivers* (Cambridge: Harvard University Press).

Marsh, D. & Rhodes, R. A. W. (Eds) (1992) *Policy Networks in British Government* (Oxford: Clarendon Press).

Martin, R. (2002) *Financialization of Daily Life* (Philadelphia, PA: Temple University Press).

Miliband, R. (1969) *The State in Capitalist Society* (New York: Basic Books).

Mills, C. W. (1956) *The Power Elite* (New York: Oxford University Press).

Mitchell, N. J. (1997) *The Conspicuous Corporation: Business, Public Policy, and Representative Democracy* (Ann Arbor, MI: University of Michigan Press).

Moore, G. (1979) The structure of a national elite network, *American Sociological Review*, 44(5), pp. 673–692.

Moran, M. (2009) *Business, Politics and Society: An Anglo-American Comparison* (Oxford: Oxford University Press).

Morton, R. & Cameron, C. (1992) Elections and the theory of campaign contributions: a survey and critical analysis, *Economics and Politics*, 4(1), pp. 79–108.

OECD (2008) *Growing Unequal? Income Distribution and Poverty in OECD Countries* (Paris: OECD Publications).

Olson, M. (1965) *The Logic of Collective Action: Public Goods and the Theory of Groups* (Cambridge, MA: Harvard University Press).

Page, B. I., Shapiro, R. Y. & Dempsey, G. (1987) What moves public opinion? *American Political Science Review*, 81(1), pp. 23–43.

Peltzman, S. (1973) An evaluation of consumer protection legislation: the 1962 Drug Amendments, *Journal of Political Economy*, 81(5), pp. 1049–1091.

Peston, R. (2008) *Who Runs Britain . . . and Who's to Blame for the Economic Mess We're In?* (London: Hodder and Stoughton).

Przeworski, A. & Wallerstein, M. (1988) Structural dependence of the state on capital, *American Political Science Review*, 82(1), pp. 11–29.

Quinn, D. P. & Shapiro, R. Y. (1991) Business political power: the case of taxation, *American Political Science Review*, 85(3), pp. 851–874.

Redford, E. S. (1969) *Democracy in the Administrative State* (New York: Oxford University Press).

Rhodes, R. A. W. & Marsh, D. (1992) New directions in the study of policy networks, *European Journal of Political Research*, 21(1–2), pp. 181–205.

Richardson, J. (2000) Government, interest groups, and policy change, *Political Studies*, 48(5), pp. 1006–1025.

Richardson, J. & Jordan, G. (1979) *Governing under Pressure: The Policy Process in a Post-Parliamentary Democracy* (Oxford: Martin Robertson).

Roscoe, D. D. & Jenkins, S. (2005) A meta-analysis of campaign contributions' impact on roll call voting, *Social Science Quarterly*, 86, pp. 52–68.

Salisbury, R. H. (1975) Interest groups, in: F. I. Greenstein & N. W. Polsby (Eds) *Nongovernmental Politics, Handbook of Political Science,* Vol. 4 (Reading, MA: Addison-Wesley).

Salisbury, R. H. (1984) Interest representation: the dominance of institutions, *American Political Science Review*, 78(1), pp. 64–76.

Salisbury, R. H., Johnson, P., Heinz, J. P., Laumann, E. O. & Nelson, R. L. (1989) Who you know versus what you know: the uses of government experience for Washington lobbyists, *American Journal of Political Science*, 33(1), pp. 175–195.

Sayre, W. S. & Kaufman, H. (1965) *Governing New York City: Politics in the Metropolis* (New York: Norton).

Schlozman, K. L. & Tierney, J. T. (1986) *Organized Interests and American Democracy* (New York: Harper & Row).

Schmidt, V. (2003) French capitalism transformed, yet still a third variety of capitalism, *Economy and Society*, 32(4), pp. 526–554.

Skinner, G., Mortimor, R., Coombs, H., Cameron, D., Cormick, P. & Edminston, D. (2010) *Politics, Public Services and Society. Context for the General Election 2010* (London: Ipsos MORI).

Smith, A. (1776) *An Inquiry into the Nature and Causes of the Wealth of Nations*, Vol. 2 (Dublin: Eighteenth Century Collections Online, Gale).

Smith, M. A. (2000) *American Business and Political Power: Public Opinion, Elections, and Democracy* (Chicago: University of Chicago Press).

Stigler, G. J. (1975) *The Citizen and the State: Essays on Regulation* (Chicago: University of Chicago Press).

Sunstein, C. (1998) Health–health trade-offs, in: J. Elster (Ed.) *Deliberative Democracy*, pp. 232–259 (Cambridge: Cambridge University Press).

Truman, D. B. (1951) *The Governmental Process. Political Interests and Public Opinion* (New York: Knopf).

van der Brug, W., van der Eijk, C. & Franklin, M. (2007) *The Economy and the Vote: Electoral Responses to Economic Conditions in EU Countries* (Cambridge: Cambridge University Press).

Wilson, G. K. (2006) Thirty years of business and politics, in: D. Coen & W. Grant (Eds) *Business and Government: Methods and Practice* (Opladen: Barbara Budrich Publishers).

Wilson, G. K. (2011) The crisis of capitalism and the downfall of the Left, in: T. Casey (Ed.) *Legacy of the Crash: How the Financial Crisis Changed America and Britain* (Basingstoke and New York: Palgrave Macmillan).

Wilson, J. Q. (1981) Democracy and the corporation, in: R. Hessen (Ed.) *Does Big Business Rule America?* (Washington, DC: Ethics and Policy Center).

Financial and Economic Crisis: Explaining the Sunset over the Celtic Tiger

RAJ CHARI* & PATRICK BERNHAGEN**

*Trinity College Dublin, Ireland; **University of Aberdeen, Scotland

ABSTRACT *This article examines the causes of the financial and economic crisis in the Republic of Ireland. It first reviews the crisis in advanced capitalist democracies and then situates the Irish case in this context. In the section thereafter, it relates existing narratives and other evidence to the different theoretical explanations surveyed by Bernhagen and Chari (in this issue) in order to identify the most useful approaches to explaining the Irish crisis. It concludes that explanations focusing on the role of mass preferences and varieties of capitalism do not aid our efforts to understand the causes of the crisis or how it unfolded. By contrast, an explanation focusing on the role of lobbying is of some value, as are analyses of elite integration and the structural dependence of the Irish state on a thriving financial and property market. The article closes with lessons to be drawn from the study, with a particular emphasis on future policy responses and remedies.*

Introduction

The objectives of the article are twofold. The first is to examine the failure of financial regulation in Ireland and other advanced capitalist democracies during the global financial and economic crisis of 2007 onward. The second objective is to focus specifically on Ireland and evaluate different theoretical explanations of the crisis in the light of this case, which exhibits extreme values on several aspects of the global financial and economic crisis. A first approach identified by Bernhagen and Chari (in this issue) focuses on lobbying by financial actors aimed at coaxing governments into producing light touch regulation. Theories of elite integration, secondly, emphasise how policymakers, regulators and financial market actors form common perspectives on policy and regulation, couched in a neo-liberal ideology of unfettered markets and deregulation. A third approach points to the role of mass preferences in Western democracies, highlighting how voters have consistently returned parties to office whose policies promised homeownership for ever larger sections of society and never-ending increases in personal wealth and consumption. Fourth, theories of structural state dependence focus on the reliance of governments on thriving financial markets for tax revenues and electoral support. Fifth, the 'varieties of capitalism' literature suggests that the crisis has been generated primarily in the context of liberal market economies as well as affecting these economies more severely than coordinated market economies.

The first section of the article briefly reviews the main aspects of the worldwide crisis and, in context of this, examines the case of Ireland with a focus on the weaknesses of Irish financial markets and services regulation. In the second section we consider more explicitly the interplay and symbiotic relationships between three key actors: the state, the banks and developers.[1] This evidence will serve as a basis to evaluate better the main theoretical contributions put forward in the literature. Our analysis of the crisis in Ireland suggests that explanations focusing on elite integration, structural state dependence and the role of lobbyists and their contributions can jointly explain the workings of a triumvirate of the state, the banks and developers and their role in furthering the causes of the financial and economic crisis in Ireland. By contrast, explanations focusing on the role of mass publics and varieties of capitalism appear to be of little use. The article closes with lessons to be drawn from the study, with a particular emphasis on the need to curb the political influence of economic elites as a precondition for a sustainable and sustained regulatory framework for financial markets.

The Role of Regulation in the Financial and Economic Crisis

Although different interpretations exist of what caused the global financial and economic crisis, commentators have noted considerable agreement on the main events that marked its unfolding. Thus, in order to provide the necessary background for an analysis of the causes of the crisis in Ireland, we provide a concise summary of the main events both globally and in Ireland.[2]

In early 2007, banks and mortgage lenders involved in the sub-prime housing markets in the USA experienced difficulties triggered by defaulting homeowners struggling with increasing interest rates. Gradually, these institutions began to realise not only how much bad debt they were carrying but also how overextended they were (Gamble, 2010: 4). In the UK, this became obvious in September 2007 when Northern Rock experienced market-liquidity failure, which triggered the first physical bank run since the 1930s, and the first in the UK in 150 years. After having tried in vain to coordinate a private rescue, the British government decided to nationalise Northern Rock. Around that time, central banks around the world began to cut interest rates drastically in an attempt to prevent large-scale financial defaults, stimulate inter-bank lending and generally make money available cheaply (Gamble, 2010: 4). None the less, during 2008 numerous bank failures and rescues took place, implicating investment banks such as Bear Stearns and household names among mortgage lenders such as Fannie Mae and Freddie Mac.

By the summer of 2008 it had become clear that the crisis was not confined to sub-prime mortgages but in fact permeated the entire financial system. This has been a direct result of the way in which debts had been transformed into a complex array of diverse securities and sold on to other financial institutions (Gamble, 2010: 4). As in previous speculative bubbles, leveraging had taken on gargantuan dimensions and a complex web of legal Ponzi schemes had been created. At some point, uncertainty among bankers about the real value of the assets on their books took over. It became apparent that an enormous mountain of debt had been erected on insufficient capital bases and unfounded expectations of infinite, or at least indefinite, growth in financial and real estate markets (Gamble, 2010: 4). Once these expectations were called into question, the entire structure unravelled. The collapse of the investment bank Lehman Brothers in September 2008 marked only the tip of the iceberg. When the US financial authorities decided not to bail out Lehman Brothers they triggered a wave of panic selling that temporarily threatened the stability of the entire global financial system. Without the swift intervention of governments that stepped in to underwrite and even nationalise many institutions, this could have led to the collapse of some of the leading banks around the globe, though mainly in Britain, Ireland and the USA.

In Ireland, banks went from a Celtic Tiger 'roar' to a stray cat 'meow' within a short period starting in 2008. The collapse represented the iconic story of a country having gone boom to bust once again. The bust unfolded in three main stages.

First, when the dire state of the banks was becoming apparent in autumn 2008 the government implemented a 'life-support' system that consisted of bank bailouts by taxpayers organised through the newly created National Assets Management Agency (NAMA). This institution effectively acted as a state-owned bank, whose principal task was to absorb the bad loans made by Irish banks during the boom, estimated at over €80 billion (*The Guardian*, 30 March 2010). The 29 September deal 'put in place a guarantee arrangement to safeguard all deposits (retail, commercial, institutional and interbank), covered bonds, senior debt and dated subordinated debt (lower tier II)'[3] with all major Irish financial institutions. In order to finance this deal, as well as later capital injections into Bank of Ireland (BoI) and Allied Irish Bank (AIB) in February 2009 and the nationalisation of Anglo Irish Bank the previous month, the state had to find billions of euros (*New York Times*, 22 December 2008, 12 February 2009). Consequently, state spending would need to be slashed, including a public service pay cut of 20 per cent and a freeze on promotions in the public sector. More alarming was the forecasted siphoning of funds out of the already fumbling education and health services.

Second, Ireland's troubles became even worse with the Central Bank announcement on 30 September 2010 that the Anglo Irish bailout would cost an additional €34 billion on top of the €23 billion already injected previously. The Central Bank also stated that AIB would need a further €3 billon in addition to the €7.4 billion already received (*Irish Times*, 30 September 2010).

Third, shortly before the December 2010 budget that targeted more cuts to social welfare and pensions, the Irish state agreed to a rescue package from the IMF and EU to the amount of €85 billion. Of this amount, €45 billion was loaned by the EU, €10 billion was earmarked towards further bank recapitalisation and €50 billion was targeted towards budgetary requirements over the next 4 years (*Irish Times*, 28 November 2010). The total interest payment for the package was estimated at €5.6 billion for 2011 alone.

Even though many EU states had to 'bail out' banks during the crisis, the Irish situation was particularly significant. Writing in 2009, Pagoulatos and Triantopoulos (2009: 47) contended that the overall bank support package was one of the highest in the EU as a percentage of GDP. Consolidated figures presented in June 2011 by Joaquin Almunia (Vice-President of the European Commission) confirm this point and demonstrate the almost shocking nature of the Irish situation in comparative perspective: 'Ireland's bank bailout has been by far the most expensive in the EU ... reaching 33 percent of GDP' where comparative figures for the Netherlands (with the second most costly bank bailout), Belgium and the UK were at 6.6, 5.4 and 4.4 per cent of GDP, respectively (*Irish Times*, June 18, 2011).

One of the leading economists in Ireland, and Governor of the Central Bank since 2009, Patrick Honohan (2009: 208), explains that '(t)he cause of the problem was classic: too much mortgage lending (financed by heavy foreign borrowing from the banks) into an unsustainable housing price and construction boom'. This statement is intriguing: if the problem was a 'classic' one, the consequences of the financial institutions' behaviour were foreseeable. Why, then, were they allowed to proceed?

Throughout the 1990s, and more so following the 1997 Asian financial crisis, many analysts had warned of the dangers of what was happening in the financial markets (Strange, 1998; Krugman, 2000; Stiglitz, 2002). Almost everyone agrees now that there was over-borrowing and under-saving in both the public and private sectors, and that the markets ran ahead much too far and too fast (Soros, 2008; Gamble, 2009). Bankers and traders were ingenious at creating new financial instruments – most famously the 'collateralised debt obligation' – that entailed the inextricable pooling of 'prime' and 'sub-prime' mortgages. While lending expanded and the asset price bubbles continued inflating, an expansive non-bank financial system (or 'shadow banking system') was effectively in operation, channelling vast amounts of largely fictional assets.[4] The majority of influential people in the financial markets, including their regulators, believed that the markets had become so sophisticated that they were able to price any risk, and adjust to any shock (Krugman, 2008: 139–152). As Gamble (2010: 6) put it, '[t]he complexity of the system and the fact that no one mind could grasp it or understand what was going on was held to be a virtue, because it meant that the order created by the markets was spontaneous and unplanned and all the more robust because of it'.

In contrast to the international markets, complexity of financial instruments does not seem to have been an important factor in the Irish case. Here, commentators locate the failure of regulators on two dimensions (Honohan, 2009; Connor *et al.*, 2010). On the one hand, banks became involved in large amounts of speculative loans, thereby increasing systemic risk. On the other hand, regulators turned two blind eyes to the banks' full accounting details.

On the first dimension, Honohan (2009: 209) argues that '... banks got caught up in the mass psychology of an unprecedented property bubble ... (and) began to increase the share of their assets in property related lending from less than 40 percent before 2002 to over 60 percent from 2006'. In order to explain this bubble, the impact of economic and monetary union entry on long-term interest rates is essential. Honohan (2009: 209–210) contends that being part of the eurozone

> ... really started the housing price surge by sharply lowering nominal and real interest rates, thereby lifting equilibrium asset prices ... The combination of higher population, higher income and lower actual and prospective mortgage interest rates clearly provided a straightforward upward shift in demand, i.e. the willingness and ability to pay for housing.

Low rates helped spur on demand, which subsequently saw an increase in construction, where '... house completions soared and, overall, the share of the growing workforce engaged in construction jumped from 7 percent in the early and mid-90s to over 13 percent by 2007 ...' (Honohan, 2009: 212).

The boom was effectively financed by high amounts of foreign borrowing by the banks, which themselves had no intention of 'tightening credit conditions as the prices rose' (Honohan, 2009: 212). Yet, recourse to foreign funds quickly diminished by early 2007 when 'foreign investors started dumping Irish bank shares because of the banks' heavy exposure to a property sector that had all the hallmarks of a bubble' (Ross, 2009: 83).

It has been widely known at least since the early 2000s that Ireland exhibited extreme house price inflation from 1996 onward and that such a development might have undesirable consequences for the economy as a whole (*The Economist*, 30 March–5 April 2002). Fears of 'negative equity' looming over new homeowners were discussed in Irish radio shows in 2003. Thus, the potential consequences of the way the market was allowed to develop were not at all unknown at a time when it would have still been possible to steer the ship around.

Turning to the second dimension, we have to ask what the Irish regulatory authorities did in order to identify whether or not Irish banks were placing themselves in a risky position. The answer is: not much. Irish regulators ignored simple but important warning signs of increased risk exposure, such as rapid balance sheet growth. For example, if an annual growth rate of 20 per cent is a threshold, Anglo Irish exceeded this at an average of over 35 per cent every year between 1998 and 2007 (Honohan, 2009: 217).

One tool regulators have at their disposal is stress tests aiming to model the condition of banks in an 'extreme but plausible' scenario. The problem in the Irish case is that it is not at all clear whether these analyses were ever carried out by the regulator regarding the massive loans to developers (Honohan, 2009: 219). The financial regulators apparently also overlooked strange loans from banks such as Anglo Irish. Connor *et al.* (2010: 15) argue that

> ... the regulatory regime for domestic Irish banks during the pre-crisis period was extremely weak and ineffective ... the only aggressive actions of the Irish Financial regulator seemed to be directed at media leaks; its relationship with the financial services sector was very accommodating and compliant. For example, for eight years, the board chairman and other Directors of Anglo Irish Bank hid very large personal loans by temporarily transferring them just prior to the accounting year-end to other banks complicit in the scheme and then by pre-agreement rolling the loans back into Anglo Irish immediately after the publication of the annual accounts. It is not yet clear whether the regulator approved, ignored or missed this subterfuge, but no regulatory action was taken.

By October 2008 – well into the crisis – the continued light-touch regulation meant that the regulators had effectively done nothing to regulate the sector. For example, there were no unannounced inspections of banks and no fines imposed for bad banking practises, such as overcharging clients (Ross, 2009: 81).

Why Did the Irish Regulators Fail to Act?

If the above helps us understand that the Irish Financial Regulator failed, then this section has as its main goal to elucidate the factors that explain this failure, expanding on Ross's (2009: 112–137) idea of the 'deadly triumvirate' of the banks, developers and the Fianna Fáil-led government. We do so by arguing that the third element of the triumvirate is not the party in power *per se*, but the role of the *state apparatus*, which includes the government in power, the regulatory authorities and the Central Bank. Figure 1 presents a schematic outline of the symbiotic relationship between banks, developers and the state apparatus. While the term 'symbiosis' historically has its roots in biology, the term 'symbiotic relationship' as used in this article refers to any interdependent or mutually helpful relationship between two actors; or, in common parlance, 'you scratch my back and I scratch yours'. The following three subsections will thus examine the symbiosis at play, focusing on the two main dimensions found in the different pairwise relationships.

The Symbiotic Relationship between the Banks and the State Apparatus

Historically there has been a close relationship between the banks and the state apparatus, in particular the Central Bank, highlighting the importance of elite integration. Ross points to the network of interests involved in financial policy, explaining that:

> Central bank directors had often moved comfortably onto the boards of commercial banks once their terms of office in the service of the state were over.

Professor James Meenan, an early Central bank Director, moved to the Bank of Ireland . . . [as did] Dr. Ken Whitaker and Professor Louden Ryan. At one point, the relationship between the regulator and the regulated was so close that there were instances of AIB and BoI directors sitting simultaneously on the board of the Central Bank. (Ross, 2009: 70–71)

Thus, historically, there has been a direct and strong relationship between finance capital and the state. This relationship has been facilitated and strengthened by a revolving door between senior positions within these institutions. Moreover, as Ross's observation highlights, agency capture has taken on an extreme form here, as the leaders of financial institutions have taken it upon themselves to man the Central Bank directly. Unlike in the UK and USA, common educational experience does not seem to play a major role in generating elite integration. To an extent, the size of Irish society would have made it likely that members of the elite all went to the same universities. University College Dublin has traditionally supplied most of the legal and to some extent civil service and political elite (especially in Fine Gael). Trinity College was less relevant because of its reputation as a Protestant university, and even to date not that many politicians have attended Trinity College Dublin. Finally, quite a high proportion of both the economic elite (self-made business people) and politicians would not have gone to university at all.

The result has been a historical lack of regulation of the sector by the Central Bank. For example, when banks were regulated by the Central Bank, they encouraged their clients to invest in offshore accounts in the Cayman Islands (referred to as Ansbacher accounts) in order to avoid having to pay tax. As Ross notes, this is something that senior Central Bank staff had known about since 1976 but did nothing about for years. When Central Bank investigators looked into the matter, they were surprised

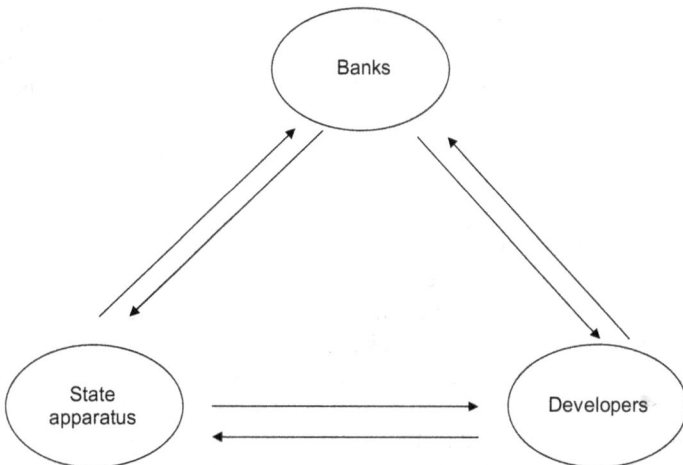

Figure 1.   The banks–state apparatus–developers triumvirate

to learn that an appointee on the Central Bank's board, Ken O'Reilly-Hyland, was actually on the Ansbacher list (Ross, 2009: 73). Rather than act on this, however, directors of the Central Bank had this information swept under the rug (Ross, 2009: 74).

The Central Bank's failure to regulate financial services adequately was also manifest after the Irish Financial Services Regulatory Authority (IFSRA) was set up in 2003. Like the Central Bank, this regulator was ineffective and did not show great interest in the levels of systematic risk. As a result, it did not instruct banks to reduce the volume of property loans. The regulator also failed to recommend ceilings to the exponentially growing salaries of bankers.

To understand this continuity we have to look back to when the IFRSA was established in 2003. From the point of inception, the new regulator shared the Central Bank's sympathy for bankers: IFRSA was never meant to be an 'independent agency' *per se* that was going to 'clean house'. One may even argue that it was really set up for 'optics'. As Ross argues, the 'new financial regulator was given limited autonomy' (Ross, 2009: 76) and the directors and board of the new regulator were a continuation of the Central Bank's leadership. For example, the Financial Regulator's first and second chief executives, Liam O'Reilly (2003–2006) and Patrick Neary (2006–2009), who rarely made any public appearances during their tenure, were former high-level officials in the Central Bank (Ross, 2009: 76–79).

This history must be understood as a path-dependent development of the Irish regulatory regime. As a result, the newly established IFSRA did not need to have been 'directly' captured. Rather, it had already started out 'captured' even before being established given dynamics in pre-existing institutions (particularly the Central Bank). A similar capture from birth applies to the encompassing Central Bank of Ireland, created in autumn 2010.[5]

Rather than being directly 'lobbied' by financial capital – and assuming that the regulators themselves were not 'on the take' and accepting (corrupt) bribes from the banks as there is no evidence for this to date – the regulators simply ignored doing their job both before and during the crisis. From this perspective, they were 'captured', but no one was strangling them to act in the interests of finance capital. This can in part be explained by the lack of outsiders beyond the Central Bank, let alone Ireland, who may have cared to monitor and police the banks any more strictly than the 'mother institute'.

Acting relatively autonomously in what it assumed was the interests of finance capital, the regulatory authority took an 'eye off the ball' approach to regulation, couching its behaviour as being reflective of a 'principles based approach' to regulation (*Irish Times*, 26 April 2010). This supports the structural dependence explanation. In the words of the second chief executive of IFSRA, Patrick Neary, the eye off the ball approach really meant that the regulator 'places responsibility for the proper management and control of a financial service provider, and the integrity of its systems, on the board of directors and its senior management' (Neary, 2007: 4). In other words, Neary believed that financial service providers were basically to regulate themselves. In his view, 'banks must assess the most appropriate stress tests and scenario analysis to be applied to their own exposures and operations. This approach is in line with best practice and ensures that proper risk assessment is conducted rather than a tick box approach' (Neary, 2007: 5).

In addition, there has been a close relationship between corporate actors and the main governing party in Ireland, Fianna Fáil, pointing to the importance of corporate lobbyists, as seen in party financing. For example, relying on data from the Standards in Public Office Commission, Byrne (2010) shows that 'Fianna Fáil received £10,000 in political donations from Anglo Irish Bank from 1999–2000 ...; [and] £10,000 from AIB in 1999 and £35,000 from Irish Life in 1998' (Byrne, 2010). However, these sums do not seem very significant compared with the benefits received by the state apparatus from tax revenues drawn from rapidly growing real estate and financial sectors.

In sum, there is evidence that the regulators acted as they did without being actively coaxed into doing so by financial capital. Unlike the Central Bank, which had been 'directly' influenced by capital when it regulated financial services, the experience of the new regulator saw this type of direct influence replaced by an 'indirect', or assumed, influence over time: by promoting self-regulation, the regulator acted in what it assumed were the interests of financial actors without these actors' direct participation. This means that private interests effectively captured the agency without any direct, tangible participation, thus benefiting from what we term 'hands-free regulatory capture'.

The Symbiotic Relationship between the State Apparatus and Developers

A first dimension of the symbiotic relationship between the state actors and developers becomes evident in the late 1990s, when the Fianna Fáil government brought in different tax rules that would encourage the building barrage from which developers benefited. As Ross explains, 'the taxes on profits from residential development land were ... halved to 20 percent, in 1998 and 1999 respectively' (Ross, 2009: 123). Further, alongside were special tax incentives for 'regeneration' schemes that 'allowed for up to 100 percent of the costs of construction of a building to be deducted from the owner's tax bill over a number of years' (Ross, 2009: 124). In more detail, in his report on the Irish banking crisis, Central Bank Governor Honohan (2010: 30–31) states that:

> ... the Government made extensive use of taxation incentives aimed at the construction sector. The rates of stamp duties, which were high, were lowered several times in recent years (in 2001, 2002, 2003, 2005, and 2007), sometimes with the aim of improving the affordability of housing to first time buyers ... In addition, different classes of construction investment have attracted sizeable income tax concessions extending over long periods. At the height of the boom, in 2004–06, schemes existed for ... buildings used for third level educational purposes ... [to] holiday cottages ...

Additionally, even though developers would directly benefit from the tax breaks, perhaps more significant for the state were the tax revenues that were generated given the thriving markets, pointing to the importance of state dependence in explaining the crisis. Throughout the early 2000s, stamp duty (property sales tax) revenues increased almost exponentially, as demonstrated by O'Leary (2006: 2). Having represented slightly less than 4 per cent of total revenues for the state in 1995, property-related taxes underwent a fourfold increase to 17 per cent at their peak in 2006.

A second dimension of the symbiotic relationship was that Irish developers shared close relationships with the main government party by way of party financing. Ross (2009) shows that several top builders during the economic boom were directly related to financing Fianna Fáil, something that is also demonstrated by McDonald and Sheridan (2009) in *The Builders*. This includes top property developers such as Sean Dunne, Bernard McNamara, Paddy McKillen (Clarendon Properties), Sean Mulryan (Ballmore Properties) and Seamus Ross (Menolly Homes; for more detail, see Ross, 2009: 113, 117). Developers' direct links with and donations to the party facilitated access to policymakers, leading to participation in a policy network that shaped the country's tax regime, with dramatic consequences. Once again, this points to the importance of the 'elite integration' explanation. Even though there are campaign financing limits and regulations, it is hard to say with certainty how much of this 'extra' financing was declared by the party. Nevertheless, Byrne's study of the records in the Standards in Public Office Commission's from 1997 to 2007 is illustrative in this regard: her data 'reveal 40 percent of Fianna Fáil's disclosed donations came from developers and construction-related donors' (Byrne, 2010). Thus, in addition to tax revenues, party donations played a considerable role in the symbiotic relationship between developers and the state apparatus.

The Symbiotic Relatiosnhip between the Banks and Developers

Irish banks gave massive volumes of (speculative) loans to developers, relying on heavy foreign borrowing. Such loans came not just from the effective duopoly of AIB and BoI in the Irish market; they included several others, such as Anglo Irish Bank and Irish Nationwide (Byrne, 2010). Manipulating their balance sheets, banks such as Anglo Irish had become perceived 'champions' in the sector in a relatively short period of time during the boom. 'The Banks, almost unchecked by the financial regulator, had embarked on a competitive lending frenzy. Anglo Irish led the way ...', but others such as BoI, AIB, Ulster Bank, Irish Nationwide and EBS 'all competed for the business of property developers' (Ross, 2009: 84). One particular constructor whose business all banks sought was Bernard McNamara, who has built a barrage of houses, hotels and car-parking lots (Ross, 2009: 125). The consequence of the appearance of solid performance in the sector resulted in inflated bonuses and seven-figure salaries.

Conversely, Irish developers become billionaires through the inflated property boom and invested further, fuelling in turn more business with banks. With increasing loans from banks, developers could build – and charge – as they saw fit. For

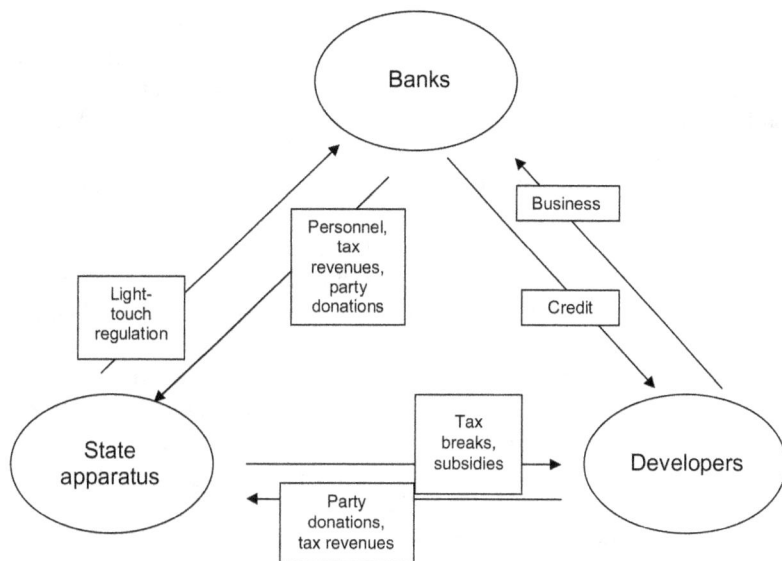

Figure 2. The nature of the symbiotic relationships among banks, state and developers

example, the country witnessed an incredible inflation of the cost of housing, with property prices doubling between 2000 and mid-2007, when it reached its peak. Of all areas in the country, Dublin witnessed the highest prices and hikes during the good days; and the sharpest fall during the slump.[6] From a comparative perspective with other countries in the world, real house prices in Ireland increased higher than in other states that saw considerable growth between 1997 and 2006: the UK, Spain, Sweden, France, Norway, Italy, Denmark, Finland and the USA (Glick & Lansing, 2010: 3). Prices in Ireland rose well over 170 index points on their scale (from 1997 levels) at its peak in 2006, compared with roughly 50 index points at its peak in 2006 in the USA (*ibid.*). Such staggering increases help put in comparative context the profits made by developers, landowners and estate agents in Ireland before the crisis.

We are now able to flesh out the symbiotic connections between the embers of the triumvirate that drove the political developments leading to the crisis in Ireland. Figure 2 summarises what each party provided for the other in this triangular relationship, which was mutually beneficial for the three main actor types involved but ultimately led to the near collapse of the entire Irish economy.

Discussion

Our analysis of the Irish experience of the financial and economic crisis in the context of global developments suggests that financial capital had a symbiotic relationship with the Irish state apparatus, as did developers. What does the analysis of this triangular symbiosis tell us about the explanatory capacities of the approaches described by Bernhagen and Chari in this issue? The initial relationship that set the foundation for the Irish version of the crisis, particularly the network between the Central Bank and financial capital before the IFSRA was set up, can best be understood in terms of the 'elite integration' approach. First, a revolving door between regulatory authorities and financial institutions has had high traffic volumes, leading to one-sided information about the health of financial institutions and perspectives on appropriate regulation. Second, donations from developers to politicians and parties, mainly Fianna Fáil, served to facilitate preferential access to policymakers. There is also some evidence of the importance of lobbying. The exchange-based nature of the symbiosis between the state and developers involves the state delivering an attractive tax regime for developers in return for both banks and developers financing parties. Thus, all three actors formed part of an institutionalised cluster, or network, of special interests within a given policy area.

Despite the relevance of the elite integration and lobbying approaches, however, it is important to note that when the financial regulator was set up it was never envisaged to provide independent regulation, given the historical ties between the Central Bank and financial capital. In other words, resulting from the historically close ties of state structures to the banks, the Irish financial regulator was 'captured' from the point of its inception. 'Hands-free regulatory capture' was manifest: banks did not need to participate much directly to create a regulator that acted in the interests of financial capital without the latter's direct participation. Furthermore, incessant construction and the banks' desire to lend to homebuyers (frequently offering 100 per cent financing) meant that financial markets were also essential in providing rapidly increasing tax revenues to the state. From this perspective, this experience also suggests, over time, the importance of the structural dependence on capital for understanding the crisis.

To be sure, bankers and developers may have genuinely believed that their activities were key to national wealth creation and that the universal financialisation of citizens through private homeownership and credit was also beneficial to consumers and homeowners who sought increased personal wealth during the boom. But what can be said of the argument that underlines the role of mass beliefs and preferences in society – are the people to blame? Many Irish citizens seem to accept readily the blame. So far, public anger about the pay cuts, dispossessions and rising unemployment has been remarkably restrained (*The Guardian*, 30 September 2010). The general mood that is cast in the media is that everyone has lived beyond their means while times where good – and now it is payback time. Martin Mansergh explained to *The Guardian* (30 September 2010) the public's stoicism with a mixture of fear and lack of a clear alternative:

> You can feel anger towards the developers, the bankers, but that doesn't provide a constructive solution. Most unions have advised their members: Don't rock the boat or we might all sink. I think the public understand that to protest will make the situation worse.

By contrast, Honohan (2010: 15–16) argues that:

> macroeconomic and budgetary policies contributed significantly to the economic overheating, relying to a clearly unsustainable extent on the construction sector and other transient sources for Government revenue (and encouraging the property boom via various incentives geared at the construction sector). This helped create a climate of public opinion which was led to believe that the party could last forever.

Regling and Watson (2010: 27) went on to say that:

> ... the Irish taxation system favours systematically, and more than in other EU countries, property and particularly home ownership. Ireland is one of very few countries where interest payments on mortgages can be deducted from income tax yet there is no property tax (which would provide a stable source of revenue for the public sector). While this approach narrowed – again – the tax base, it also interacted in a negative way with the emerging real estate bubble by giving additional incentives to households to invest in real estate.

These observations suggest that mass beliefs were neatly aligned with the ideology of the political and economic elites.

Finally, when turning to the varieties of capitalism approach, we note that the impact of the crisis in Ireland was as significant (perhaps even more so in terms of its long-term impact on the future of the country) as that suffered by liberal market economies (LMEs) such as the UK and the USA. However, the weakness of the explanation lies in the question of whether or not Ireland is in fact an LME or a coordinated market economy (CME). Although Hall and Soskice (2001: 20) claim that Ireland has features of an LME, its corporatist traditions with an institutionalised 'social partnership' since the late 1980s (which lasted until its recent debacle during the crisis in the later part of the first decade in the 2000s) means that it is difficult to classify Ireland as an LME. Certainly, in order to understand the crisis in Ireland, our evidence shows that institutions do matter; but it is not so much the institutional distinction between LMEs and CMEs that seems to have mattered here. Rather, the empirical information reviewed by us points to the integration between state actors and financial elite.

What lessons, and potential remedies, can be taken from this study? Students of Irish politics will no doubt be aware of those lessons highlighted by the Central Bank Governor (Honohan, 2010) or by Regling and Watson (2010) in their Report to the Commission of Investigation into the Banking Sector in Ireland. The latter call for 'the introduction of independent institutional sources for economic and fiscal projections ...' and also suggest that the 'light-touch' approach to regulation has to be abandoned (Regling & Watson, 2010: 43). Without doubt, the establishment of a truly independent body that promotes effective regulation as well as increased public surveillance is necessary. The question is just how likely a political scenario this is.

To address that question, this article has sought to identify some of the reasons why the crisis occurred: only if the political problems are identified can any lessons be translated into an unwavering resolve to pursue remedies to prevent this from happening again. While international factors of course played a role, one of the main reasons for the crisis in Ireland as seen in this article is 'home-grown', namely, the symbiotic relationships between the state, bankers and developers. The dynamics of all three symbiotic relationships highlighted the lack of transparency and accountability in Irish politics. With this in mind, one lesson to be learned is that as long as there are opaque networks operating relatively insulated from any serious form of scrutiny, poor decisions by political actors may be repeated. One remedy for this is to enact legislation that increases the public's knowledge of *who* is influencing government policy and regulatory bodies and their activity, and why, not simply after the fact but on a day-to-day basis. Lobbying legislation is seen in over 10 countries at present, and some of the countries that have enacted such legislation, such as Canada, were far less severely affected by the global financial and economic crisis (Chari *et al.*, 2007, 2010).

With appropriate regulation of interest representation, private actors seeking to influence either politicians or civil servants when economic and financial policy is made would have to register with an independent regulatory authority, fully disclose both individual and employer spending reports, and, if there are 'revolving-door' provisions, be banned from lobbying state institutions if the lobbyists were themselves politicians in their previous career. More importantly, such a registry would be open to the public who can then trace who is seeking to influence whom and with regard to which issues. Such a lobbyist registry may prevent those private actors with undue influence from exercising it in opaque networks; and it may eventually help politicians who are not necessarily performing in a transparent fashion from being re-elected. Although not a panacea, such a remedy would increase citizens' confidence in the political system, boost international investors' confidence in the economic system and, with a bit of luck, encourage the sun to rise, once again, over a Celtic Tiger in Ireland. Speculative bubbles are an inherent feature of capitalist economies (Kindleberger, 1989). To ensure that the next burst is a long time away and of limited proportions, a decrease of the social, economic and political influence of financial capital is needed.

Acknowledgements

A previous version of this paper was presented at the 60th Political Studies Association Annual Conference, 29 March–1 April 2010, Edinburgh, UK. The authors thank Heinz Brandenburg, Michael Gallagher, Brendan Howe, Eddie Hyland, Colm McKeogh, Laura Sudulich and Benigno Valdés for insightful comments as well as those civil servants and lobbyists consulted during the study who offered frank and honest comments in anonymity.

Notes

1. By 'state' we mean the various branches of government, regulatory authorities, government parties and the civil service.
2. For our overview of the global developments, we draw closely on Gamble (2009, 2010). For Ireland, we rely on recent accounts by Connor *et al.* (2010), Honohan (2009) and Ross (2009).
3. See http://www.ntma.ie/IrishEconomy/bankGuaranteeScheme.php
4. In early 2007, the combined assets of the five major US investment banks accounted for $4 trillion – or roughly 40 per cent of the total assets of the entire US banking system (Krugman, 2008: 161).
5. The Central Bank Reform Act, 2010, created a new single unitary body – the Central Bank of Ireland – to replace the previous related entities: the Central Bank, the Financial Services Authority of Ireland and the Financial Regulator.
6. For an analysis of the housing market in Ireland, see Department of the Environment, Heritage and Local Government (2009) as well as the graph that can be found on the Ireland After NAMA website: http://irelandafternama.files.wordpress.com/2009/12/new-house-prices-2000-092.jpg

References

Byrne, E. (2010) Blind optimism cannot hide that crisis is just starting, *Irish Times*, 5 January, available at: http://elaine.ie/?p=578 (accessed 6 October 2011).

Chari, R., Murphy, G. & Hogan, J. (2007) Regulating lobbyists: a comparative analysis of the US, Canada, Germany and the European Union, *Political Quarterly*, 78(3), pp. 422–438.

Chari, R., Hogan, J. & Murphy, G. (2010) *Regulating Lobbying: A Global Comparison* (Manchester: Manchester University Press).

Connor, G., Flavin, T. & O'Kelley, B. (2010) *Irish Economy Note No. 10 – The US and Irish Credit Crisis: Their Distinctive Differences and Common Features*, available at: http://www.irisheconomy.ie/Notes/IrishEconomyNote10.pdf (accessed 27 June 2011).

Department of Environment, Heritage and Local Government (2009) *Housing Market Overview 2009*, available at: http://www.environ.ie/en/Publications/StatisticsandRegularPublications/HousingStatistics/FileDownLoad,23310,en.pdf (accessed 29 June 2011).

Gamble, A. (2009) *The Spectre at the Feast: Capitalist Crisis and the Politics of Recession* (Basingstoke: Palgrave Macmillan).

Gamble, A. (2010) The political consequences of the crash, *Political Studies Review*, 8(1), pp. 3–14.

Glick, R. & Lansing, K. (2010) Global household leverage, house prices and consumption, *FRBSF Economic Letters 2010-01*, available at: http://www.frbsf.org/publications/economics/letter/2010/el2010-01.html (accessed 27 June 2011).

Hall, P. A. & Soskice, D. (Eds) (2001) *Varieties of Capitalism* (Oxford: Oxford University Press).

Honohan, P. (2009) Policy paper: resolving Ireland's banking crisis, *The Social and Economic Review*, 40(2), pp. 207–231.

Honohan, P. (2010) *The Irish Banking Crisis Regulatory and Financial Stability Policy 2003–2008: A Report to the Minister for Finance by the Governor of the Central Bank*, 31 May, available at: http://www.bankinginquiry.gov.ie (accessed 6 October 2011).

Kindleberger, C. P. (1989) *Manias, Panics and Crashes: A History of Financial Crises* (New York: Basic Books).

Krugman, P. (2000) *The Return of Depression Economics* (New York: Norton).

Krugman, P. (2008) *The Return of Depression Economics and the Crisis of 2008* (London: Allen Lane).

MacDonald, F. & Sheridan, K. (2009) *The Builders* (Dublin: Penguin).

Neary, P. (2007) A principles led approach to regulation – striking the right balance while regulating over 10,000 firms in the financial sector. Paper presented at the *Public Affairs Ireland, Regulating Ireland Conference*, 16 July, available at: http://www.financialregulator.ie/press-area/speeches/Pages/AddressbyPatrickNearyChiefExecutiveFinancialRegulatorRegulatingIrelandConference.aspx (accessed December 2010).

O'Leary, D. (2006) *Goodbody Stockbrokers Irish Economic Commentary, Economics, Q4, 2006*, available at: http://www.finfacts.ie/biz10/ForgingAhead.pdf (accessed 27 June 2011).

Pagoulatos, G. & Triantopoulos, C. (2009) The return of the Greek patient, *South European Society and Politics*, 14(1), pp. 35–54.

Regling, K. & Watson, M. (2010) *A Preliminary Report on the Sources of Ireland's Banking Crisis*, 31 May, available at: http://www.bankinginquiry.gov.ie (accessed 6 October 2011).

Ross, S. (2009) *The Bankers: How the Banks Brought Ireland to Its Knees* (Dublin: Penguin).

Soros, G. (2008) *The New Paradigm for Financial Markets: The Credit Crisis of 2008 and What It Means* (London: Public Affairs).

Stiglitz, J. E. (2002) *Globalization and its Discontents* (New York: W.W. Norton).

Strange, S. (1998) *Mad Money* (Manchester: Manchester University Press).

Why Vote-seeking Parties May Make Voters Miserable

MICHAEL LAVER
New York University, USA

ABSTRACT *This paper explores an unexpectedly hard question for representative democracy, which is usually thought to be enhanced when political parties compete with each other for the support of voters in free and fair elections. Defining optimal representation in terms of the probability that a voter will find a party to support at election time that promotes a policy position close to his/her ideal point, it transpires that vote-seeking parties do not deliver optimal representation. They tend to locate 'too close' to the centroid of voter ideal points to minimize the aggregate distance between party positions and voter ideal points. Instead, optimal representation in this sense will be delivered if parties set policy positions using 'aggregator' rules, which seek to represent the views of current party supporters, but not to attract new supporters. One policy implication is that the representativeness of inter-party politics is increased by enhancing the representativeness of intra-party politics.*

Overview

Working definitions of democracy in real countries typically include a requirement for regular 'competitive' elections. Working definitions of real competitive elections cover many matters, including the probity of election officials, the franchise, access by prospective candidates to the ballot, regulation of political financing and information flows, the drawing of district boundaries and the formula used to convert votes cast into seats won. If all of these matters are in order, then the presumption is that the preferences of the (typically huge) set of people who vote in elections will be well-represented by the (typically small) set of public representatives who are elected.

In this paper, I show that this may not be the case. Specifically, while the notion of 'well-represented' preferences is vague and subjective, I show that elections contested by vote-seeking parties typically do *not* result in a set of public representatives with policy positions that generate an *optimal* representation, specified precisely below, of voters' ideal policy positions. Following from this, I identify an internal decision-making regime for political parties that does indeed imply such an optimal representation.

My argument is constructed as follows. First, I specify a voter utility function and then use results from a subfield of geometry that deals with what are called Voronoi tessellations to identify the 'optimal representation' of a larger set of points (on my interpretation voters' ideal points) by a smaller number of representative points (on my interpretation representatives' policy positions). Second, I draw on a computational model of multiparty competition in multidimensional policy spaces to show that there is one, and only one, internal party decision-making rule for setting party policy such that, if all parties use this rule, then the configuration of party policy positions that emerges from party competition generates an optimal representation of voter ideal points. This is the Aggregator rule, specified in the context of spatial models of party competition by Laver and explored in depth by Laver and Sergenti (Laver, 2005; Laver & Sergenti, 2012). Aggregators always set party policy at the centroid of the ideal points of their *current* supporters; *they make no attempt to win new supporters*. Thus, when vote-seeking parties who continually seek new supporters are involved in party competition, the configuration of party policy positions that typically emerges from competitive elections will not be optimal, in this strict but intuitively meaningful sense. In a nutshell, we only expect competitive elections to generate optimal representations of voter ideal points if all parties contesting the elections are *internally* 'democratic', in the sense that they focus exclusively on representing the preferences of their current supporters. Perhaps counter-intuitively, we do not expect competition between vote-seeking parties to result in an optimal representation of voters' preferences.

Optimal Representations of Voters' Preferences

Voter Utility Functions

The argument in this paper is set in the context of the vast intellectual project, inspired by the work of Hotelling and Downs, of building spatial models of party competition (Hotelling, 1929; Downs, 1957). There is no space here to review this enormous body of work; Adams *et al.* provide an excellent survey, while Austen-Smith and Banks offer a comprehensive technical treatment (Austen-Smith & Banks, 2000, 2005; Adams *et al.*, 2005). One common assumption about voters in such models, including the seminal models of Downs and Hotelling, is that they use a 'proximity' rule when deciding which candidate to support. This implies that voters care only about their own policy preferences, have an 'ideal' policy position and support the candidate whose declared policy position is closest to their own ideal position.

Being more precise about this involves defining a voter utility function. In what follows, I assume a very simple utility function in widespread use by scholars who specify Downsian spatial models of party competition. Voter utility for any candidate is assumed to be an inverse function of the distance between the voter's ideal point and the candidate's policy position. Specifically, I assume the utility $U(i, j)$ of a policy at j for a voter with an ideal point at i is:

$$U(i, j) = -d(i, j)^2$$

The expression $d(i, j)$ stands for the Euclidean distance between i and j. The quadratic form of this voter loss function, typically held to encode risk-aversion among voters, is the most commonly used and convenient, but the argument in this paper also follows through if linear rather than quadratic policy loss is assumed. Humphreys and Laver have recently shown that key theoretical results are affected by assuming voters' perceived policy distances should be measured using the city block metric, as opposed to making the orthodox Euclidean assumption (Humphreys & Laver, 2009). In the context of the current argument, I take this as a point to be explored in future work.

Voronoi Tessellations

The problem of analyzing multiparty competition in a multidimensional policy space is a realization of a much more general class of problems of 'competitive spatial location'. These belong to a subfield of geometry that deals with 'tiling' or 'tessellation'. This is most easily seen using an example.

Figure 1 shows the Irish party system in 2003. Party positions on the horizontal axis concern economic policy (left to right in the conventional sense); those on the

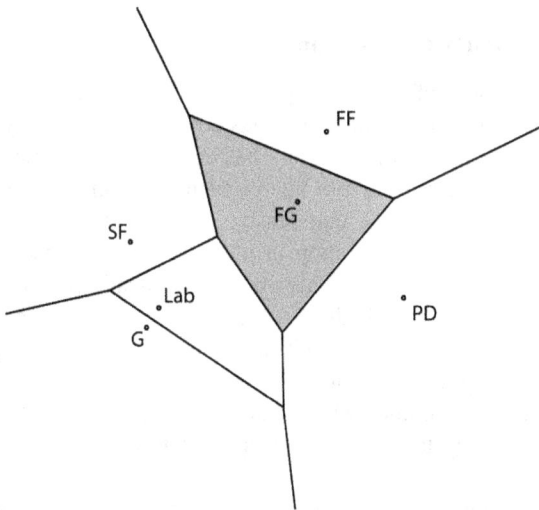

Figure 1. Voronoi tessellation of the Irish party positions, c2003
Note: This and all other figures in this paper are adapted from Laver and Sergenti (2011).

vertical axis concern the liberal (bottom) versus conservative (top) dimension of social policy. These positions are derived from an expert survey (Benoit & Laver, 2003, 2006). The parties are: Fianna Fáil (FF); Fine Gael (FG); Progressive Democrats (PD); Labour (Lab); Greens (G); and Sinn Féin (SF). The shaded region around FG shows where we will find the ideal points of Fine Gael voters who use a proximity rule; ideal points in this region are closer to FG than to any other party policy position. Similar regions around FF, PD, Lab, G and SF show potential locations for the ideal points of proximity voters for these parties. Each line in the figure bisects a line between two party policy positions. The set of lines generates a tiling, or tessellation, of the space into regions. Each region has a generating point and every locus in the region is closer to that region's generating point than to any other generating point. The result is a Voronoi tessellation of the space.[1]

Note that the generating points (e.g. Lab, G and SF in Figure 1) need not be, and indeed typically are not, at the center of their Voronoi regions. There is, however, a special sort of Voronoi tessellation, known as a centroidal Voronoi tessellation (CVT), such that each generating point is at the centroid of its Voronoi region, the point that minimizes the sum of the squared distances between itself and all other points in the region. Du *et al.* define an 'optimal representation' of the space as one minimizing aggregate quadratic (or linear) distances between all points in the space and their closest generating point. They show that a set of generating points that is in a CVT is an optimal representation in this sense (Du *et al.*, 1999). This tells us that the representativeness of any configuration of party policy positions is maximized when party positions are in a CVT.

Decision Rules for Party Competition

Although spatial models of party competition have been subjected to extensive analytical investigation, little of this work has concerned multiparty competition in multidimensional policy spaces. Even less has concerned dynamic versions of this problem. Results derived by scholars interested in the computational geometry of Voronoi tessellations show that one reason for this is that the more general problem of competitive spatial location in multidimensional spaces is analytically intractable (Teramoto *et al.*, 2006). There is no analytically provable best response strategy in any given situation. If this problem is intractable for analysts it is also intractable for real human agents. This in turn means that real people making decisions in multiparty competition must rely on informal decision heuristics, decision-making rules-of-thumb, which can in practice be very effective but can never be proven formally to be the best responses to any conceivable state of the world.

There has been extensive research into decision rules used by real humans faced with another classic intractable decision problem, the Travelling Salesmen Problem (TSP), which sets agents the task of finding the shortest route that visits all of an arbitrary number of arbitrarily located cities. Despite its intractability, many real humans quickly come up with very good solutions to particular realizations of the TSP, even if these solutions are not strictly optimal.[2] The TSP is thus used in experiments designed to investigate how real humans make decisions in intractable settings (Dry *et al.*, 2006). In such settings, different real humans typically use different decision rules to tackle the same intractable problem, and may well come up with quite different solutions to it (MacGregor*et al.*, 2006). This implies that different real humans are likely to use different decision rules when approaching the intractable problem of setting party policy positions in multiparty competition in a multidimensional policy space.

Laver and Sergenti specified a variety of decision rules for choosing party policy positions in this setting and investigated the interaction of these rules in extensive computational work (Laver & Sergenti, 2012). One of the decision rules they specified was 'Sticker' – never change position. Three families of decision rules, each with a wide range of parameterizations, were focused in increasing party vote shares. These were Hunter (a Pavlovian rule that reacts to rewards and punishments), Predator (which attacks other parties with higher vote shares) and Explorer (a hill-climbing rule that explores a local neighborhood for higher vote shares).[3] A fifth family of decision rules specified by Laver and Sergenti was Aggregator (move party policy to the centroid of the ideal points of your current supporters). Aggregator rules model parties that are concerned exclusively with satisfying current members as best they can, and are not concerned at all with winning votes. Unsurprisingly, but crucially for my current argument, Aggregator rules are relatively ineffective at vote maximization; they are after all not programmed to do this. Thus, parties using the Aggregator rule will tend not to prosper in evolutionary settings where fitness is denominated in vote shares.

One important finding in computational geometry is that a method called Lloyds Algorithm is very effective at finding the (CVTs), which, as we have seen, are optimal representations of the set of voter ideal points (Lloyd, 1982). Lloyds Algorithm involves starting with a random scatter of generating points and then moving one generating point at a time to the centroid of its own Voronoi region. As the process is iterated continuously in a dynamic system, the configuration of generating points always converges on a steady-state CVT. The crucial implication of this for my argument is that the implementation of Lloyds Algorithm is identical to a dynamic process of party competition in which all parties use an Aggregator rule, each party constantly adapting and readapting, using this rule, to policy movements made by the other parties. We thus know from Lloyds Algorithm, as well as from extensive computational work conducted by Laver and Sergenti (2012), that party competition in a system in which all parties use the Aggregator rule, in which all move their policy positions to the centroid of their current supporters' ideal points, will result in a steady-state configuration of party positions that is a CVT and thus an optimal representation of the space. This is not true when parties use other internal decision rules, for example vote-seeking rules, for setting party policy positions.

Why does Competition between Vote-seeking Parties Result in Suboptimal Social Welfare?

My core theoretical argument is now established, though it does of course come with many *caveats*. The most important of these concern voter utility, which has been specified as deriving entirely from Downsian proximity voting. Downsian proximity voters get utility from supporting their closest party at election time; the closer this party, they better they like it. Voters are not, for example, assumed to get utility from any non-policy 'valence' attribute of the various candidates on offer (Stokes, 1963; Ansolabehere & Snyder, 2000; Groseclose, 2001; Aragones & Palfrey, 2004; Schofield, 2008); neither are individual voters assumed to be trying to influence the partisan composition of the government that forms after the election (Kedar, 2009). On Downsian proximity voting assumptions, voters are more satisfied if they find parties to support at election time that offer policies relatively close to their ideal points, and less satisfied if this is not the case. In this particular sense, we can see that, *for a given number of parties*, the voting population as a whole will be happiest when all parties use the Aggregator rule for setting party policy. When this happens, party policy positions in a dynamic party system evolve into a CVT; and, when party positions are in a CVT, we know that this is an optimal representation of voter ideal points.

When parties do not all use the Aggregator rule, and in particular when some parties use vote-seeking rules, we expect the representation of voters' ideal points to be suboptimal. The substantive reason for this was presaged by Downs's original results predicting the convergence of parties in a one-dimensional two-party system. Vote-seeking parties tend to locate 'too close' to the center of the policy space to generate an optimal representation of voter ideal points. In the classical one-dimensional Downsian spatial model, for example, it is well known that competition between two vote-seeking parties leads them to adapt their policy positions in a manner that causes them to converge, all else equal, on the ideal point of the median voter. This is far from an optimal representation of voter ideal points which, as it happens in this setting given the utility function specified above and a normal distribution of voter ideal points, would place parties at about -0.8 and $+0.8$ standard deviations from the mean voter ideal point.[4]

Laver and Sergenti (2012) define party system representativeness in terms of the mean utility of all voters. They specify voter utility as above, as the negative quadratic distance between the ideal point of each voter and his or her closest party, and denominate policy distances in terms of standard deviations of the distribution of voter ideal points. The maximum possible value of party system representativeness is zero, though this can happen only if there is a party with a policy position at the ideal point of every voter. Representativeness, thus measured, becomes more negative as party positions diverge from voter ideal points. Figure 2 reports results from computational work by Laver and Sergenti (2012), showing benchmark results for party systems that are exogenously specified as having a fixed number

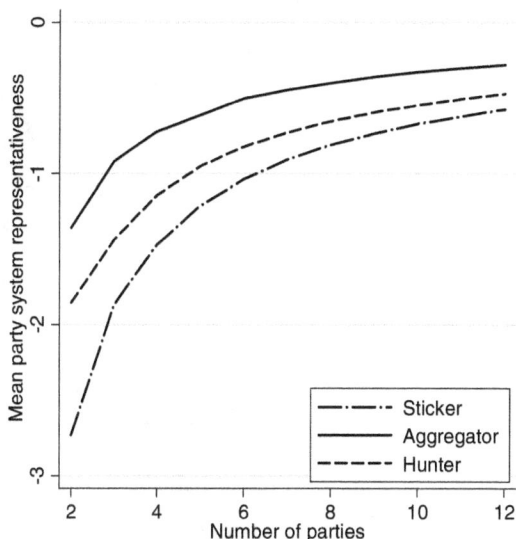

Figure 2. Party system representativeness, by number of parties and party decision rule

of political parties (between two and 12), all parties using the same decision rule. It thus shows the evolved representativeness of 33 different party systems, 11 each for all-Aggregator, all-Sticker and all-Hunter systems.

The solid line shows the representativeness of the all-Aggregator party systems. Recall that we know from Lloyds Algorithm that this line thus also plots the optimal level of representativeness that can be achieved in party systems of differ-ent sizes. The central dashed line plots the typical representativeness of party systems in which all parties use the vote-seeking Hunter rule. The results are crisp, informative and statistically significant at a very high level of confidence. All-Aggregator party systems of any size evolve to have configurations of party positions that are substantially more representative than all-Hunter or all-Sticker systems of equivalent size.

Laver and Sergenti (2012) define policy 'eccentricity' as the distance of any policy position from the centroid of voter ideal points, again measuring distance in terms of standard deviations of the distribution of voter ideal points. Figure 3 reports their computational finding that parties in all-Aggregator systems typically choose much more eccentric policy positions than the vote-seeking parties in all-Hunter systems, which tend to locate much closer to the center of the policy space. Lloyds Algorithm tells us that the solid line plots the mean eccentricity of policy positions in a CVT – in other words, the mean eccentricity of party policy positions when these optimally rep-resent voter ideal points. Crudely speaking, vote-seeking rules such as Hunter tend to locate parties too close to the center of the policy space to achieve an optimal rep-resentation of voter ideal points.

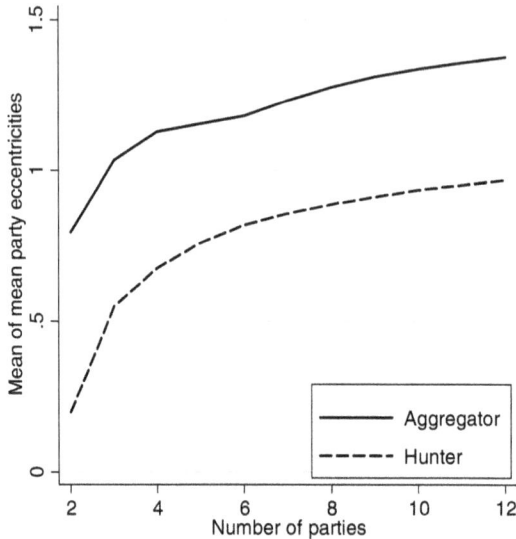

Figure 3. Mean party policy eccentricity, by number of parties and party decision rule

Engineering Enhanced Social Welfare in Competitive Elections

More Parties

The upward-sloping curves in Figure 2 show us that, regardless of the decision rule party leaders use to set their party's policy position, the more parties there are, the more representative is the evolved configuration of party policy positions. Even though all-Aggregator party systems tend to be significantly more representative than all-Hunter systems *of the same size*, party systems with five Hunters, for example, tend to be significantly more representative than those with two Aggregators. Axiomatically, for any *n*-party system, adding a new party and holding everything else constant will make the configuration of party positions more representative, unless the new party takes a position identical to that of some existing party. Crudely, the more parties there are, the more possible it is for party positions to be distributed around the distribution of voter ideal points, thereby pleasing more voters.

The number of parties is never fixed exogenously in real democratic party systems. Indeed, it is integral to many working definitions of democracy that new parties can enter the fray and compete at will if the demand arises. The net result is that the number and identity of competing parties is an *endogenous output of party competition*, not an exogenously determined input. All party systems have thresholds, some formal and some informal, that set the minimum vote share necessary for continued representation in the legislature. Even the very permissive Dutch system of representative democracy with the list-PR electoral system used with a single national constituency with 150 seats, for example, has a formal threshold of $1/150 = 0.67$ per cent of the vote before a party can win a single seat in the legislature. Many representative thresholds are, however, *de facto* rather than *de jure*. For example, any number of parties can compete in a national election with a single member plurality electoral formula, but, if votes are in practice distributed more or less evenly around the country, only two parties will tend to be represented in the legislature. Looking at things from a completely different perspective, partisan control of the media of mass communication, or particular regimes for political finance, may make it very difficult for more than a few parties to get their messages across.

Laver and Sergenti (2012), who model party systems with endogenous parties, assume that each party system has a *de facto* threshold that takes account of the many different factors that might limit the number of competing parties. A party system with a *de facto* 20 per cent threshold, for example, is axiomatically constrained to have at most five parties, but this can happen only if all parties are of absolutely equal size. When parties vary in size the number of real parties may be considerably less than this.

Figure 4 shows results from computational work by Laver and Sergenti (2012) on endogenous parties systems in which parties 'die' when they fall below the *de facto* threshold and new parties are 'born' into the party system at spatial locations ill-served by existing parties, in this application choosing their decision rules at random from a predefined set of possibilities.[5] This sets up a simple evolutionary system in which party leaders may use different decision rules, but where parties using decision rules that keep them over the threshold are more likely to survive. The top panel of Figure 4 shows the relationship between the *de facto* threshold and the total number of surviving parties, as well as the number of parties using Aggregator and Hunter rules. The upper dotted line shows that a *de facto* threshold of 0.10 of the total vote typically implies between five and six surviving parties,[6] whereas a threshold of 0.15 tends to imply about four parties. As we saw in Figure 2, the number of parties affects the representativeness of the evolved configuration of party positions. Given the effect of the *de facto* threshold on the number of surviving parties, this means that the *de facto* threshold has a direct effect on the representativeness of the evolved party system; this is shown in the clearest possible terms in the bottom panel of Figure 4. Lower *de facto* survival thresholds imply more representative party systems; higher thresholds imply less representative systems.

This is relevant to the extent it is possible to engineer the *de facto* survival threshold in any competitive party system. The electoral formula can be changed, as can district magnitude; these two factors, *ceteris paribus*, very directly affect the threshold in any real party system. Campaign finance laws, or the regulation of political broadcasting, can be made friendlier to small parties. If these changes have the effect of lowering the *de facto* threshold, they should tend to increase the number of surviving parties and thereby to increase the representativeness of the typical evolved configuration of party policy positions.

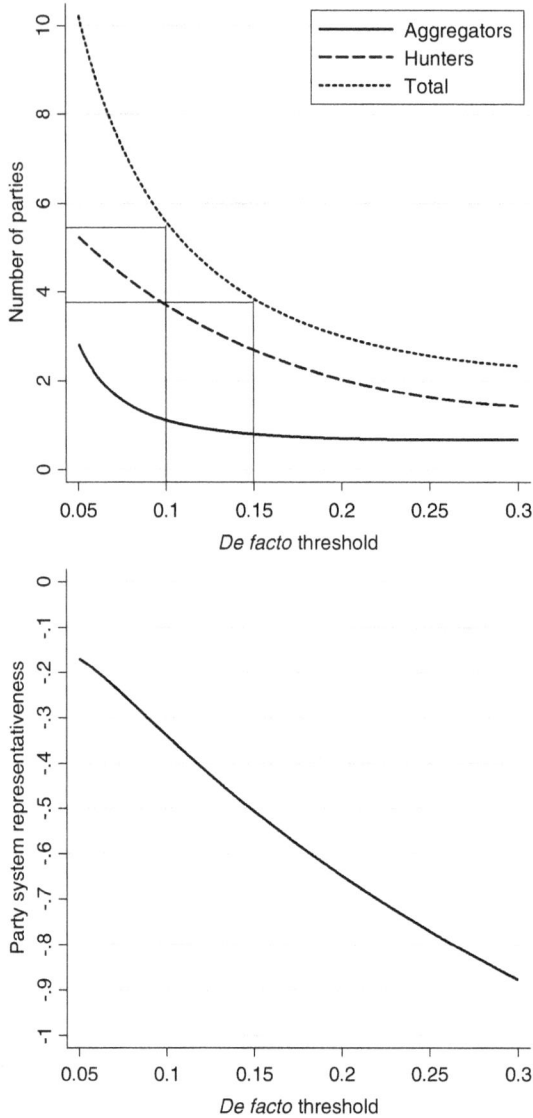

Figure 4. Mean number of surviving parties, by *de facto* threshold and party decision rule

More Internal Party Democracy

The top panel of Figure 4 also shows that, in the competitive environment under investigation, parties using the Aggregator rule, which is not programmed to seek more votes, have significantly lower survival prospects than parties using the vote-seeking Hunter rule. The typical number of surviving Aggregators is therefore significantly less than the typical number of surviving Hunters – lowering the representativeness of the evolved configuration of party policy positions. Competition between parties using different decision rules tends to favor parties using vote-seeking rules, to the detriment of parties using more internally 'democratic' decision rules. If a situation could be brought about in which all parties use Aggregator rules, then representativeness of the party system would be enhanced. More generally, legislation to make *intra*-party politics more democratic might, other things equal, generate dynamic systems of *inter*-party competition that result in emergent configurations of party policy positions that better reflect the preferences of ordinary voters. While this might conflict with other aspects of working definitions of democracy that stress principles of freedom of association, and might therefore be taken to imply non-intervention in the internal workings of political parties, forcing parties to privilege the preferences of their current supports over those potential future supporters should, other things equal, result in more 'representative' party competition.

In the End

The arguments in this paper offer a new angle on what it might take to engineer representative democracy, interpreting representation in terms of the likelihood that voters are able to vote for parties with policy positions that are relatively close to their own ideal points. In the extreme, it is easy to see that, if the institutional arrangements are such that nearly all voters typically hate all of the policy party positions that are put before them at election time, then the resulting election is in some sense less 'democratic' than one in which nearly all voters can find some party policy position that is close to their own personal preferences. More generally, we might feel that the more 'democratic' elections are, the more likely it is that the typical voter is offered some policy position that he/she would like to support. The paradox highlighted here is that vote-seeking party competition, whereby parties continuously seek policy positions that appeal to voters who do not currently support them, is not necessarily the most 'democratic' in this sense. Voters as a whole may be better served by sets of parties who pay special attention to the views of their *current* supporters rather than tirelessly seeking *new* supporters.

The bottom line is that, if we are interested in representative democracy, we should not confine ourselves to considering whether arrangements for *inter*-party politics meet certain specified 'democratic' criteria. We should also pay attention to whether arrangements for *intra*-party politics lead to evolved configurations of party policy positions that tend to make voters happy.

Notes

1. Named after the Russian mathematician Georgy Voronoi (1868–1908); a student of Andrey Markov.
2. By 'very good' in this context we mean solutions with a route length for the salesman that is close to that of the optimal route for a particular solved case.

3. Laver and Sergenti (2012) provide formal definitions of these rules, and computer code for implementing them.
4. Author's calculation.
5. The possibilities were Hunter, Aggregator and Sticker. Other work by Laver and Sergenti endogenizes rule reproduction probabilities as a function of the past success of each rule, for a much-expanded set of decision rules.
6. Other party system parameters, discussed by Laver and Sergenti (2012), also have a significant effect on the number of surviving parties. The scale of such effects, however, is nowhere near as large as that of the survival threshold, shown in Figure 4.

References

Adams, J. F., Merrill, S. & Grofman, B. (2005) *A Unified Theory of Party Competition: A Cross-national Analysis Integrating Spatial and Behavioral Factors* (Cambridge: Cambridge University Press).

Ansolabehere, S. & Snyder, J. M. (2000) Valence politics and equilibrium in spatial election models, *Public Choice*, 103, pp. 327–336.

Aragones, E. & Palfrey, T. (2004) The effect of candidate quality on electoral equilibrium: an experimental study, *American Political Science Review*, 98, pp. 77–90.

Austen-Smith, D. & Banks, J. S. (2000) *Positive Political Theory I: Collective Preference* (Ann Arbor, MI: University of Michigan Press).

Austen-Smith, D. & Banks, J. S. (2005) *Positive Political Theory II: Strategy and Structure* (Ann Arbor, MI: University of Michigan Press).

Benoit, K. & Laver, M. (2003) Estimating Irish party policy positions using computer wordscoring: the 2002 election – a research note, *Irish Political Studies*, 18, pp. 97–107.

Benoit, K. & Laver, M. (2006) *Party Policy in Modern Democracies* (London: Routledge).

Downs, A. (1957) *An Economic Theory of Democracy* (New York: Harper).

Dry, M., Lee, M. D., Vickers, D. & Hughes, P. (2006) Human performance on visually presented traveling salesperson problems with varying numbers of nodes, *Journal of Problem Solving*, 1, pp. 20–31.

Du, Q., Faber, V. & Gunzburger, M. (1999) Centroidal Voronoi tessellations: applications and algorithms, *Society for Industrial and Applied Mathematics Review*, 41, pp. 637–676.

Groseclose, T. (2001) A model of candidate location when one candidate has a valence advantage, *American Journal of Political Science*, 45, pp. 862–886.

Hotelling, H. (1929) Stability in competition, *The Economic Journal*, 39, pp. 41–57.

Humphreys, M. & Laver, M. (2010) Spatial models, cognitive metrics, and majority voting equilibria, *British Journal of Political Science*, 40, pp. 11–30.

Kedar, O. (2009) *Voting for Policy, not Parties: How Voters Compensate for Power Sharing* (New York: Cambridge University Press).

Laver, M. (2005) Policy and the dynamics of political competition, *American Political Science Review*, 99, pp. 263–281.

Laver, M. & Sergenti, E. (2012) *Party Competition: An Agent-based Model* (Princeton, NJ: Princeton University Press).

Lloyd, S. P. (1982) Least squares quantization in PCM, *IEEE Transactions on Information Theory*, 28, pp. 129–137.

MacGregor, J. N., Chronicle, E. P. & Ormerod, T. C. (2006) A comparison of heuristic and human performance on open versions of the traveling salesperson problem, *Journal of Problem Solving*, 1, pp. 33–43.

Schofield, N. (2008) *The Spatial Model of Politics* (London: Routledge).

Stokes, D. E. (1963) Spatial models of party competition, *American Political Science Review*, 57, pp. 368–377.

Teramoto, S., Demaine, E. & Uehara, R. (2006) Voronoi game on graphs and its complexity, *2nd IEEE Symposium on Computational Intelligence and Games*, Reno, NV, pp. 265–271.

What Gives Politics Such a Bad Name?

HEINZ BRANDENBURG
University of Aberdeen, Scotland

ABSTRACT   *This paper discusses the erosive impact of a shift from a politics of conflict, of polarised partisan representation to valence politics, a politics of performance, delivery and widespread policy consensus in advanced Western democracies. It is argued that consensus politics undermines the structuring role of political parties in the representation of societal conflict and hence results in diminishing interest, intensity and respect for politicians, parties and parliaments. It points towards a political rather than a sociological explanation of declining political trust.*

Introduction

> Why the politician should be so often condemned, so seldom praised, is not difficult to discern in some of his roles, but in others the reasons for his unpopularity are more elusive and, possibly, instructive. (Lundberg, 1968: 15)

David Easton argued over 35 years ago that '[p]olitical discontent is not always, or even usually, the signal for basic political change' (Easton, 1975: 436). In a way, that statement can serve well to characterise the current trend in political disaffection in advanced Western democracies, which is spreading but shows little signs of threatening order or indeed breeding rebellion against democratic regimes;[1] but while at face value Easton's statement seems to fit the current trend of unthreatening discontent, this trend tellingly defies Easton's core distinction between specific and diffuse support. Easton argued that specific support is related to 'satisfactions that members of a system feel they obtain from the perceived outputs and performance of the political authorities' (Easton, 1975: 437) and specified that such support is 'object-specific'. Any dissatisfaction with current office holders would constitute discontent that remains unthreatening and unlikely to breed rebellion in the continuing presence of what he described as 'diffuse support', i.e. general, long-term trust in the system and perceived legitimacy of the regime.

I think a strong argument can be made that current trends in growing discontent are not limited to declining specific support but actually characterised by significant erosion in diffuse support. However, instead of rebellion that erosion of trust breeds nothing but contempt.

Of course, Easton himself, while emphasising that what he called 'alienation' should be treated as conceptually different and separate from diffuse support, did proclaim a causal relationship between the two, arguing that certain elements of alienation (powerlessness, normlessness, meaninglessness and isolation) can be both causes and consequences of declining trust and legitimacy (Easton, 1975: 455–457). In general, however, he understood alienation as a melange of disparate frustrations that does not, even if widespread, suffice to undermine systematically the support for democratic institutions. However, what we are currently witnessing in advanced Western democracies questions his assertion that in the long run only an accumulated 'reserve of goodwill' can enable a regime to sustain itself (Easton, 1975: 445). That is why he insisted on the notion of 'support': because it is a concept that bridges from the attitudinal domain into the behavioural. Any serious withdrawal of support for democratic institutions would render these institutions not just disliked but essentially unsustainable.

But what if democratic institutions were now on the verge of becoming increasingly unsupported while remaining perfectly sustainable? Peter Mair (2006: 25) spoke about an emerging 'notion of democracy that is being steadily stripped of its popular component – democracy without a demos', and to a large extent this article shares much with Mair's analysis. At its core his argument was that

> parties are failing as a result of a mutual withdrawal, whereby citizens retreat into private life or more specialized and often *ad hoc* forms of representation, while party leaderships retreat into institutions, drawing their terms of reference ever more readily from their roles as governors or public-office holders. The traditional world of party democracy – as a zone of engagement in which citizens interacted with their political leaders – is being evacuated. (Maie, 2006: 33)

In the following, I put forward the related argument that what we are witnessing is best characterised as spreading contempt for politics, and that it is a popular response to a significant decline in the representative and ideological function of political parties – a gradual downgrading of feelings towards democratic politics that is a response to the downgrading of partisan polarization and politics in general in modern democratic governance.

What is Political Trust?

If one reads Lundberg's (1968) book *Politicians and Other Scoundrels* from which the introductory quote to this article is taken and which collates examples of the not so fine art of politics and politician-bashing by philosophers and intellectuals through the ages, one wonders not so much why the public has lost trust in politicians and the political system in advanced democracies, but rather why there had ever been higher levels of trust in the first place.

That trust in politicians and confidence in political institutions has declined over recent decades has been documented most comprehensively by Dalton (2004: 25–31, 34–41), who uses various data sources (from national election studies to world values surveys) to show that over recent decades the public in most if not all Western democracies has come to distrust politicians, lose confidence in political institutions and be disenchanted about how the democratic system works (Dalton, 2004: 39–41).[2] There are of course some dissenting voices, challenging the idea of a systematic time trend indicating growing dissatisfaction with politics (Clarke et al., 2004, Norris, 2011). However, apart from remaining questions about the reliability of the data used in these cases,[3] the overwhelming picture from the literature is one that indicates a serious problem (see summary in Norris, 2011: Ch. 1). Corroborating evidence also comes from increasingly apparent trends in declining turnout across established democracies (see Mair, 2006). There are of course substantial differences in trends between countries, with some, most notably the UK, appearing at the one extreme where trust and turnout have been declining most rapidly, while some Scandinavian countries show at best modest levels of declining trust. Interestingly, Ireland, otherwise often seen as an outlier in modern electoral politics (especially where cleavage systems are concerned), emerges as the median case in almost all such studies into declining political trust (see Newton & Norris, 2000; Dalton, 2004).

This paper aims to discuss the nature and root cause of this problem that the public apparently has with politics as such; and I propose a deep explanation, i.e. one that goes beyond blaming the media (Capella & Jamieson, 1997; Newton, 1999), or treating declining political trust as epiphenomenal, a mere further symptom of declining social capital (Newton, 2001; Zmerli & Newton, 2008), or indeed beyond claiming that this is indicative of a 'critical public' that politics needs to re-engage with (Dalton, 2004).

Such a deeper explanation is to be found by trying to understand what essentially distinguishes the political process nowadays from what politics was and meant a generation ago. What seems to be missing from current debates about political apathy, public disenchantment with politics or however else the problem is framed, is any deeper discussion of why political institutions and the political profession were not always treated with as much suspicion and disdain as they are now. As mentioned before, if we look at the collection of statements from philosophers, writers and thinkers from Plato to Ambrose Bearce that Lundberg (1968) compiled, the exercise of politics and the activities and driving motives of politicians were frequently treated with contempt. So what was it then that generated not overwhelming but at least comparatively decent levels of trust in politicians and institutions during the mid-twentieth century?

There are two fallacies in how political trust has been measured and how it is being framed and discussed nowadays. The first fallacy is embedded in the phrasing of a typical political trust question sometimes posed in, for example, British Election Study surveys: 'How much do you trust politicians/parties to put the national interest before partisan interests?' This implies that trust in the political system is predicated on the ability of governments or lawmakers to act in non-partisan or bipartisan fashion. However, there is no evidence to suggest that more consensual politics results in more contented citizens. It will be argued later in this paper that the exact opposite might be the case.

The second fallacy is to misinterpret political trust as either a question of character-based individual trustworthiness of office holders or indeed as a matter of conditional trust that results from delivery in office. As Ruscio (1999) points out, political trust is indeed more conditional than personal trust, but it is conditional on perceived institutional guarantees that reassure citizens about their polity not being inherently corrupt or unfair. I would propose that trustworthiness of office holders or satisfactory delivery in office would constitute sufficient but not necessary conditions for widespread political trust, much in line with Easton's (1975) arguments about the role of specific support. That is to say that if everyone was to perceive all parliamentarians and government ministers as generally trustworthy, things would be fine. Similarly, if government were understood by citizens to deliver excellent policies, everything would be fine too; but there is no reason to expect all politicians ever to measure up to such high standards or to expect government actions ever to be universally beneficial, so any discussion that focuses on how to ensure outstanding behaviour in office or better delivery remains futile (or at least beside the point of trying to explain why politics has become so unpopular), especially since there were times when political trust was higher even though there is little reason to assume that politicians were of a better moral standard in the 1960s or 1970s than they are now, or indeed that government delivery was more universally beneficial back then than it is now.

The literature on political trust tends to emphasise the notion of trust at the expense of contemplating the political nature of the supposed relationship between those who trust and those who are being trusted.[4] An obvious starting point is to go back to basic definitions of politics. Irrespective of whether we look at Easton's (1965) more elaborate definition of politics as 'the authoritative allocation of values' or Laswell's (1936) more mundane definition of politics being about 'who gets what when and how', politics is essentially about distribution. This does not necessarily always involve distribution of material values, as Easton's definition implies, but whether we talk about the allocation of resources or the acknowledgement and consideration of non-material values; neither are those resources ever abundant, nor are values or beliefs mutually inclusive or compatible. It is worth noting that the potentially conflicting or even mutually exclusive nature of political allocations and popular acceptance of that fact lies at the heart of Easton's definition of diffuse support:

> reservoir of favorable attitudes or good will that helps members to accept or tolerate outputs to which they are opposed or the effects of which they see as damaging to their wants. (Easton, 1965: 273)

Indeed, Schattschneider's (1960) understanding is helpful here as he stated that matters become political whenever conflicts can no longer be solved privately but become socialised. Politics is the organisation of conflict, and in Schattschneider's view such organisation can be provided only by political parties determining what are the core fault lines or cleavages that divide society. The reliance of the public on parties to help structure societal conflict and on that basis effectively to compete over the running of government is a necessary representative substitute, not actual 'government by the people' but 'government by consent of the governed' (Schattschneider, 1967: 58). This substitute is necessary because of the nature and scale of modern societies and serves to structure political conflict in mass societies.

> The immobility and inertia of large masses are to politics what the law of gravity is to physics. This characteristic compels people to submit to a great channelization of the expression of their will, and is due to numbers, not to want of intelligence. An electorate of sixty million Aristotles would be equally restricted. (Schattschneider, 1942: 52)

Schattschneider invoked the notion of responsible parties (Adamany, 1972: 1,325), which together with the idea of people being compelled to 'submit to a great channelization of the expression of their will' circumscribes the meaning of political trust. Democracy is an exercise in community-building, and 'the boundaries of voting ... correspond roughly to the boundaries of social community – that segment of the population who share values as well as goods' (Adamany, 1972: 1,332). In this model of democracy, social conflict and partisanship are not eroding community, but quite the opposite; they are structuring politics, and if parties are successful in adequately organising the different sides in the major social conflicts, political trust emerges as an individual and collective understanding of one's own or one's own side's stakes being adequately represented and voiced. This idea is also reflected in the picture that Mair (2006) paints of the traditional cleavage-based model of mass politics, which means that political parties are rooted within society, allowing individuals to have their interests and stakes in the social distribution of values and goods adequately represented, because they share their interests and stakes with their fellow partisan constituents. Schattschneider (1967) was already concerned with the exclusion and alienation of 40 million Americans, which he understood to result from the political system not adequately working to organise their grievances into meaningful political representation.

Representation and Trust

Dalton's (2004) analysis of increasing political discontent over recent decades across many if not all developed democracies highlights an important point: citizens have lost trust in politicians, in institutions and in how the political system in their country works, but they have not lost belief in the superiority of democracy as a political system. Like many other scholars, Dalton concludes this to mean that we are dealing with more critical and demanding citizens (see also Coleman, 2005; Norris, 2011). However, serious doubts can be raised about the idea of a more demanding democratic citizenry. Van Deth (2009) points out that all evidence points towards citizens not being willing to invest more time and energy in additional forms of participation, and also the findings from the Hansard audit of political engagement in Britain (Hansard, 2010: 57) are that most of the discontented citizens are best characterised as either bored or apathetic, disengaged and distrustful or some even openly hostile. There is little reason to assume that the problem of declining trust in politics could be rectified by engaging citizens more, consulting more, or by increasing possibilities of direct involvement. An alternative interpretation of Dalton's (2004) finding is rather that distrust in politicians, institutions and the working of the system amounts to an increasing rejection of the representative model of democracy, as advocated most forcefully by Schattschneider. Citizens continue to like the idea of democracy but appear increasingly unsatisfied with the system of representation, however, without indicating that a move to more direct democracy would be the solution.

It seems reasonable to understand declining trust as synonymous with a feeling of no longer being adequately represented, hence a reduced willingness of citizens to make that giant leap and 'submit to a great channelization of the expression of their will' (Schattschneider, 1942: 52). The concept of representation is rarely invoked in discussions about declining political trust; arguments centre on external factors such as media images, or social change (decline of social capital), or indeed the quality of delivery in government; and in surveys, respondents are in various forms being asked what they expect or want from politicians and parties, never what they expect from politics. One might even argue that a disregard for the importance and meaning of representation is why Downsian models of voting have not been overly successful in modelling voting and party behaviour:

> Directional voters ask of their parties 'Are you on my side?' and 'Can I trust you to be responsible' – as opposed to the classic proximity question: 'How close is your position to mine?' (Macdonald & Rabinowitz, 1998: 282)

What I am trying to argue in the remainder of this paper is that politics in the Schattschneiderian sense, namely the partisan organisation of societal conflict, has lost its significance, and that as a result political trust has not so much declined but rather morphed into a distinctly non-political form of institutional trust that is decidedly more and differently conditional than its political predecessor. The partisan political systems of Britain and other Western democracies have essentially been depoliticised. This process shares some similarities with Downs's predictions about party convergence but derives less from deductive premises about utility maximisation and more from a historical understanding of the interconnected and mutually exacerbating processes of social change and partisan professionalisation and modernisation.

Valence Politics

Partisan dealignment is widely understood to be a result of social change, of people being less likely to regard themselves as members of a particular social class, of individualization, value change, etc. (Butler & Stokes, 1974; Inglehart, 1990; Clark & Lipset, 1991). However, the political parties' response to this, by professionalising their campaign activities, adopting modern marketing strategies, in the Downsian sense converging on median policy positions, has reinforced this process, raising important questions about causal direction.

Such questions have been particularly raised in recent debates in which electoral research as well as reconceptualisations of spatial models of voting have emphasised Stokes's older notion of valence issues or indeed valence politics (Stokes, 1963; Macdonald & Rabinowitz, 1998; Schofield, 2003; Clarke et al., 2004, 2009, Whiteley et al., 2005; Green, 2007). Stokes (1963) argued that not all issues are positional issues, but that some issues are non-controversial with regard to their outcomes – everyone wants less crime, a better environment; and economic growth is increasingly also named as one such issue 'on which there is agreement on the end of politics' (Green, 2007: 629). However, the argument of proponents of the idea of valence politics goes much further in that they propose that almost all issues are by now valence issues, so that consensus exists about ends of politics, whereas conflict surrounds questions of means, i.e. how best to accomplish these ends, and indeed questions of competence and delivery (Clarke et al., 2004, 2009; Whiteley et al., 2005).

Crucially, the valence politics model is different from the Downsian insofar as it is argued that not only parties but also voters agree on these ends, so it is not the parties who just converge on one position because it is a median one; but, it is argued that an emerging world of valence politics can be understood as a result of Downsian strategies, because converging parties 'eliminate any spatial differences between them, so voters can no longer choose between them on spatial grounds' (Whiteley et al., 2005: 804). Politics becomes a matter of 'who can best deliver the equilibrium policy' (*ibid.*) where the equilibrium policy is being determined by preceding party convergence to which the public responds by assimilating their preferences. Explicitly, partisans are predicted and empirically found to become over time more similar in their preferences on issues on which parties have previously converged (Green, 2007: 632). This is also understood as consensus politics, and is claimed to render voter evaluations into retrospective judgements about performance rather than prospective judgements about promises that would be more in line with a positional model of party competition (Whiteley et al. 2005: 805). This definition of consensus politics differs substantially from Lijphart's (1984) earlier model of consensus government. Valence-based consensus is not about compromise, concessions, give and take between different parties or sectoral interests, but rather about streamlining and adaptation of public preferences predicated on the minimisation of policy alternatives in the party system.

It is interesting to note that the developing paradigm about valence politics has remained limited in scope, insofar as it has been applied only to discuss and explain electoral change or revise the spatial model of voting. It has not been noted and applied by proponents of the 'political marketing' framework (even though with its focus on performance and delivery it appears ideally suited for exploration within a management studies approach to political competition). Nor has anyone yet pointed to a possible connection between this significant alteration of the essence of what politics is and is about and the coincidentally occurring substantial decline in public trust in and engagement with politics. If we grant any credence to Schattsch-neider's claim that politics is essentially about the socialisation of conflict, then valence politics no longer qualifies as politics at all; and we do not even have to sub-scribe to Schattschneider's party-centred model of what politics is in order to come to this conclusion. Equally, if one thinks through Laswell's definition of politics as a question of 'who gets what when and how' or Easton's idea of politics as 'the author-itative allocation of values', it is obvious that politics, being about distribution, is inherently about temporarily creating winners and losers. This is inherent in earlier understandings of politics, and certainly in the Schumpeterian model, namely that democratic politics creates winners and losers but deserves to be called democratic insofar as it is truly and continuously competitive, offering current losers the prospect of moving to the winning side in the future.

Not only is valence politics no longer about taking sides in social conflicts, but also it is not about distinguishing winners from losers. Evaluative criteria of performance, competence and delivery are bereft of any such political content. These criteria render political evaluation similar to how citizens evaluate and respond to performance of social and administrative services – a topic that is of course at the heart of modern political marketing theory (see Henneberg et al., 2009; Henneberg, 2006). In the realm of valence politics, the citizen morphs into a political consumer who is judging governments on the same terms as he/she judges civil servants or front line staff in the NHS or the educational sector. Then, of course, customer service cri-teria such as better communication, accessibility and response to feedback become paramount (Coleman, 2005); but remember that this only ever amounts to what Easton (1975) called 'specific support'. This is certainly in line with some narrow definitions of political trust 'as a basic evaluative orientation toward the government founded on how well the government is operating according to people's normative expectations' (Hetherington, 2005: 791); but it remains object-specific. Also, in line with Mair's (2006) contention that the popular, electoral element of democratic politics is increasingly devalued, one might point to a potential paradox here: namely that such specific support could only possibly translate into diffuse support if succes-sive governments (of varying partisan composition) were to perform satisfactorily, creating general trust that whoever is voted in will govern competently and expertly. Such a scenario would, however, necessarily devalue elections, because opposing parties that no longer differ in their policy platforms can only be evaluated on valence grounds. Only if those valence grounds were to minimise could diffuse support emerge. Essentially, such performance and delivery-based diffuse support would necessarily remain disconnected from electoral, mass politics, because it would render parties ultimately exchangeable and remove reasons for voting and choosing.

This has two further consequences that combine to explain low levels of political trust and increasing disaffection with and disquiet about politics. First, trust in corporations or trust in administration or other institutions cannot and should not be equated with political trust. Civil servants, companies, nurses or teachers are not representatives but politicians still are; but a trend towards valence politics may imply that representation is no longer at the heart of statements about political trust; or worse yet, if they still are part of public expectations then office holders who aim solely to perform and deliver will, even if they perform and deliver well, fall short by not fulfilling any additional demands that political trust encapsulates. Second, a remaining and quite crucial contrast between politicians and other service providers is that politicians hold power, which demands that they are held to other and most probably higher standards than civil servants or nurses. No level of customer service, good communication and responsiveness can substitute for a substantially political trust, a feeling of being meaningfully represented that alone can justify in any citizen's mind the transferral of public sovereignty on to parties and politicians to act on the their behalf that is theoretically at the heart of democracy.

To put it bluntly, communication, good customer service, competence, performance and delivery can result in satisfaction but never in consent.

Acknowledgement

The author would like to thank Eddie Hyland not only for his comments on this paper, but also for his support, intellectual stimulation and critical insights over the past 15 years.

Notes

1. Admittedly, the financial crisis and budgets cuts have led to mass protests in some European countries, most notably Greece, Spain and France, but there is little to suggest that these protests are threatening regimes, or indeed that any of these protests are related to long-term trends of growing disaffection with politicians, parties and parliaments.
2. The distinction between trust in people and confidence in institutions is emphasised strongly in the literature on social and political trust (see Zmerli & Newton, 2008: 709), although the wording in questionnaires does not systematically use 'trust' whenever measuring attitudes towards people, and 'confidence' whenever measuring attitudes towards institutions. Also, principal component analysis (carried out by the author on British and Irish Election Studies) indicates that measures of 'trust in politicians', 'trust in parties' and 'trust in parliament' tend to load heavily on a single underlying component, which is distinctive from a second component that comprises items such as 'duty to vote' and 'satisfaction with democracy'. Hence, there is good reason to believe that political trust is a single dimension that contains attitudes to office holders and institutions but is separate from general appreciation of democracy.
3. While Clarke et al. (2004) can certainly not be faulted on their methodology in testing attitudes to democracy, they do seem to understate the problem resulting from changes in British Election Study survey questions that measure trust in institutions. These have varied substantially over recent

decades and render any claim of time trends in general questionable. In Norris's (2011: Ch. 4) case, she presents a picture of volatility rather than any systematic trends in attitudes towards politicians and institutions across European countries, but the Eurobarometer data she uses appear overly noisy, producing inexplicably upwards or downwards movements from one year to the next of up to 20%. Why, for example, would 'trust in parliament' in West Germany rise by 18% from 2006 to 2007 (36–54%) and fall again by as much as 11% in the following year? Nothing happened in Germany at that time that could possibly account for such extreme movements in public opinion.

4. Newton (2001: 204) does point out that whereas 'social trust is associated, if at all, with social variables measuring social and economic success, political trust is rather more strongly associated with a set of political variables measuring interest in politics, pride in the national political system, a belief in open government, a low priority given to social order and the left-right scale'.

References

Adamany, D. (1972) The political science of E. E. Schattschneider: a review essay, *The American Political Science Review*, 66(4), pp. 1321–1335.

Butler, D. & Stokes, D. (1974) *Political Change in Britain: The Evolution of Electoral Choice* (London: Macmillan).

Cappella, J. N. & Jamieson, K. H. (1997) *Spiral of Cynicism: The Press and the Public Good* (Oxford: Oxford University Press).

Clark, T. N. & Lipset, S. M. (1991) Are social classes dying?, *International Sociology*, 6(4), pp. 397–410.

Clarke, H. C., Sanders, D., Stewart, M. C. & Whiteley, P. (2004) *Political Choice in Britain* (Oxford and New York: Oxford University Press).

Clarke, H. C., Sanders, D., Stewart, M. C. & Whiteley, P. (2009) *Performance Politics and the British Voter* (Cambridge: Cambridge University Press).

Coleman, S. (2005) *Direct Representation. Towards a Conversational Democracy* (London: Institute for Public Policy Research).

Dalton, R. J. (2004) *Democratic Challenges, Democratic Choices. The Erosion of Political Support in Advanced Industrial Democracies* (New York: Oxford University Press).

Easton, D. (1965) *A Systems Analysis of Political Life* (New York: Wiley).

Easton, D. (1975) A re-assessment of the concept of political support, *British Journal of Political Science*, 5(4), pp. 435–457.

Green, J. (2007) When voters and parties agree: valence issues and party competition, *Political Studies*, 55, pp. 629–655.

Hansard (2010) *Audit of Political Engagement 7. The 2010 Report* (London: Hansard Society).

Henneberg, S. C. M. (2006) Leading or following?, *Journal of Political Marketing*, 5(3), pp. 29–46.

Henneberg, S. C. M., Scammell, M. & O'Shaughnessy, N. J. (2009) Political marketing management and theories of democracy, *Marketing Theory*, 9(2), pp. 165–188.

Hetherington, M. J. (2005) *Why Trust Matters. Declining Political Trust and the Demise of American Liberalism* (Princeton, NJ and Oxford: Princeton University Press).

Inglehart, R. (1990) *Culture Shift in Advanced Industrial Society* (Princeton, NJ: Princeton University Press).

Laswell, H. (1936) *Politics: Who Gets What When and How* (New York: McGraw Hill).

Lijphart, A. (1984) *Democracies: Patterns of Majoritarian and Consensus Government in Twenty-one Countries* (New Haven: Yale University Press).

Lundberg, F. (1968) *Politicians and Other Scoundrels* (Secaucus, NJ: Lyle Stuart).

Macdonald, S. E. & Rabinowitz, G. (1998) Solving the paradox of nonconvergence: valence, position, and direction in democratic politics, *Electoral Studies*, 17(3), pp. 281–300.

Mair, P. (2006) Ruling the void? The hollowing of Western democracy, *New Left Review*, 42, pp. 25–51.

Newton, K. (1999) Mass media effects: mobilization or media malaise?, *British Journal of Political Science*, 29(4), pp. 577–599.

Newton, K. (2001) Trust, social capital, civil society, and democracy, *International Political Science Review*, 22(2), pp. 201–214.

Newton, K. & Norris, P. (2000) Confidence in public institutions: faith, culture, or performance?, in: S. Pharr & R. Putnam (Eds) *Disaffected Democracies: What's Troubling the Trilateral Countries?* (Princeton, NJ: Princeton University Press).

Norris, P. (2011) *Democratic Deficits: Rising Aspirations, Negative News, or Failing Performance* (New York and Cambridge: Cambridge University Press).

Ruscio, K. P. (1999) Jay's pirouette or why political trust is not the same as personal trust, *Administration & Society*, 31(5), pp. 639–657.

Schattschneider, E. E. (1942) *Party Government* (New York: Holt, Rinehart and Winston).

Schattschneider, E. E. (1960) *The Semi-Sovereign People* (New York: Holt, Rinehart and Winston).

Schattschneider, E. E. (1967) *Two Hundred Million Americans in Search of a Government* (New York: Holt, Rinehart and Winston).

Schofield, N. (2003) Valence competition in the Spatial Stochastic Model, *Journal of Theoretical Politics*, 15(4), pp. 371–383.

Stokes, D. E. (1963) Spatial models of party competition, *American Political Science Review*, 57(2), pp. 368–377.

Van Deth, J. (2009) The 'good European citizen': congruence and consequences of different points of view, *European Political Science*, 8, pp. 175–189.

Whiteley, P., Stewart, M. C., Sanders, D. & Clarke, H. C. (2005) The issue agenda and voting in 2005, *Parliamentary Affairs*, 58(4), pp. 802–817.

Zmerli, S. & Newton, K. (2008) Social trust and attitudes toward democracy, *Public Opinion Quarterly*, 72(4), pp. 706–724.

Can Compactness Constrain the Gerrymander?

MACARTAN HUMPHREYS

Columbia University, USA

ABSTRACT *Gerrymandering – the manipulation of electoral boundaries to maximize constituency wins – is often seen as a pathology of democratic systems. A commonly cited cure is to
require that electoral constituencies have a 'compact' shape. But how much of a constraint
does compactness in fact place on would-be gerrymanderers? The author operationalizes compactness as a convexity constraint and applies a theorem of Kaneko, Kano and Suzuki to the
two-party situation to show that for any population distribution a gerrymanderer can always
create equal (population)-sized convex constituencies that translate a margin of k voters into a
margin of at least k constituency wins. Thus, even with a small margin a majority party can win
all constituencies. In addition, it is shown that there always exists some population distribution
such that all divisions into equal-sized convex constituencies translate a margin of k voters into
a margin of exactly k constituencies. Thus, a convexity constraint can sometimes prevent a gerrymanderer from generating any wins for a minority party. These results clarify that the heart
of the problem with outcomes that deviate from proportionality in single member constituency
systems is not the manner in which constituencies are drawn but the mode of preference
aggregation.*

Introduction

Gerrymandering is the art of manipulating electoral constituencies in order to maximize vote shares for a favored party. In principle, the scope for gerrymandering is
large and for this reason lawmakers and courts have advanced criteria to limit it.
Perhaps the three most common criteria are that electoral constituencies should
possess equality of population (equinumerosity), contiguity and compactness
(Niemi *et al.*, 1990; Polsby & Popper, 1991). The arguments for equinumerosity
and contiguity are relatively simple; the arguments for compactness are more difficult. Without something like compactness anything goes: it is possible to satisfy

contiguity and place any set of people together in a single constituency subject only to the size constraint (Polsby & Popper, 1991). Advocates also argue the converse, however: that 'a requirement of compactness would prevent effective gerrymandering' (Polsby & Popper, 1991: 333) and that compactness acts as a 'prophylactic measure that limits the possibility of legislative gerrymandering' (Stern, 1974: 411). Thirty-five US states now require that constituencies be compact (Chambers & Miller, 2009).

There is, however, considerable disagreement over what is meant by 'compact' (the mathematical notion of compactness for this space – closed and bounded – is of limited application for this problem). Niemi *et al.* (1990) list nearly two dozen compactness measures and advocate the use of multiple measures to capture different features of compactness (see also Young, 1988). Two prominent features discussed in the literature are the extent to which an area is 'elongated' and the extent to which it is irregularly shaped (Chambers & Miller, 2009). Dispersion measures focus on the former, convexity measures focus on the latter (where an area is convex if the shortest path between two points in the area lies entirely within the area) (Taylor, 1973; Chambers & Miller, 2009).

There are also criticisms of the use of compactness as a criterion for limiting gerrymandering. Vickrey (1961) notes that shape considerations alone cannot rule out gerrymandering. Lowenstein and Steinberg (1985) argue that compactness constraints are biased, in the USA benefiting Republicans over Democrats (but more generally harming parties whose support base is more clustered). The argument is dismissed for lack of supporting evidence by Polsby and Popper (1991) but is supported by simulations provided by Altman (1998).

Following Taylor (1973) and Chambers and Miller (2009), I focus on convexity as a simple requirement for constituency compactness and ask what scope there is for gerrymandering given such a constraint. One might expect that convexity could impose formidable constraints because it rules out the tentacled shapes traditionally associated with gerrymandering. Moreover, by most measures, compactness is maximized by convex shapes even if convexity is not an explicit part of the measure. For measures that focus on minimizing dispersion within districts, for example (see Fryer & Holden, 2007, and related measures in Niemi *et al.*, 1990), convexity is a necessary but not a sufficient condition for compactness.

An application of a theorem from computational geometry due to Kaneko *et al.* (2004), however, yields a striking result. In general, a convexity requirement has no effect on the scope for gerrymandering for majority parties; narrow numeric margins are sufficient to ensure that a gerrymanderer can bank all constituencies and still comply with convexity. In addition, it is shown here that convexity may have an adverse effect on the ability of minorities to gerrymander. For some population distributions the convexity constraint can prevent a minority party from gaining any seats, even if it fully controls constituency designs and the margin between majority and minority is small. These results suggest that shape-based constraints are unlikely to resolve the problems associated with gerrymandering; moreover, 'anonymous' procedures may be no better at ensuring even a modicum of proportionality. These results shed light on a key difference between single member constituency systems – in which the quality of boundaries is sometimes assessed by the ability to produce proportionality at an aggregate level – and systems like Ireland's single transferable vote – which seeks to achieve proportionality at the constituency level. The heart of the problem with outcomes that deviate from proportionality in single member constituency systems is not the manner in which constituency boundaries are established but the poverty of the information that is aggregated.

Results

The setting examined here is idealized in a number of ways. It is assumed that all voters support one of two parties in single member constituencies; and these voters are taken to have fixed locations that can be represented as points in 'general position' on a convex two-dimensional space.[1] It is assumed that the number of voters is fixed at n, that the number of constituencies is fixed at k and that the number of voters in each constituency, n/k, is an odd integer.

I consider designs for the location of constituency boundaries and say that a design is 'admissible' if it partitions the space into k convex areas with n/k voters in each area. Implicitly, then, 'wholesale' gerrymandering is examined in which constituency design does not depend on pre-existing designs. Under these conditions, the first result follows from a theorem due to Kaneko *et al.* (2004).

Theorem 1. *(Kaneko, Kano and Suzuki) Let $a \geq 1$, $g \geq 0$ and $h \geq 0$ be integers such that $g + h \geq 1$. Let R be a set of $ag + (a + 1)h$ red points and B a set of $(a + 1)g + ah$ blue points in the plane such that $R \cup B$ is in general position. Then there exists a subdivision $X_1 \cup X_2 \ldots X_g \cup Y_1 \cup Y_2 \ldots Y_h$ of the plane into $g + h$ disjoint convex polygons such that every X_i $(1 \leq i \leq g)$ contains exactly a red points and $a + 1$ blue points and every Y_j $(1 \leq j \leq h)$ contains exactly $a + 1$ red points and a blue points.*

The theorem generalizes a result due to Bespamyatnikh *et al.* (2000), which is in turn a generalization of the ham sandwich theorem in two dimensions. Proposition 1 follows as a direct implication of the theorem.

Proposition 1. *Let $-k \leq m_i \leq k$ denote the margin of voters that party i commands. Then for any population distribution in general position there exists an admissible design such that party i commands a margin of m_i constituencies.*

Proof. Follows immediately from Theorem 1, setting $g = \frac{k-m}{2}$, $h = \frac{k+m}{2}$, $a = \frac{n-k}{2k}$. ◆

Proposition 1 provides a minimum number of constituencies that a gerrymander can guarantee a party.[2] A k vote margin is sufficient to guarantee 100% of constituencies. The proposition extends in the obvious way to parties with a margin greater than k or less than $-k$.

With a margin of $-k$ votes the proposition does not provide a guarantee that a gerrymanderer can control any constituencies. Yet clearly it is sometimes possible for a gerrymanderer controlling margin $m_i < k - 1$ to control more than m_i constituencies. Indeed, it is easy to see that a party that controls v votes could control up to $\min\left(\left\lfloor \frac{2k}{n+k}v \right\rfloor, k\right)$ constituencies. Thus, for example, in a $n = 90$ person polity with $k = 6$ constituencies each containing 15 voters, a party with 40 supporters could in some circumstances organize boundaries so that it has eight members in each of five convex constituencies, thereby translating a share of 44% and a margin of -10 votes into a constituency share of 83% and a margin of four constituencies. In general is it always possible for parties to use gerrymandering to ensure that their constituency margin exceeds their vote margin (subject to the limit of k constituencies)?

The next result answers this question in the negative and establishes that the gains guaranteed in Proposition 1 are in general the greatest gains that can be guaranteed by a gerrymanderer.

Proposition 2. *Let m_i, $-k \le m_i \le k$, denote the margin of voters that party i commands. Then there exists a population distribution in general position such that for every admissible design, party i commands a margin of m_i constituencies.*

Proof. See the Appendix.

The proposition establishes that, for some distributions, convexity ensures that there is no scope for gerrymandering. In such cases the margins guaranteed by Proposition 1 can be returned but cannot be improved upon by gerrymanderers working for either side.

The proof strategy of the proposition exploits features of points arranged in convex position (that is, as vertices of a polygon). Fix n and k and let $s = n/k$ denote the number of voters in each constituency. Consider a set of points arranged in this way and count them off in order into k sequences of length s, $\{1, 2, \ldots, s\}$ (see Figure 1). Thus, each index in $\{1, 2, 3, \ldots, s\}$ is shared by k points. The key element of the proof is a demonstration that any admissible design must have in each constituency one point labeled '1', one point labeled '2' and so on up to s. As a result any assignment of points to sides such that points with indices below $\frac{1}{2}(s + 1)$ belong to one group, points with indices above $\frac{1}{2}(s + 1)$ belong to the other group and all other points have index $\frac{1}{2}(s + 1)$ achieves the desired distribution.

Figure 1 illustrates both propositions. We see from the top two figures that for a given division of votes, for some populations each group can, through gerrymandering, achieve up to $\min\left(\left\lfloor \frac{2k}{n+k}v \right\rfloor, k\right) = \frac{v}{3}$. Note in particular that the minority can win two constituencies; but for another distribution, illustrated in the lower figures, the maximum win for the majority provided in Proposition 1 is also a minimum – under all admissible arrangements the majority wins all constituencies.

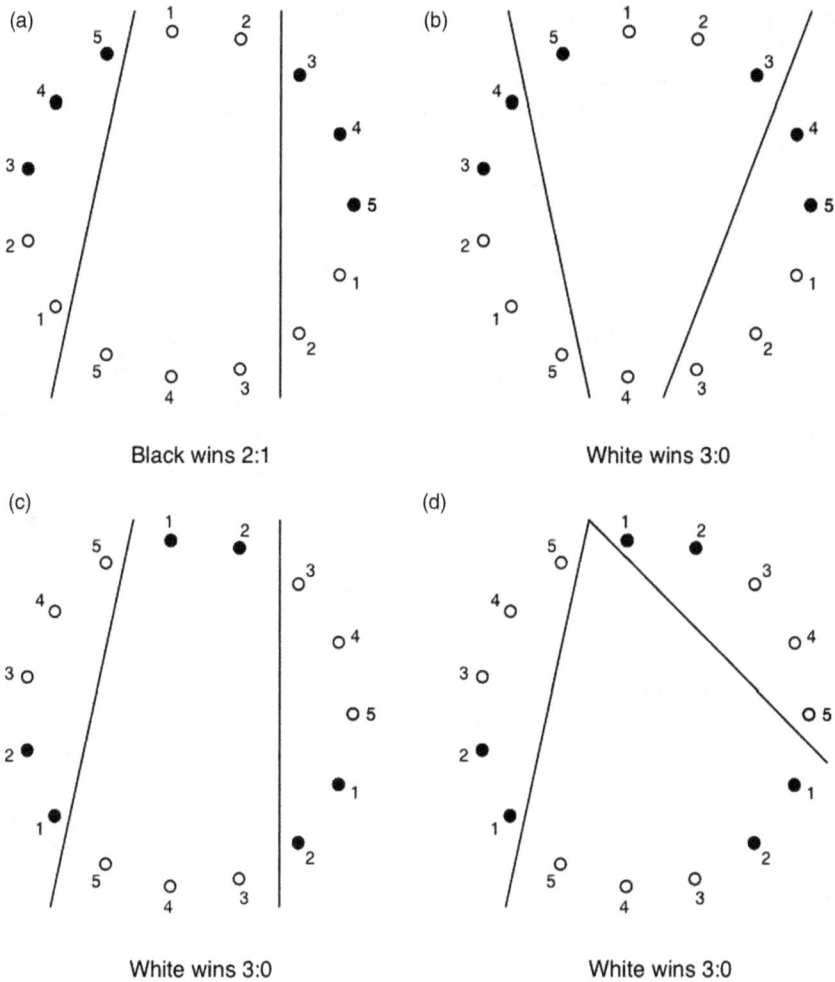

Figure 1. Polities with six black points, nine white points and three constituencies
Notes: For some configurations outcomes can range from 2:1 majorities for Black (a) to 3:0 majorities for White (b). For others White wins by a majority of 3:0 for all admissible designs (c and d); in such cases there is no scope for gerrymandering. Note that all admissible constituencies include one point marked '1', one marked '2' and so on up to '5'.

Conclusion

Consistent with the argument of Vickrey (1961), it was found that a shape constraint on constituency boundaries provides little insurance against gerrymandering. Whereas the classic image of a gerrymandered constituency involves tortured shapes, majority parties can generally ensure that vote leads translate into constituency leads even if they constrain themselves to regular shapes. This allows for very large distortions. In the UK, for example, with approximately 650 constituencies and 50 million voters, full control over constituency boundaries is sufficient to convert a one-thousandth of a per cent vote lead into 100% constituency control.

Do the results support the claim that compactness favors majority parties and more dispersed parties (Lowenstein & Steinberg, 1985)? The results do support the argument that a convexity constraint hurts minorities. Convexity does not prevent gerrymanderers supporting a party with a k seat lead from controlling all constituencies, but it can prevent a minority party with a k seat lag from gaining any (even if such a party could otherwise control up to $k - 1$ seats). There are, however, some benefits for minorities: in close races (with margins between $- k$ and k) minorities can translate their vote margin into a seat margin and, for some distributions, they can be guaranteed that a majority gerrymanderer cannot force an even worse outcome upon them. However, these benefits arise only for a very constrained set of contexts.

The results do not support the argument that compactness disadvantages more concentrated minority or majority groups confronted with gerrymandering by majority groups because, at least when operationalized as a convexity constraint, majority gerrymandering is unconstrained by distributions except for exceptionally close races. Whether compactness constrains gerrymanderers working for concentrated minorities more than it does gerrymanderers working for dispersed minorities remains an open question.

I close by emphasizing a final, deeper, implication of this analysis. At the outset it was noted that convexity is a necessary but not a sufficient criterion for an optimal design under a wide range of compactness measures. Thus, one might argue that the results of Proposition 1 may be avoided for designs that require more than convexity (such as the dispersion requirement in Fryer & Holden, 2007). This is correct. However, the results of Proposition 2 are relevant for all criteria that include convexity: if all convex designs award all constituencies to one side then so do all designs that require more than convexity. Moreover, for such distributions, this is the case no matter which side controls the districting. This has important implications for normative assessments of gerrymandering. Perhaps the most prominent normative critique of gerrymandering is that it results in seat shares that poorly reflect vote shares (see e.g. the discussion in Gelman & King, 1994). Yet as is clear from Proposition 2, distributions exist such that *any* division into convex districts will produce such a mismatch. In such cases having 'fairer' outcomes *requires* a gerrymandering that violates compactness. This clarifies the fact that the problem of mismatch cannot simply be attributed to the gerrymander but is inherent in the use of single member districts in the mapping from votes to seats.

Acknowledgements

The author is deeply grateful to Eddie Hyland for opening a universe of questions on aggregation and representation and forcing the author to put some discipline on his thinking about them. The author also thanks Mikio Kano for very generous advice on this work.

Notes

1. Note that other recent work on gerrymandering allows for more continuous party affiliation but removes geographical constraints (Friedman & Holden, 2008).
2. Note that g, h and a are all guaranteed to be integers here because k odd (even) implies n odd (even), which in turn implies m odd (even).

References

Altman, M. (1998) Modeling the effect of mandatory district compactness on partisan gerrymanders, *Political Geography*, 17, pp. 989–1012.

Bespamyatnikh, S., Kirkpatrick, D. & Snoeyink, J. (2000) Generalizing ham sandwich cuts to equitable subdivisions, *Discrete and Computational Geometry*, 24, pp. 605–622.

Chambers, C. P. & Miller, A. D. (2009) A Measure of Bizarreness, *Working Paper*, California Institute of Technology.

Friedman, J. N. & Holden, R. T. (2008) Optimal gerrymandering: sometimes pack, but never crack, *American Economic Review*, 98(1), pp. 113–144.

Fryer, R. G. J. & Holden, R. T. (2007) Measuring the Compactness of Political Districting Plans, *NBER Working Papers 13456*.

Gelman, A. & King, G. (1994) Enhancing democracy through legislative redistricting, *American Political Science Review*, 88(3), pp. 541–559.

Kaneko, A., Kano, M. & Suzuki, K. (2004) Path coverings of two sets of points in the plane, in: J. Pach (Ed.) *Towards a Theory of Geometric Graphs*, Vol. 342, pp. 99–111, Contemporary Mathematics Series of AMS.

Lowenstein, D. H. & Steinberg, J. (1985) The quest for legislative districting in the public interest: elusive or illusory?, *UCLA Law Review*, 33, pp. 1–75.

Niemi, R. G., Grofman, B., Carlucci, C. & Hofeller, T. (1990) Measuring compactness and the role of a compactness standard in a test for partisan and racial gerrymandering, *The Journal of Politics*, 52(4), pp. 1155–1181.

Polsby, D. D. & Popper, R. D. (1991) The third criterion: compactness as a procedural safeguard against partisan gerrymandering, *Yale Law and Policy Review*, 9, pp. 301–353.

Stern, R. S. (1974) Political gerrymandering: a statutory compactness standard as an antidote for judicial impotence, *The University of Chicago Law Review*, 41, pp. 398–416.

Taylor, P. J. (1973) A new shape measure for evaluation electoral district patterns, *The American Political Science Review*, 67, pp. 947–950.

Vickrey, W. (1961) On the prevention of gerrymandering, *Political Science Quarterly*, 76, pp. 105–110.

Young, H. P. (1988) Measuring the compactness of legislative districts, *Legislative Studies Quarterly*, 13, pp. 105–115.

Appendix

A constructive proof is provided of Proposition 2 in which a distribution of points that are in 'convex position' is constructed that satisfy the claim of the proposition. A set of points is in convex position if no point lies in the convex hull of the other points.

Proposition 2. *Let m_i, $-k \leq m_i \leq k$, denote the margin of voters that party i commands. Then there exists a population distribution in general position such that for every admissible design, party i commands a margin of m_i constituencies.*

Proof. Let P denote a set of n points (voters) to be divided into k cells (constituencies) and P_i and P_{-i} the subsets belonging to group i and its rival. Let $s = n/k$ denote the number of points in each cell. Label the n points x_0 to x_{n-1} such that j (mod s) $< (s - 1)/2 \rightarrow x_j \in P_i$ and j (mod s) $> (s - 1)/2 \rightarrow x_j \in P_{-i}$. Arrange them sequentially such that each point is a vertex of a convex polygon. Associate with each vertex a group K_h according to j (mod s) $= h \rightarrow x_j \in K_h$. To establish the proposition it is demonstrated that for any admissible design, each cell contains exactly one point from each group in $\{K_0, K_1, \ldots, K_{s-1}\}$.

For any point x_j in the collection A we say that $x_{(j+z) \pmod{n}}$ is 'next' to x_j in A if $z = \{\min_s \in \{1, 2, \ldots, n - 1\} \mid x_{j+s \pmod{n}} \in A\}$. Thus, x_2 is next to x_0 in A if x_2 is in A but x_1 is not.

Now consider some admissible partition that places s points in each of k cells. It is shown that for any point x_g in cell C, if $x_g \in K_h$ then the point next to x_g in C is in $K_{(h+1) \pmod{s}}$. Without loss of generality set $g = 0$. Now assume to the contrary that x_w is next to x_0 in C but is not an element of K_1. Let $\bar{X} = \{x_1, x_2, \ldots, x_{w-1}\}$ and $\underline{X} = \{x_{w+1}, x_{w+2}, \ldots, x_{n-1}\}$ denote the collections of points between x_0 and x_w (moving in different directions around the polygon). As the points in P are vertices on a convex polygon, the collection $\bar{X}$ lies on one side of the line that contains x_0 and x_w and the collection $\underline{X}$ lies on the other. As x_w is next to x_0 in C but is not an element of K_1 the cardinality of $\bar{X}$ is not evenly divisible by k and so at least one point in $\bar{X}$ is in a cell together with some point in $\underline{X}$. Let a denote some such point in $\bar{X}$ and b a point from $\underline{X}$ in the same cell as a. As points $\{x_0, a, x_w, b\}$ are in convex position we have that the line segment joining a and b intersects with the line segment joining x_0 and x_w; but then the (convex) cells containing a and b and x_0 and x_w are not disjoint. This yields a contradiction, thus x_w lies in K_1. By induction each point in K_0 shares a cell with a point in $K_1, K_2, \ldots, K_{s-1}$, the number of constituencies commanded by group i corresponds exactly to the number of elements in collection $K^{\frac{s-1}{2}}$, and so i's margin in constituencies is equal to its margin in voters.

Electing Women to the Dáil: Gender Cues and the Irish Voter

GAIL McELROY & MICHAEL MARSH

Trinity College Dublin, Ireland

ABSTRACT   At no time in history has the number of women elected to Dáil Éireann surpassed 14 per cent of the total membership. In spite of significant social changes, the use of a proportional electoral system and no obvious bias among voters, the number of female TDs remains stubbornly low by international standards. This paper examines why, if the prospects for women's election are relatively good, so few women end up in public office. Using both aggregate and survey data, the issues of incumbency advantage, the electorate's attitudes and the candidates' differing experiences of the political process are explored. The evidence suggests that, all else equal, female candidates have as good a chance of being elected as their male counterparts, and the real difficulties in achieving equitable representation lie elsewhere, in the candidate emergence and nomination stages of the election game.

Introduction

In the 2011 Irish general election, just 23 of the 165 members elected to Dáil Éireann were women, just one more than had been elected in 2002 and 2007. Despite significant social changes and an exponential growth in women's labour force participation, the percentage of women elected as TDs has remained static over the course of the past two decades. Furthermore, there has been no breakthrough in representation at the local level either, with women achieving a mere 16 per cent of seats in the city and county council elections of 2009. Within the European Union (EU), only Hungary, Romania, Cyprus and Malta have lower proportions of women in their national parliaments. In what follows we explore a series of factors that might help us resolve the puzzle of why Ireland elects so few women.

The literature on gender and politics explains cross-national variation in election rates largely in terms of contextual and structural factors. One of the most consistent findings to emerge from this voluminous body of work is the very positive impact of proportional electoral systems (PR) on women's representation, with PR almost universally acknowledged to increase the number of women in elected office (Kenworthy & Malami, 1999; McAllister & Studlar, 2002; Salmond, 2006). While closed-list PR systems are generally recognized best to facilitate large numbers of women in Parliament (Lakeman, 1994), the multi-member nature of PR-STV (single transferable vote) constituencies should provide selectorates with more opportunities to nominate women than single member district (SMD) systems (Rule, 1987; Matland & Brown, 1992). None the less, it is striking that Ireland has been overtaken in the past decade by the UK and France, two single member district electoral systems, in the international rankings of women in parliament.

A second key finding in cross-national studies is the strong relationship between women's rates of labour force participation and levels of representation, particularly in the industrialized world (Matland, 1998; McDonagh, 2002); but the dramatic changes in rates of employment of women in Ireland in the past three decades, from historically very low levels to above the EU average, do not appear to have had knock-on effects in parliament. Cultural differences are also frequently invoked in the literature to explain cross-national trends in representation levels, particularly religious heritage (Inglehart, 1981; Rule, 1987); but other, more recent, research suggests that such differences are significant only when comparing dominant Christian countries (whether Protestant or Roman Catholic) with non-Christian ones (Reynolds, 1999) or when comparing post-industrialist and more traditional societies (Inglehart & Norris, 2003). Thus, cultural explanations appear to fall short in explaining Ireland's poor showing in electing women.

In what follows, we attempt to answer why Ireland performs worse than one might expect, given the contextual and structural factors, through an examination of both aggregate and survey evidence from the election of 2007. We first explore the performance of women candidates in terms of their overall electoral performance. We then examine the evidence in the Irish National Election Study (INES) (www.tcd.ie/ines) to see whether we can identify the profile of voters most likely to vote for female (or male) candidates. Finally, we examine the evidence from the 2007 candidate survey to discover whether male and female candidates experience the nomination and electoral process in a similar fashion.

Female Candidates and the Vote

As is clear from Figure 1, the number of women candidates in Irish elections has never risen above 20 per cent; and although there was a marked increase in female candidatures in the 1980s, this upward trajectory has since levelled off. Of the 566 candidates who contested the 2011 national election, a mere 86 (15%) were women, although the proportion of female candidates does vary quite significantly across the political parties. Both of the main parties, Fianna Fáil and Fine Gael, typically run significantly more male candidates than the smaller parties (see Table 1 for a breakdown by party for the three most recent elections). The low number of candidates for Fianna Fáil and Fine Gael may simply reflect the realties of the incumbency

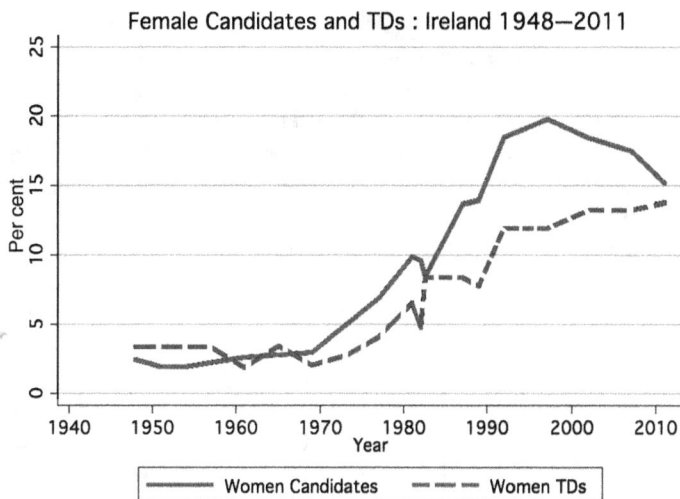

Figure 1. Women candidates and members

Table 1. Number of women candidates by party 2002–2011

Party	2002		2007		2011	
	Per cent female	Total candidates	Per cent female	Total candidates	Per cent female	Total candidates
Fianna Fáil	12.26	106	13.20	106	14.66	75
Fine Gael	16.47	85	16.50	91	15.38	104
Labour	25.53	47	22.00	50	26.47	68
Green Party	25.81	31	25.00	44	18.60	43
Sinn Féin	18.92	37	24.40	41	19.51	41
Progressive Democrats	30.00	20	23.30	30	–	–
Others	12.20	43	12.90	31	15.25	59
Independents	20.00	95	12.98	77	7.95	176
Total	18.24	464	17.45	470	15.19	566

advantage that operates in Ireland rather than a systematic bias against women (Gallagher, 2007), and we explore this possibility below. Where incumbency is one of the best predictors of re-election, the fact that most incumbents are male serves as an obstacle to the election of women (Schwindt-Bayer, 2005).

We begin our analysis by exploring whether women candidates performed systematically worse than male candidates in terms of their first preference vote totals. While PR-STV does involve the transfer of votes, the safest route to election is to ensure as large a first preference count as possible. The dependent variable in this analysis is *VOTE*, which is a count of the number of first preference votes a candidate obtained relative to his or her fellow competitors. Specifically, the dependent variable measures a candidate's deviation from the average first preference vote in his or her constituency. This approach captures how well a candidate does relative to other candidates in the election, while controlling for the different number of votes cast in each constituency.[1]

The key independent variable of interest in the model is the *GENDER* of the candidate (a dichotomous variable coded 0 for men and 1 for women). In addition, several other candidate characteristics are controlled for through the variables *SPENDING, INCUMBENT* and *MINISTER*. The *INCUMBENT* variable measures whether or not the candidate was a sitting member of the Dáil (0 if no, 1 if yes). The incumbency rate in Ireland is high by international standards, with around three-quarters of sitting TDs getting re-elected (Schwindt-Bayer, 2005). *MINISTER* captures whether or not the candidate was a sitting minister (0 if no, 1 if yes), as it is theorized that such candidates are additionally advantaged in their vote-getting abilities. *SPENDING* is the standardized euro expenditure of the candidate over the course of the campaign period. Money is increasingly important in Irish campaigns (Benoit & Marsh, 2010) and women tend to have slightly smaller war chests than their male counterparts. Also included in the full model are the interactions of all of these variables with the key variable of interest, *GENDER*, to capture whether the impact of incumbency, ministerial office and spending varies as a function of a candidate's sex. Finally, dummies are also created for the party affiliation of the candidate.

The results of the regression analysis are presented in Table 2. Four separate models are estimated but in none of these models does the gender of the candidate prove significant in predicting the number of first preferences received, even in the most parsimonious model. Indeed, in three of the four models the sign on the *GENDER* variable is positive (though not significant), contrary to expectations. In the full model in column 2, *SPENDING, INCUMBENT* and *MINISTER* are included, along with the party dummies and interaction terms. All three variables, not surprisingly, achieve significance and in the expected direction. Candidates who spend more money, have served already as a TD or (better still) as a minister get more votes than their more impoverished, non-incumbent challengers. Being a female minister has, however, a negative impact on the number of first preferences achieved (significant interaction of *GENDER* × *MINISTER*), though, given there were only three candidates in this position, we should not read too much into the results. The simple and full models were rerun on the subset of non-incumbent candidates (models 3 and 4) in order to check whether the impact of gender is moderated by incumbency, but no differences emerged.

There is nothing particularly advantageous or disadvantageous about being a woman candidate *per se*. When controlling for all of the standard variables, we found no evidence that female candidates perform worse (or better) than their male counterparts in terms of their first preference votes. However, there is clearly a

Table 2. Performance of candidates in 2007 election

	All candidates		Non-incumbents	
	(1) Vote	(2) Vote	(3) Vote	(4) Vote
Gender	−0.0804	0.0751	0.1014	0.0875
	(−0.82)	(0.49)	(1.17)	(0.64)
Minister		1.269***		
		(9.92)		
Spending		0.0000252***		0.0000267***
		(9.21)		(9.53)
Incumbent		0.514***		
		(9.67)		
Gender × Minister		−0.939**		
		(−3.12)		
Gender × Spending		−0.00000526		−0.00000284
		(−0.81)		(−0.45)
Gender × Incumbent		0.0837		
		(0.60)		
Fianna Fáil (FF)		0.762***		0.912***
		(9.83)		(10.00)
Fine Gael (FG)		0.644***		0.622***
		(8.88)		(8.42)
Labour		0.191*		0.0486
		(2.20)		(0.57)
Greens		0.0985		0.0976
		(1.17)		(1.22)
Progressive Democrats (PDs)		−0.308**		−0.251**
		(−2.93)		(−2.61)
Sinn Féin (SF)		0.338***		0.294***
		(3.79)		(3.55)
Gender × FF		−0.0527		−0.365
		(−0.29)		(−1.90)
Gender × FG		−0.00318		−0.0701
		(−0.02)		(−0.42)
Gender × Labour		0.162		0.147
		(0.82)		(0.65)
Gender × Greens		0.0678		0.0377
		(0.35)		(0.22)
Gender × PDs		−0.0760		−0.0241

(*Continued*)

Table 2. (Continued)

	All candidates		Non-incumbents	
	(1) Vote	(2) Vote	(3) Vote	(4) Vote
		(−0.33)		(−0.10)
Gender × SF		−0.124		−0.123
		(−0.63)		(−0.70)
Constant	0.0140	−0.952***	−0.354***	−0.965***
	(0.34)	(−20.37)	(−9.39)	(−23.65)
R-squared	0.00	0.75	0.00	0.69
N	470	470	324	324

Note: t-Statistics in parentheses.
*$p < 0.05$, **$p < 0.01$, ***$p < 0.001$.

strong incumbency bias that militates against large changes in the overall profile of TDs. In the next section, we explore in some more detail whether or not the impact of candidate gender is conditional on voter characteristics. While the aggregate evidence suggests that women candidates are not systematically underperforming in their vote returns, we explore whether there is a particular profile of voter that systematically votes for women (or men) at the ballot box.

Voter Survey Analysis

The Irish National Election Study survey data matched with the candidate data permit us to consider voter characteristics and candidate characteristics, as well as the interactions between the two, to see whether there is a set of voters who are systematically more likely to vote for women (or men). We make use of three separate dependent variables in the analysis that follows. The first, *PREFERENCE*, captures whether or not the respondent expressed any preference for a female candidate and if so which preference; the second, *THERM*, measures on a 1–10 thermometer scale the rating score given to each candidate by the respondent, and the third, *PREF1–3*, captures whether or not the respondent gave a high preference (a one, two or three) to the candidate in question. The independent variables in the analysis include the demographic and attitudinal characteristics of voters that might influence their propensity to vote for a woman candidate: *WOMAN, AGE, EDUCATION, FEMINIST, KNOWLEDGE, PARTY CANDIDATE, PARTY ID* and *PARTY CENTRED VOTER*.

The key variable of interest is *WOMAN*, which is intended to capture the propensity of women to vote for women (measured as a standard dichotomous variable: zero if the respondent is male and unity if female). *AGE* is measured in years, with the expectation that younger people will be more likely to vote for women. *EDUCATION* is a dichotomous variable that distinguishes those with secondary school education (or less) from those with a tertiary-level qualification, with the latter theorized to be more likely to vote for women. Political *KNOWLEDGE* is intended to capture political engagement and uses the political knowledge scale from the INES. This comprises five factual closed ended questions with four options provided with each. *PARTY CANDIDATE* is a simple dichotomous variable that captures whether the candidate under consideration is from a party with which the respondent self-identifies, i.e. reports himself as feeling close to. We also include a variable, *PARTY ID*, which measures the strength of the respondent's party identification; we reason that where this is strong, the voter will be driven to vote the party line regardless of the gender of the candidate. *PARTY ID* is measured as a dichotomous variable, where unity is feeling close to a particular party and zero is not. Finally, *PARTY CENTRED VOTER* captures how important the candidate rather than the party is for the respondent. This measure is a three-point scale and ranges from -1 (candidate centred) to 1 (party centred).[2]

A specific attitudinal question on gender and politics was included for the first time in the 2007 INES. Respondents were asked whether or not they agreed with the statement 'In general things would improve if there were more women in politics'. We label this variable *FEMINIST*, which is a simple dichotomous measure distinguishing between those who agree with and those who disagree with (or are neutral about) the statement. We expect that voters who have more politicized attitudes to gender issues in politics will be more inclined to vote for women. Finally, for the *PREFERENCE* model we control for the number of preferences cast as some respondents express only one preference and others complete the full ballot. For the *THERM* models we also control for a respondent's mean rating of other candidates as respondents may treat these scales differently and we are interested in the relative ratings of women and men by the respondent in question.

Table 3 presents the results of this analysis for six separate models using both a parsimonious and a full model for each of the three dependent variables. It is important to stress that although the analysis was confined to female candidates, the results are equivalent to a model in which both male and female candidates were included.[3] The first column in Table 3 reports the results of the parsimonious linear regression model with *PREFERENCE* as the dependent variable and *WOMAN* and *PARTY CANDIDATE* as independent variables. As is clearly evident from the results in column 1, the only substantive variable that is significant is whether or not the candidate under consideration is from a party the respondent identifies with. In model 5, where a high preference for the candidate is the dependent variable, *PARTY CANDIDATE* is yet again the only variable to reach significance. Similar results are found with the thermometer scores, though here it seems women respondents are slightly more likely to rate women candidates highly.

The results from the fuller models (models 2, 4 and 6) also fail to find any evidence in favour of the hypothesis that women favour female candidates; nowhere does *WOMAN* reach significance; nor do we find evidence that any particular subgroup of women respondents is more inclined to vote for women candidates (the interaction terms are not significant). The only exception to this is that women with low levels of party identification are less likely to assess women candidates favourably on the

Table 3. Explaining votes for and thermometer ratings of female candidates

	(1) Preference	(2) Preference	(3) Therm	(4) Therm	(5) Preferences 1–3	(6) Preferences 1–3
Woman respondent	0.0836	−0.250	0.418**	0.726	0.181	0.508
	(0.87)	(−0.71)	(2.41)	(1.09)	(1.57)	(0.93)
Own party candidate	−0.484***	−0.921***	2.849***	3.468***	2.523***	3.151***
	(−2.67)	(−4.29)	(7.54)	(7.90)	(7.85)	(8.68)
Woman × Own party candidate	0.0578	−0.136	−0.0385	0.618	−0.406	−0.0934
	(0.26)	(−0.46)	(−0.072)	(0.99)	(−0.88)	(−0.18)
Weakness of Party ID		0.541***		−0.867***		−0.756***
		(3.22)		(−3.16)		(−3.46)
Education		0.00397		0.129		0.0191
		(0.030)		(0.58)		(0.11)
Knowledge		−0.0942		0.0598		0.127
		(−1.50)		(0.53)		(1.47)
Age		−0.000938		0.00259		0.00171
		(−0.25)		(0.36)		(0.31)
Feminist		−0.171		0.687***		0.570***
		(−1.36)		(3.06)		(3.27)
Party-centred voter (PCV)		0.160*		−0.00883		−0.0530
		(1.87)		(−0.057)		(−0.47)
Woman * Weak Party ID		0.202		−0.827**		−0.418
		(0.79)		(−2.09)		(−1.30)
Woman * Education		−0.141		0.0603		0.0722
		(−0.81)		(0.19)		(0.29)
Woman × Knowledge		0.0110		0.0146		−0.167
		(0.14)		(0.094)		(−1.49)

Woman * Age	0.00261			−0.00710		0.00254
	(0.49)			(−0.69)		(0.32)
Woman * Feminist	0.252			0.0227		−0.156
	(1.37)			(0.066)		(−0.63)
Woman * PCV	−0.0831			−0.148		0.0247
	(−0.72)			(−0.70)		(0.16)
Number of preferences	0.587***	0.578***				
	(26.7)	(27.6)				
Mean rating of male candidates			0.331***	0.381***		
			(5.67)	(6.63)		
Constant	0.898***	1.224***	1.843***	0.940	−1.523***	−2.098***
	(8.73)	(4.07)	(3.74)	(1.53)	(−18.3)	(−5.68)
Observations	756	756	1370	1370	2090	2090
R-squared	0.57	0.59	0.09	0.13		

Notes: Robust *t*-statistics in parentheses. Robust *z*-statistics for models 5 and 6. ***$p < 0.01$, **$p < 0.05$, *$p < 0.1$.

thermometer scales, but the effect is small: less than four points on the thermometer scale (range 0–100) across the range of the variable. Moreover, that evaluation does not appear to translate into actual electoral support (preferences cast) – a result that perhaps underlines the difference between thermometer scores and voting behaviour. The variable *FEMINIST* is, however, significant in models 4 and 6, suggesting that respondents (male and female) who favour the entry of more women into politics are more likely to rate women candidates highly and also to give them a higher preference.

On the whole, the analysis in this section suggests that female candidates are neither systematically favoured nor discriminated against by voters. These results echo much international research, which finds that voters do not differentiate between candidates on gender grounds. In the next section we explore further the question of why, if all the evidence so far suggests that the Irish political system is not rife with gender bias, there is such a large gender disparity in elective office in Ireland.

Evidence from the 2007 Candidate Survey

While the incumbency advantage is an impediment to raising the overall number of women in the Dáil, this factor cannot explain why there are systematic differences in the numbers of male and female challengers at election time, especially given that there is no systematic voter bias against women candidates. In 2007, of the 324 non-incumbent candidates who contested the election, fully 262 (81%) were men. International research suggests that women are less likely than men to be recruited into politics (Burns *et al.*, 2001), they are less likely to receive encouragement and support to run for office from party and elected officials and even among highly educated professionals they are less likely to think they are qualified to run (Lawless & Fox, 2005). To explore the possibility that there is a gender gap in political ambition or that parties fail to recruit and encourage women to run for office, we turn to the 2007 Candidate Survey.[4]

The survey was conducted in the immediate aftermath of the election and was sent to every candidate. The response rate was just under 40 per cent, which is not out of line with international experience. The incumbent–non-incumbent response rate exactly mirrored the split in the overall universe of candidates and the gender split in response rates was similarly reflective of the overall population. However, the response rate from Labour Party candidates was somewhat higher than average; while they constituted 11 per cent of candidates, they comprised 17 per cent of respondents, which may bias the results somewhat. Furthermore, we also have a sample selection problem in that we did not survey the pool of 'potential' candidates, but have only those who were nominated. Absent from the sample are all of the 'potential' legislative candidates – those who were discouraged from running or opted out at the initial decision stage. The sampling of only those who entered the race will almost certainly underestimate the impact of gender on political recruitment. On a more positive note, for the first time in an Irish Candidate Survey, the candidates

Table 4. Candidate perceptions of the political and electoral process

	Male candidates agreeing (%)	Female candidates agreeing (%)	Difference (%)
Women are not given the opportunity by parties	29	73	44***
Women do not have the confidence to stand	17	50	33***
Not enough women come forward to be considered	91	74	16**
Most voters prefer male candidates	17	31	14
Women put families above a career in parliament	82	93	11
Women do not fit into parliament	3	3	0
Women do not have right experience and education	2	6	4
Women are not interested in politics	8	6	2

Note: Chi-square significance level: **0.01, ***0.001.

were presented with a battery of statements that explicitly tapped their beliefs about the reasons for the under-representation of women. These statements attempt to capture open manifestations of gender bias but also differences in the opportunity structure of men and women. Respondents were asked either to (strongly) agree or to disagree with a statement such as 'Not enough women come forward to be considered as candidates'. In Table 4, the results from a comparison of the responses of male and female candidates to these statements are presented.

The first notable element to be taken from this analysis is that there does not appear to be a traditional view among candidates of politics being a male-only preserve. Very few male or female respondents believed that women were not qualified for political careers, that they did not fit into parliamentary life or that they were not interested in politics. Interestingly, more women than men agreed with the statement that 'Women don't have the right experience and education', though the number is small and the difference is not statistically significant. The second striking result is that female candidates are much more likely to believe strongly that parties do not give women adequate opportunities. Seventy-three per cent of female candidates in the survey felt that this was the case, compared with only 29 per cent of male candidates. The highly significant difference hints at the very different experiences of male and female candidates in getting nominated. Both male and female candidates tended to subscribe to the supply-side model explanation for the under-representation of women, though male candidates were more likely (91 per cent versus 74 per cent) to agree with the statement that 'not enough women come forward to be considered'.

Another interesting finding, which hints at the political ambition and socialization thesis for the continued under-representation of women, is the finding that far more women candidates ascribe to the view that 'women don't have the confidence to stand'. One in two female respondents agreed with this statement compared with less than one in five men. Women candidates seem to believe that gender plays a role at the critical candidate emergence phase of the electoral process. Both male and female candidates believe that family responsibilities inhibit women's political careers, echoing research findings that the traditional division of labour in households may lead women to consider their family obligations more carefully than their male counterparts (Conway *et al.*, 1997). Interestingly, and despite our earlier findings, 17 per cent of male respondents and almost one in three women respondents believe that voters prefer male to female candidates.

While we should not read too much into these findings, given the sampling problems and the fact that they reflect perceptions of the process, the stark differences in women's and men's faith in political parties to recruit and promote female candidates suggests that there may well be nomination bias at play in Irish political parties. Furthermore, there is clearly much scope for further investigation of women's self-perception of their qualifications to run for office. If women rule themselves out of the game at the candidate emergence phase of the process there is unlikely to be a radical change in the numbers of female TDs in the near future.

Conclusion

This paper takes the significant case of Ireland to explore how far voters are responsible for the low proportion of women in parliaments. The Irish case combines a very low number of women in representative office with an electoral system that provides voters with the opportunity to support women strongly if they so wish, or vote against them, or simply ignore any gender cues that might be offered. We have examined several aspects, looking first at the relative success of women in elections and then at whether women discriminate in favour of, or even against women candidates. Our findings are overwhelmingly negative. We found almost no evidence at all that women, as women, fared worse than men, or that voters discriminated for or against candidates on grounds of gender. In looking at candidate success we are mindful of the difficulties in assessing the importance of gender when men and women rarely run against one another when all other things are equal. There are plenty of instances of parties running multiple candidates where at least one is a woman, but these contests are still a relatively small minority of races. We attempted to ensure all other things were equal by using a dependent variable that was itself adjusted for variations in districts. We found nothing, at least with respect to gender, although most other factors were significant in accordance with expectations. We also explored the behaviour of voters directly, calculating how far women favoured female candidates over male ones when they had a choice. Favouring could be defined in a number of ways, but regardless of the operationalization, there was little evidence of bias. We then turned to a study of the views of candidates, and found that they located most of the blame for the absence of women in the Dáil on parties, who do not encourage women to the extent that they should, although a significant number of women candidates also thought voters were less supportive of women candidates. Women are not nominated by the larger, more successful parties. It is the smaller, less successful ones who are more likely to have women run, partly for ideological reasons, but also because they have fewer incumbents and more rapid turnover. Getting nominated is no good if it is not by a successful party. Party matters most, and so needs to be an important part of making other things equal.

The main conclusion here is that the strong role that the Irish electoral system gives to voters in deciding not just which parties sit in parliament but also who represents those parties in the Dáil does not seem to provide an explanation of why so few of those seated should be women. This does not seem to be a finding that is essentially an artefact of our methodology. While serious questions can be raised about the difficulties of assessing the importance of gender when there are relatively few instances of comparable men and women candidates running against one another, our best efforts to estimate who would triumph if that did occur suggest that there would be no clear winner. Whichever way we slice up the data they continue to tell the same story. If there are too few women in Dáil Éireann, it is not down to the voters.

Notes

1. Further details on the measure can be obtained from McElroy and Marsh (2010). This measure is very highly correlated (0.95) with an alternative dependent variable, proportion of a quota received.
2. For more details, see Marsh *et al.* (2008, Ch. 8).
3. By including male as well as female candidates, however, we would have to include third-order interaction terms, which only serve to obfuscate the central findings, not to mention making an already large table of output considerably larger.
4. This was carried out in the Department of Political Science in Trinity College Dublin by a team of graduate students, including Laura Sudulich, Matt Wall and Jane Suiter under the primary direction of Michael Marsh. The data is lodged with the Comparative Candidate Study archive at the University of Mannheim.

References

Benoit, K. & Marsh, M. (2010) Incumbent and challenger campaign spending effects in proportional electoral systems: the Irish elections of 2002, *Political Research Quarterly*, 63(1), pp. 159–173.

Burns, N., Scholzman, K. & Verba, S. (2001) *The Private Roots of Public Action: Gender, Equality, and Political Participation* (Cambridge, MA: Harvard University Press).

Conway, M., Steuernagel, G. & Ahern, D. (1997) *Women and Political Participation* (Washington, DC: Congressional Press).

Gallagher, M. (2007) The earthquake that never happened: analysis of the results, in: M. Gallagher & M. Marsh (Eds) *How Ireland Voted* (Basingstoke: Palgrave Macmillan).

Inglehart, M. (1981) Political interest in West European women, *Comparative Political Studies*, 14, pp. 299–326.

Inglehart, R. & Norris, P. (2003) *Rising Tide: Gender Equality and Cultural Change around the World* (New York: Cambridge University Press).

Kenworthy, L. & Malami, M. (1999) Gender inequality in political representation: a worldwide comparative analysis, *Social Forces*, 78(1), pp. 235–269.

Lakeman, E. (1994) Comparing political opportunities in Great Britain and Ireland, in: W. Rule & J. Zimmerman (Eds) *Electoral Systems in Comparative Perspective* (Westport, CT: Greenwood Press).

Lawless, J. & Fox, R. (2005) *It Takes a Candidate: Why Women Don't Run for Political Office* (New York: Cambridge University Press).

Marsh, M., Sinnott, R., Garry, J. & Kennedy, F. (2008) *The Irish Voter: The Nature of Electoral Competition in the Republic of Ireland* (Manchester: Manchester University Press).

Matland, R. (1998) Women's representation in national legislatures: developed and developing countries, *Legislative Studies Quarterly*, 23(1), pp. 109–125.

Matland, R. & Brown, D. D. (1992) District magnitude's effect on female representation in US state legislatures, *Legislative Studies Quarterly*, 17, pp. 469–492.

McAllister, I. & Studlar, D. (2002) Electoral systems and women's representation: a long-term perspective, *Representation*, 39(1), pp. 3–14.

McDonagh, E. (2002) Political citizenship and democratization: the gender paradox, *American Political Science Review*, 96(3), pp. 535–552.

McElroy, G. & Marsh, M. (2010) Candidate gender and voter choice: analysis from a multimember preferential voting system, *Political Research Quarterly*, 63(4), pp. 822–833.

Pitkin, H. (1967) *The Concept of Representation* (Berkeley, CA: University of California Press).

Reynolds, A (1999) Women in the legislatures and executives of the world: knocking at the highest glass ceiling, *World Politics*, 51(4), pp. 547–572.

Rule, W. (1987) Electoral systems, contextual factors and women's opportunity for election to parliament in twenty-three democracies, *Western Political Quarterly*, 40, pp. 477–498.

Salmond, R. (2006) Proportional representation and female parliamentarians, *Legislative Studies Quarterly*, 31(2), pp. 175–204.

Schwindt-Bayer, L. A. (2005) The incumbency disadvantage and women's election to legislative office, *Electoral Studies*, 24, pp. 227–244.

Parties and Referendums in Ireland 1937–2011

MICHAEL GALLAGHER
Trinity College Dublin, Ireland

ABSTRACT   *Political parties are central to democracy, but according to some arguments their capacity to discharge their functions is weakening in many countries. Moreover, the institution of the referendum is sometimes perceived to pose particular problems for political parties, impinging on their centrality in political life and on their internal cohesion. Ireland is one of Europe's heaviest users of the referendum, so in that light it may be expected that parties in Ireland are weaker than those in most other countries. Consideration of the available evidence produces a mixed picture, however, with Irish parties conforming to expected trends in some respects but not in others.*

Introduction

Democracy, as we know, is a contested concept, but the regimes that claim liberal democracy as their underlying ideology operate on the basis of a fairly common set of political institutional arrangements. Democracy in what is sometimes termed the first world is essentially representative democracy, in which power rests primarily with a government, which is elected by a parliament, or sometimes appointed by a president, elected in turn by the people. The people's elected representatives, rather than the people themselves, make political decisions and are accountable to the people through regular competitive elections.

Political parties play a central and crucial role in this process. In the much quoted statement of Schattschneider, 'modern democracy is unthinkable save in terms of the parties' (Schattschneider, 1977: 1). *Inter alia*, they structure the political world, recruit and socialise the political elite, provide linkage between rulers and ruled, and aggregate interests (Dalton & Wattenberg, 2000: 5–10). Without them, it seems, the political process would be dominated by individual political entrepreneurs and by ever-shifting alliances among these. The policymaking process would lack all coherence, accountability would vanish because it would become impossible to attribute responsibility for decisions to any particular actor, and making decisions on any issue would entail negotiating a series of *ad hoc* deals with individual MPs, who themselves would be under pressure from a range of local and national interests. With all their faults, parties are an indispensable part of modern politics. If at times we find it difficult to live with them, we cannot imagine living without them.

Yet, parties are widely perceived to be in difficulty, held in increasing disregard by citizens and becoming ever more weakly implanted in and engaged with civic society. These tendencies affect parties everywhere, but if our focus is on parties in Ireland specifically, it becomes relevant to consider that one aspect of the Irish political system might mean that Irish parties face even greater difficulties than their counterparts elsewhere. This is the extensive use of the referendum as a means of deciding major political questions.

In this short paper I shall establish the centrality of parties to politics in Ireland, discuss their arguably weakening grip and consider whether the frequency of referendums has particular implications for the cohesion and salience of parties in Ireland.

The Role of Parties in Irish Politics

Parties in Ireland, as elsewhere, dominate political life, albeit less than totally. Their dominance is unquestioned at government level. Since the foundation of the state only one minister has not belonged to a party: an independent who, with a few supporters, was part of the coalition making up the 'makeshift majority' government of 1948–1951 (McCullagh, 1998). Even he, James Dillon, was a former TD, and future leader, of one of the established parties, Fine Gael. In Ireland's government-centred system of decision-making (O'Malley & Martin, 2010), parties occupy the positions of greatest power. One important aspect of party control of government is that the Irish parties, including the government parties, act very cohesively in parliament, with any deviation from party block voting being rare indeed (Gallagher, 2010: 135–142).

At other levels of governance parties have less of a monopoly. Whereas parliaments across Europe tend to consist only of party MPs, independent TDs have been a continuous presence in the Dáil since 1922, regularly winning between 5 and 10 per cent of the seats (Weeks, 2010: 146–147). While Dillon remains the only independent to become a minister, a number of minority governments – the most recent examples are those of 1997–2002 and, in its last months, 2007–2011 – have been reliant upon the support of independent TDs to remain in office, support that is usually linked to particularistic spending in those TDs' constituencies.

The presidency might be seen as an institution that is still further removed from party control. Two of the eight presidents of the period 1938–2011 (Hyde and Ó Dálaigh) were independents, and a case that might be made that other presidents should be seen as independents rather than as party nominees; Mary Robinson (1990–1997) was an independent backed by Labour and other left-wing parties, while Seán T. O'Kelly, Patrick Hillery and Mary McAleese nominated themselves for their second term, emphasising their independence of the party to which they had once belonged. The presidency, though, is an almost entirely symbolic office.

Local government, too, can hardly be seen as party-controlled. While it is true that most councillors belong to one of the main parties, independents are even more prominent here than in the Dáil, and, in any case, power at council level lies firmly with the centrally appointed county or city manager rather than with elected representatives (Collins & Quinlivan, 2010: 362–368).

Finally, it should be noted that some important aspects of policymaking are no longer controlled by parties and their representatives because of the extent to which the power formerly in the hands of governments is now shared with other actors. Interest groups have been heavily involved in economic policymaking since the late 1980s (Murphy, 2010). In addition, an increasingly important role in the governance of its 27 member states is played by the European Union (EU). The individuals who occupy the positions of power within the EU's main institutions are selected by parties, or by party-controlled bodies such as governments, but parties do not themselves control the way in which members of the Commission or the Council behave (Lindberg *et al.*, 2008). The result is, clearly, to weaken the centrality of parties, as the bodies that they control wane in power while those outside their control wax, leading, it has been argued, to a degree of 'politics without policies' at national level (Schmidt, 2006: 223). This applies *a fortiori* to Ireland since the December 2010 'memo of understanding' with the European Central Bank and the International Monetary Fund, bodies to which government policies have to be explained and justified and that, of course, are not controlled by political parties.

None the less, the 'partyness of government' at national level is total. In practice, all ministers are TDs of the government party or parties. This is not constitutionally obligatory; Article 28.7.2 of the constitution allows the appointment of two government members who belong to the Seanad rather than to the Dáil, and given that the Taoiseach has the right to nominate 11 of the 60 senators, this provides a route to bringing non-party technocrats into government. Yet, this has not happened, even at a time of national crisis; only twice (in 1957 and in 1981) since the coming into operation of the constitution in 1937 has a senator been made a minister, and in each case he was a party member and a former member of the Dáil or Seanad. In short, parties are central to governance in Ireland.

The Weakening of Parties

If parties are as strong as ever when it comes to having their hands on the levers of government, even if governments themselves may now have less freedom to make choices than once they did, the same cannot be said for parties' roles elsewhere. There is a familiar distinction, first introduced in the 1960s, between parties in public office, parties as organisations and parties in the electorate (Mair, 1997: 120–154). Regarding the first of these, as we have seen, parties remain central, and in the second, too, parties in most countries, including Ireland, seem to be thriving, with party head offices ever more strongly resourced, due in particular to the introduction and expansion of state financing and the fact that this money is paid to party centres rather than to local organisations. It is at the third level, the 'party in the electorate', that parties seem to be becoming ever more peripheral rather than more central. There are three aspects of this: the ability of parties to inspire loyalty among voters, stability in the party system and the degree of parties' implantation in civic society.

Party identification in Ireland is, in brief, low and declining. Analysis of the 2002 Irish National Election Study data shows that the percentage of those feeling 'close to' a party was lower in Ireland than in 13 of the other 14 countries in the Comparative Study of Electoral Systems (CSES) project and at the same level as that in Denmark (Marsh *et al.*, 2008: 63). Moreover, the trend in Ireland is one of steady decline. In 1978 around 65 per cent of respondents said they felt close to a party, but by 2002 this figure had dropped to only 26 per cent (Marsh *et al.*, 2008: 64). The relative stability in voting behaviour during the 1990s and 2000s raised questions as to whether party identification might be stronger and more stable than these data suggested, but the dramatic drop in Fianna Fáil support at the 2011 election bears out the argument that an increasing proportion of the electorate is willing to vote instrumentally and is largely free of any strong emotional attachment to any particular party.

On the other hand, the Irish party system, viewed over the long term, has been remarkably stable, with Fianna Fáil, Fine Gael and Labour occupying, in that order, the first three places at every election from 1932 to 2007. While Fianna Fáil's dramatic loss of support at the 2011 election put an end to that sequence, it was striking that the main beneficiaries were Fine Gael and Labour rather than a new party. The three main parties collectively are weakening, but only slightly: an average of 87 per cent of the votes at the elections of the period 1923–1982 compared with 78 per cent at those of 1987–2011.

It is over terms of parties' connections with civil society that the strongest concerns have been expressed, with suggestions that 'parties are failing in their capacity to engage the ordinary citizen' (Mair, 2006: 12). Parties' implantation in civil society is conventionally measured by examining figures on membership. As is well known, there are many difficulties here: parties may not know how many members they have, they may have different conceptions of what 'membership' means in the first place, they have an incentive to exaggerate their claimed membership numbers, and actors within the party may have intra-party incentives to overstate the membership of their units (Gallagher *et al.*, 2011: 329–330). The conventional response to this dilemma is to note the problems and then to use the best data available, with all their shortcomings.

As far as we can tell, party membership in Ireland has dropped from around 5 per cent of the electorate in 1980 to about 2 per cent by the late 2000s (van Biezen *et al.*, 2009: 28). The almost universal trend across Europe is for a downward trend in membership, but, as with party identification, the Irish figure is well below average. While it is comparable with, or even above, the figures for Britain, France and Germany, it is well below membership figures in smaller countries, which tend to have relatively high membership densities, the highest being Malta (30 per cent), Austria (17 per cent), Cyprus (16 per cent) and Finland (8 per cent) (van Biezen *et al.*, 2009: 24).

Much of the drop is accounted for by the apparent fall-off in membership of the (formerly) largest party, Fianna Fáil. When asked, the party routinely claims to have about 65,000 members, but one of its own internal reports in 2004 estimated the true figure at around a quarter of this, and mentioned other signs of organisational decline: members were elderly, most branches had not had a new member in 3 years, and it was likely that the number of existing members who were dying exceeded the number joining (Weeks, 2010: 155). However, it is not clear that things were ever any different, and the story of decline requires taking on trust the high figures claimed by Fianna Fáil in particular for earlier years while treating sceptically the same claims made today. As in most countries, a majority of members do not play an active part in intra-party affairs, though, again, this was probably always the case.

Indeed, in some respects the Irish parties might be a little better implanted than their counterparts elsewhere. A recent survey of party membership across Europe concluded, damningly, that members are now so unrepresentative of broader electorates that they could be seen not as constituting part of civil society 'but rather as constituting the outer ring of an extended political class' (van Biezen *et al.*, 2009: 10–11). As well as being predominantly male and having an average age well above that of voters, they tend to be 'connected in some way to state service', being either public sector employees or dependent on the public purse in some other way – for their pension, for example (van Biezen *et al.*, 2009: 10). Irish party members, too, are overwhelmingly male and are older than party voters, but in other respects they do not conform to this picture. Typically, they belong to other organisations: around three-quarters of Fine Gael members surveyed in 1999–2000 belonged to another association, most commonly a farmers' association or the Gaelic Athletic Association (GAA), while three-quarters of Labour members belong to a trade union (Gallagher & Marsh 2002: 65–66; Kennedy *et al.*, 2005: 173). Among Fine Gael members in employment, only 23 per cent work in the public sector, though given that nearly a quarter were aged 65 or more it is clear that many others were in receipt of the state pension (Gallagher & Marsh, 2002: 63). Information on the backgrounds of Fianna Fáil members is lacking given the continued absence of a full-scale member survey of that party.

This degree of implantation in civic society is a resource for the Irish parties, but there is a feature of Irish politics that is sometimes seen as a particular threat to parties' ability to act effectively. This is the frequency of referendums in Ireland.

Parties and Referendums

Parties are central to the practice of representative democracy, and as such the institution of the referendum could, in theory, pose problems for them, as some argue it does for representative democracy. According to critics of the referendum – some of whom equate any use of the referendum with the adoption of the ill-defined concept of 'direct democracy' – it gives ordinary citizens a power that they are ill-equipped to deploy. Sartori, for example, refers to the 'cognitive incompetence' of most citizens and argues that it is Utopian to expect them 'to express, issue by issue, articulate, informed and "rational" judgements' (Sartori, 1987: 120, 123). Michels, too, set up the straw man of 'direct democracy' only to knock it down again (Hyland, 1995: 247). Arguments along these lines are occasionally heard at Ireland's EU referendums, where some voters are perceived to vote on the basis of extraneous factors, though cross-national analysis concludes that issue voting is prevalent at EU referendums and that 'voters are smarter than they are often given credit for' (Binzer Hobolt, 2009: 248–249).

Given that parties control governments and dominate elections, the referendum has the potential to constitute a threat to their hegemony. Referendums challenge the 'partyness' of policymaking (Strøm, 2000: 186); in Ireland, citizens could be forgiven for ignoring the parties' policies on European integration at election times because they know that they will have the final say on any proposed change through a referendum. It is true that parties may under some circumstances be able to control the issues, the precise question and the timing of referendums. In these circumstances, governing parties in particular might be able to ensure that the referendums that occur do not endanger their fortunes or their unity (LeDuc, 2003: 167–169). However, some referendums may be unavoidable responses to events outside governmental control (many EU referendums fall into this category), while a referendum that seemed unproblematic when it was called might prove unexpectedly disruptive to party unity. In addition, referendums might pose problems for parties in government if they enable the electorate to derail a programme or impose impossible or contradictory demands upon the government. These risks are highest in countries where there is provision for the initiative, such as Italy, Latvia, Lithuania, Slovakia, Slovenia and Switzerland. In Italy in the early 1990s the rejective initiative played a central role in bringing about the demise of the previously dominant Christian Democrats (DC) and Socialist Party (PSI).

Party unity is most likely to be threatened by a referendum on an issue that cuts across party lines. Initiatives in particular, but all referendums to some extent, pose the risk that the issues on which they are fought are precisely the ones that do not correspond to those that structure the party system, because such issues are, almost by definition, the ones that can be assumed to be decided by general elections. Consequently, the major parties, in referendum campaigns, are liable to be confronted by issues (such as European integration) that divide them internally and that, moreover, may be particularly salient issues for minor parties for whom such campaigns are unifying and mobilising. This highlights a further problem for the parties, which is that very often referendum campaigns are dominated not by parties at all but by established interest groups or by *ad hoc* groups that bring to the campaign a commitment that the divided parties are unable to muster. On the other hand, it may be that it is an issue itself, rather than the referendum on the issue, that is divisive for a party, and thus party unity would be affected even if there were no referendum. Indeed, referendums may help to preserve party unity by enabling the party to avoid committing itself on the grounds that the decision is up to the people.

Across the EU the incidence of referendums varies significantly. While the median across member states is four referendums in the period 1945–2010, the range is large: from countries that have held none, such as Bulgaria and Germany, to Italy with 69 and, in second place, Ireland with 30. (Two states outside the EU, Switzerland and Liechtenstein, have each held more referendums than Italy.) Party membership, as we noted earlier, also varies greatly. Trust in parties is generally low, with an EU-wide survey in October–November 2009 finding that only 16 per cent of respondents said they 'tend to trust' parties, with 75 per cent tending not to trust them; the range here was from a peak of 50 per cent of Danes trusting their parties to a mere 2 per cent of Latvians sharing that feeling (Eurobarometer, 2010: QA10.7). The figures in Ireland (13 per cent tend to trust, 81 per cent tend not to trust) were a little more critical than the EU average. While levels of membership and trust in parties are positively correlated ($r = 0.29$), the relationship between the number of referendums and trust in parties is negative but weak ($r = -0.10$). Omitting the post-communist member states, where both membership levels and trust are systematically low, strengthens the latter relationship only slightly ($r = -0.13$). At the macro level, this provides no support for any suggestion that use of the referendum weakens parties or their standing in the eyes of the electorate.

Parties and Referendums in Ireland

In Ireland the referendum is strongly tied to constitutional change, which removes significant discretionary power from governments. While a government can sometimes decide whether to bring an issue forward or not – and in the case of EU referendums it does not even have this choice – it is unable to choose whether the issue should or should not be decided by referendum. Hence, it cannot, as some governments can, ensure that issues that might divide a government party internally are kept off the referendum agenda. A survey of Ireland's referendum history shows that while the dominance of the mainstream parties is regularly challenged at referendums by smaller parties and *ad hoc* groups, parties have been successful in avoiding any internal divisions becoming public in a damaging manner.

A number of Irish referendums illustrate well the general phenomenon of campaigns being dominated by *ad hoc* groups with parties relegated to the sidelines. Even at the second referendum, the 1959 vote on whether to change the electoral system, a central role was played by trade unions and small but vociferous groups on both sides (O'Leary, 1961: 71–80). This was also very apparent during the seven 'moral issue' referendums on divorce and abortion held during the period 1983–2002. The first of these, indeed, was instigated by a pressure group, the 'Pro-Life Amendment Campaign', and this referendum campaign in particular was dominated by *ad hoc* groups to an extent not witnessed since, giving many voters the impression of 'elite withdrawal' (Darcy & Laver, 1990).

In particular, all of Ireland's EU referendums have seen, at the very least, competition between the main parties and other groups over the framing of the issue at stake (O'Mahony, 2009: 435–442). In the first of these, the 1972 campaign on European Community (EC) entry, the trade unions and minor left-wing groups played a prominent role in the 'No' campaign, although the combined support of Fianna Fáil and Fine Gael for entry produced an overwhelming 'Yes' majority. Subsequent EU referendums have been made necessary by the judgment of the Supreme Court in April 1987 that the state could not, under the constitution as it stood, ratify the Single European Act (SEA). This arose from a case brought by the 'radical and nationalist' economist Raymond Crotty, himself a prominent opponent of EC entry, and it gave rise to the birth, or reactivation, of a number of groups opposed to the SEA on a variety of grounds: a sovereignty lobby opposed to EU membership *per se*, a radical internationalist lobby concerned about neutrality, and a traditional Catholic values group fearing that European integration had the potential to bring about the 'imposition' of divorce and abortion upon Ireland. In the 1980s party cues still wielded considerable sway over voters, but the decline in party identification since then – quite possibly accelerated by the incidence of referendums at which individual parties sent out mixed messages, no messages, or messages at odds with the preferences of their voters – has meant that these cues no longer have the power that they once did.

The comfortable passage of the referendums on the Maastricht Treaty in 1992 and the Amsterdam Treaty in 1998 obscured this, though the Maastricht campaign saw a marked rise in the involvement of civil society groups (O'Mahony, 2009: 436). The defeat of the Nice Treaty referendum in June 2001, despite backing for the treaty from Fianna Fáil, Fine Gael and Labour, which had won 78 per cent of the votes between them at the previous election, brought home strongly the point that voters were open to persuasion by groups other than their regularly supported party. The pattern was repeated at the three subsequent EU referendums of the 2000s, with the 'Yes' victory in the 2009 Lisbon 2 referendum being attributed partly to 'the active involvement of a number of civic society groups' such as 'Ireland for Europe' (Quinlan, 2012).

At the same time, although parties have been challenged by other actors at EU and moral issue referendums, their internal unity has rarely been seriously threatened. True, parties have not always been of one mind on referendum issues, but the electorate has rarely been presented with the spectacle of multiple voices from within a party advocating different outcomes in the way that, say, voters for the French Socialist Party were given very different cues by their leading figures at the 2005 EU Constitutional Treaty referendum. This comes about partly because there is a degree of policy convergence within parties, and also because the referendum issues on which opinions differ are less important than party unity to most of the 'dissidents', who prefer to keep silent during campaigns when they disagree with their party's line than to speak out against this line. Fianna Fáil and Fine Gael have been solidly in favour of a 'Yes' vote at all eight EU referendums, as has Labour at all but the first two of these. Labour opposed EU entry in 1972, its more Europhile wing keeping quiet during the campaign, and took no position in the SEA referendum, when most of its membership seemed to incline towards the 'No' side.

Moral issues have divided all parties, sometimes visibly so. In 1983 there was agreement between the two main parties on putting the so-called 'pro-life amendment' to the people, but there was disagreement on the precise form of words to be used. When the Dáil vote was taken, the coalition government's wording was rejected in favour of a more conservative amendment put forward by Fianna Fáil, which was passed by the Dáil owing to defections by a number of Fine Gael and Labour TDs. In 1986 the government brought forward an amendment to legalise divorce, but one cabinet minister, Patrick Cooney, spoke publicly in favour of a 'No' vote. At the second divorce referendum in 1995 it was clear that neither of the two larger parties was unanimously behind the official 'Yes' position that the party adopted, but this time the dissidents refrained from entering the fray publicly. With no sign of further such referendums on the horizon, moral issues seem to have lost their potential to do lasting damage to a party. Moreover, even in the heyday of the moral issue referendum, it was arguable that these referendums actually preserved the existing parties, insulating the existing party system from challenge 'by providing an alternative channel for the expression of this cleavage' (Sinnott, 1995: 295).

Conclusion

Parties are central to our conception of functioning liberal-democratic systems, and yet some observers believe that parties are 'failing', placing a question mark over the continuation of democracy as we know it. Given the argument that the institution of the referendum poses a threat to parties' centrality and cohesion, the fact that Ireland is one of Europe's heaviest employers of the referendum might seem to place the Irish parties at particular risk of being unable to perform the functions generally ascribed to parties. Few referendum issues run along the same lines as those that structure the party system, posing a threat to internal party unity and giving small parties and *ad hoc* groups the opportunity to challenge the hegemony of established parties.

Nonetheless, the Irish parties do not seem to have been unduly weakened by the referendum experience. They do have some concerns: party identification is exceptionally low and falling, and party membership is low (though not necessarily falling). On the other hand, party members seem to be well implanted in society, while parties in government still dominate the policymaking process and are able to act as highly cohesive actors in parliament. If parties as we know them do cease to operate as the central actors of Irish democracy, we cannot blame – or credit – referendums for this.

References

Binzer Hobolt, S. (2009) *Europe in Question: Referendums on European Integration* (Oxford: Oxford University Press).

Collins, N. & Quinlivan, A. (2010) Multi-level governance, in: J. Coakley & M. Gallagher (Eds) *Politics in the Republic of Ireland,* 5th ed., pp. 359–380 (London: Routledge and PSAI Press).

Dalton, R. J. & Wattenberg, M. P. (2000) Unthinkable democracy: political change in advanced industrial democracies, in: R. J. Dalton & M. P. Wattenberg (Eds) *Parties without Partisans: Political Change in Advanced Industrial Democracies,* pp. 3–16 (Oxford: Oxford University Press).

Darcy, R. & Laver, M. (1990) Referendum dynamics and the Irish divorce amendment, *Public Opinion Quarterly,* 54(1), pp. 1–20.

Eurobarometer (2010) *Report: Table of Results Standard Eurobarometer 72* (Brussels: European Commission).

Gallagher, M. (2010) Parliamentary parties and the party whips, in: M. MacCarthaigh & M. Manning (Eds) *The Houses of the Oireachtas: Parliament in Ireland*, pp. 129–152 (Dublin: Institute of Public Administration).

Gallagher, M. & Marsh, M. (2002) *Days of Blue Loyalty: The Politics of Membership of the Fine Gael Party* (Dublin: PSAI Press).

Gallagher, M., Laver, M. & Mair, P. (2011) *Representative Government in Modern Europe*, 5th ed. (Maidenhead: McGraw-Hill).

Hyland, J. L. (1995) *Democratic Theory: The Philosophical Foundations* (Manchester: Manchester University Press).

Kennedy, F., Lyons, P. & Fitzgerald, P. (2005) The members of Labour: backgrounds, political views and attitudes towards coalition government and the party system, *Irish Political Studies*, 20(2), pp. 171–186.

LeDuc, L. (2003) *The Politics of Direct Democracy: Referendums in Global Perspective* (Peterborough, Ontario: Broadview Press).

Lindberg, B., Rasmussen, A. & Warntjen, A. (2008) Party politics as usual? The role of political parties in EU legislative decision-making, *Journal of European Public Policy*, 15(8), pp. 1107–1126.

Mair, P. (1997) *Party System Change: Approaches and Interpretations* (Oxford: Clarendon Press).

Mair, P. (2006) *Polity-scepticism, Party Failings, and the Challenge to European Democracy* (Wassenaar: Netherlands Institute for Advanced Study).

Marsh, M., Sinnott, R., Garry, J. & Kennedy, F. (2008) *The Irish Voter: The Nature of Electoral Competition in the Republic of Ireland* (Manchester: Manchester University Press).

McCullagh, D. (1998) *A Makeshift Majority: The First Inter-Party Government, 1948–51* (Dublin: Institute of Public Administration).

Murphy, G. (2010) Interest groups in the policy-making process, in: J. Coakley & M. Gallagher (Eds) *Politics in the Republic of Ireland*, 5th ed., pp. 327–358 (London: Routledge and PSAI Press).

O'Leary, C. (1961) *The Irish Republic and its Experiment with Proportional Representation* (Notre Dame: University of Notre Dame Press).

O'Mahony, J. (2009) Ireland's EU referendum experience, *Irish Political Studies*, 24(4), pp. 429–446.

O'Malley, E. & Martin, S. (2010) The government and the Taoiseach, in: J. Coakley & M. Gallagher (Eds) *Politics in the Republic of Ireland*, 5th ed., pp. 295–326 (London: Routledge and PSAI Press).

Quinlan, S. (2012) The Lisbon experience in Ireland: 'No' in 2008 but 'Yes' in 2009: how and why? *Irish Political Studies*, 27(1), forthcoming.

Sartori, G. (1987) *The Theory of Democracy Revisited* (Chatham, NJ: Chatham House).

Schattschneider, E. E. (1977 [1942]) *Party Government* (Westport, CT: Greenwood Press).

Schmidt, V. A. (2006) *Democracy in Europe: The EU and National Polities* (Oxford: Oxford University Press).

Sinnott, R. (1995) *Irish Voters Decide: Voting Behaviour in Elections and Referendums since 1918* (Manchester: Manchester University Press).

Strøm, K. (2000) Parties at the core of government, in: R. J. Dalton & M. P. Wattenberg (Eds) *Parties without Partisans: Political Change in Advanced Industrial Democracies*, pp. 180–207 (Oxford: Oxford University Press).

van Biezen, I., Mair, P. & Thomas Poguntke, T. (2009) Going, going … gone? Party membership in Europe at the beginning of the 21st century. Paper presented at the *ECPR Joint Sessions*, Lisbon.

Weeks, L. (2010) Parties and the party system, in: J. Coakley & M. Gallagher (Eds) *Politics in the Republic of Ireland*, 5th ed., pp. 137–167 (London: Routledge and PSAI Press).

Should Irish Emigrants have Votes?
External Voting in Ireland

ISEULT HONOHAN
University College Dublin, Ireland

ABSTRACT   *Ireland is one of the few countries in Europe not to offer some form of suffrage to its citizens who live abroad permanently. By contrast, it has been a front-runner in the trend towards providing more liberal voting regimes for resident non-citizens, as since 1963 it has allowed all residents for the previous 6 months to vote and stand in local elections. This paper considers the normative case for and against external voting, the current comparative context of its increasing provision among European countries and the range of ways in which voting rights abroad combine with the extensibility of citizenship by descent abroad. Addressing the Irish case, it argues that there is no basis for a general right to vote for external citizens, but that, none the less, persisting connections and the rate of return migration give some reason to grant votes to first-generation emigrants, if differently weighted from those of resident citizens.*

Introduction

Voting is one of the central rights or obligations of democratic citizenship, but its exercise has been largely been conditional on residence, requiring citizens to be resident to register as voters and granting local voting rights to immigrants on this basis also. Whether there are grounds for granting votes to non-resident citizens (external citizens) raises hard questions for democracy: How do we define the demos? What is the fundamental ground of democratic membership?[1]

The grounds for extending voting rights can be considered from two different broad perspectives. The 'formalist' view conceives of citizenship as a unitary, all-or-nothing matter of legal status. This requires that all citizens are treated alike, and thus external citizens should be able to vote just as resident citizens. Conversely, in this view, voting rights for long-term residents are not required – though it is legitimate to encourage long-term residents to become citizens by providing reasonable access to naturalisation.

Citizenship, however, is in fact not a unity. It is a historically evolving bundle of rights and obligations. Whereas in the past the legal status of citizenship was necessary in order, for example, to own property or undertake public or even certain kinds of private employment, these are now less often restricted to citizens. What today distinguish citizenship are the right (when resident) to vote and stand in national elections, the right to enter the country, the right to the state's protection when abroad and the symbolic status of full membership. Citizenship thus provides crucial rights and protections, of which voting rights are just one.

Furthermore, the broader sense of citizenship comprises at least three different dimensions, each of which may be embodied separately, as is clear from the different terms with which they contrast. First is the rights-holding citizen, contrasted with a 'subject' who is under the command of a ruler. Second is the formal member of a particular bounded community, contrasted with an 'alien'. Finally, there is the active citizen who participates in self-government, where a simple contrast term is lacking, but something like the 'passive citizen' or 'free rider' comes close. These three dimensions are not inseparable. It is possible to enjoy membership rights without having participation rights (as in the case of children, or citizens of authoritarian states); or to have participation rights without being an active citizen. Likewise, migrants may participate in political movements – described as 'enacting citizenship' – without having formal membership (Isin, 2008).

While the legal status of citizenship has traditionally been understood in terms of a single and indivisible membership of a particular territorial polity, increasing mobility and multiple interconnections across countries have been associated with the emergence of what has been called 'disaggregated' citizenship. The way in which in many countries immigrants gain some, usually local, voting rights before they are eligible for citizenship, and voting rights have increasingly been extended to citizens living abroad, reflect this process. Likewise, the idea that a person should be a member of one state and one state only has receded, as an increasing number of states accept dual citizenship both of their own emigrants and of naturalising immigrants. These are just some of the features of what has come to be seen as the rise of 'transnational' citizenship, reflecting the way in which in a world where people increasingly move across borders, state boundaries, while still persisting, are increasingly blurred or porous with respect to citizenship.

Thus, another, 'pluralist' view identifies a variety of grounds for claims to a political voice. In this view, political rights are not inseparably linked to formal membership, but can be extended to all those with a significant interest in the polity. On this basis, voting rights both for resident non-citizens and expatriate citizens could be justified in a similar fashion. Yet, even if we adopt this view, we need to define exactly what kinds of connection count in justifying a right to political participation.

While citizenship cannot be seen as indivisible, it remains the case that voting rights are one of the key features of democratic citizenship. It thus needs to be considered whether legal membership should entail voting rights in all circumstances, and, if not, why not?

The Basis of Voting Rights

Democracy, at its simplest, is understood as the rule of the people. Participation in collective self-rule has been proclaimed as a human right: 'Everyone has the right to take part in the government of his country, directly or through freely chosen representatives' (Universal Declaration of Human Rights, Article 21). The answer to the question *who* constitutes the people and, in the case of emigrants, *which country* should be regarded as theirs, is, however, anything but simple.

This issue has attracted a number of answers in recent debates among normative thinkers. One long-standing and influential view has been to identify the 'people' with the nation, and to ground political rights in membership of the nation, expressed in terms of shared ancestry, heritage, culture or sense of belonging; but citizenship as membership of a self-governing community is distinct from and does not depend on membership of a nation, which may be either under-inclusive or over-inclusive in defining the demos. Although, within a democratic state, a shared identity may support a democratic culture, it is not clear that sharing a national identity or sense of belonging itself, without any substantial connection with the state, warrants a right to a say in the future of the polity.

Thus, an alternative way of defining the demos might be in terms of those who are substantially connected by *contributing* in some concrete way to the collective life of the polity; but this excludes those who, by dint of age or disability, for example, are unable to contribute. A contribution principle is under-inclusive in defining the demos. Rather than recognising a contribution, a vote recognises the impact of law and government on citizens' lives, and gives them a chance to bring their government to account and to shape the laws determining their common future. On this basis, it has been suggested that the demos should rather comprise all those affected by the laws and policies of the state (Goodin, 2007). Although this 'all-affected' principle has some attraction, because it includes young and disabled members and also recognises the spillover effects of government across state boundaries, it does not provide a clear enough criterion for distinguishing between those directly and substantially affected in their life course and central interests by government and law, who should have a vote, and those further removed or affected to a lesser extent.

The normative core of democratic citizenship is that those who are subject to the authority of government should have a say in bringing that government to account and in determining their collective future. Thus, a better principle may be that those – and only those – who are 'subjected' to government and the authority of law should be considered for inclusion in the demos.[2] Yet 'subjection' as it stands is in turn too inclusive, as it does not exclude tourists and temporary visitors. What is needed is a definition that includes those and only those who are significantly interdependent on a continuing basis in their joint subjection to the state (Honohan, 2002, 2007). One way of defining the continuing and substantial subjection to the state that warrants political rights is in terms of 'stakeholding', having long-term connections and central interests, as formulated by Rainer Bauböck, who argues that 'self-governing political communities should include as citizens those individuals whose circumstances of life link their individual autonomy or well-being to the common good of the political community' (Bauböck, 2009: 479).[3]

If such a principle is adopted as the grounds for political rights, it may be considered to apply only to those living within the territorial bounds of the state. Despite increasing globalisation and the spillover effects of states' actions, while the boundaries of states still define the principal limits of their governments' writ, permanent residents in a state are still those most intensively and comprehensively subject to its laws and policies.

If only those on the territory of the state can be considered stakeholders in this sense, there is no general case for voting rights for citizens abroad. Thus, Ruth Rubio Marín concludes that external voting should not be regarded as a right of external citizens, 'as they are not directly and comprehensively affected by the decisions and policies that their participation would help to bring about even if they are likely to be affected by some of those decisions, such as those concerning remittances, nationality, and military service laws' (Rubio Marin, 2006: 53).

It may even be argued that, as the territorial bounds of the state delimit the area of subjection, democratic principles not only do not require voting rights for emigrants, but also demand their disenfranchisement (López-Guerra, 2005: 217).

Yet citizens abroad are subject to some laws and government decisions at least, especially those concerning constitutional matters and citizenship itself. David Owen argues that it is the fact of subjection – not a matter of degree – that counts as sufficient grounds for voting rights for first-generation emigrants (Owen, 2009: 64). Emigrants, however, do not share in the politically determined life of the country; they are not subject to its working conditions and practices, they do not in general pay taxes, their children are not brought up in its education system, and so on. Thus, they are not subject to the authority of government in the same direct and comprehensive way; and it is hard to see their subjection as equivalent to that of residents. Thus, even if they are in a category distinct from others affected abroad, the subjection of citizens abroad is not enough to warrant a right to vote on all matters.[4]

Arguments from Contribution and Compulsion

There are further arguments to be considered. One is *contribution*-based, noting that emigrants often make a substantial financial contribution through remittances, and arguing that excluding them from voting is analogous to taxation without representation. We have already seen that contribution is not a good general basis for defining membership of the demos. Moreover, such remittances are voluntary personal payments, not contributions to the state, and are not equivalent to the payment of taxes any more than charitable donations are. Moreover, even if some recognition for an economic contribution is warranted, it is not clear that a political voice is the appropriate return (Rubio Marin, 2006: 133).

A second argument points to the *involuntary nature* of emigration, which can be a result either of expulsion or of other government actions. Enforced exile could be seen as an extreme form of subjection. On this basis, refugees and displaced persons at least may be thought of as having a right to vote (Beckmann, 2009: 78–80). Furthermore, in the context of post-conflict situations or transitions to democracy, votes for those forced into exile can be seen, if only on a transitional basis, as part of a pathway to reconciliation; but emigration is more often economically driven, and even if not wholly voluntary provides a less clear-cut justification for voting rights than cases of forced migration. Justifying voting rights for forced exiles can be seen as a special case that is not more widely generalisable.

External Voting – Even if Not Required, is Permissible or Desirable?

Even if the status of external citizens differs from that of resident citizens and there are not grounds for a right to vote, there may still be reasons why it may be permissible and even desirable to give at least some categories of emigrants a political voice.

Thus, Rubio Marin (2006: 134) argues that, given the increasing connections and communication of emigrants, it is permissible for them to be included by a democratic decision:

> under certain circumstances a country may democratically decide to allow for absentee voting of the first generation, thereby including expatriates in the political process. They may do so in recognition of the fact that it is now easier than ever to remain connected to home state politics from abroad, and thus easier to understand the set of concrete political options that a country may face. They may also do so in recognition of the fact that many emigrants live between two countries, as well as the fact that their return is increasingly becoming a real option because being abroad no longer requires the definite severing of ties that it did in the past.

More expansively, Bauböck argues that there are good reasons to grant votes to external citizens to the extent that they can be seen as stakeholders, maintaining lifelong objective ties and interests. A key indicator is the comprehensive subjection entailed in prior residence in the state. Thus, such a status can be associated most readily with those who have in the past been 'biographically subjected' (Bauböck, 2009: 483). Thus, if votes are to be granted to expatriate citizens, this should be confined to first-generation emigrants. Moreover, in this view, '[e]ven for permanent first-generation expatriates, the external franchise should not be seen as a fundamental individual right but as a permissible and often also recommendable form of including transnational stakeholders in political decisions' (Bauböck, 2009: 487).

In general, the grounds for democratic citizenship should be forward looking, based on future needs and responsibilities, rather than retrospective considerations. Thus, as Bauböck acknowledges, the backward looking characteristic of first-generation emigrants is only an indicator (Bauböck, 2009: 481). One important consideration here is the likelihood of return migration.

Prospects of Return Migration

To the extent that emigrants may return, they have a real stake in their country of origin and share future interests with other citizens. The significant extent of return migration and the historical and current inaccuracy of the image of the one-way emigrant voyage are now accepted. Return migration internationally is now estimated to average between 10 and 50 per cent (Global Development Network, 2010), and is more common among first-generation migrants than their descendants (Hirschman *et al.*, 1999).

On what basis might this be taken account of in a grant of votes to expatriate citizens? One suggestion, a declared intention to return, seems too subjective and consequently subject to discretionary recognition. While it is reasonable to exclude those who deny such an intention, using it as a criterion for voting requires others to make an undertaking that, even in good conscience, they may never be able to fulfil. Rather, we should conclude that significant contemporary probabilities of return warrant granting a vote to those first-generation citizens who show sufficient commitment, for example, to register regularly as voters.

Additional Objections: Size, Knowledge, Double Voting

Even if votes are granted to first-generation citizens only, a further important question is the weight that these should be given. Especially if voting is not to be seen as a right, and the force of government affects residents more substantially, external votes do not have to carry an equal weight to those of residents.[5] The size of a potential external vote is a significant consideration. In a small state, if resident citizens can be outnumbered by the external vote, this makes external voting problematical. Bauböck identifies two possibilities here: the external vote may be potentially larger than the territorial vote and thus liable to swamp it; or it may be smaller but still capable of exerting a tipping force on the electoral result. According to Bauböck, the possibility of swamping provides a reason for counting votes in a reserved constituency not to give special representation (as emigrants do not constitute a group needing affirmative action), but to reduce the weight of the potentially dominating external electorate. On the other hand, any group of electors may turn out to 'tip' an election, and this is not something that can be legislated against. As a tipping power may be more likely to become a matter of concern if the external vote elects a bloc of reserved seats, Bauböck suggests that in this second context, votes are better assimilated into domestic constituencies (Bauböck, 2007: 446).

Two other arguments against external voting should be mentioned. The first is that emigrants lack the necessary *knowledge* of national politics to participate meaningfully, and that for this or other reasons, emigrants are more likely to be mobilised to support extreme movements. It is true that emigrants can retain an image of the country that, if it ever applied, is now outdated; but being knowledgeable, informed or moderate are not required or guaranteed among resident citizens. It is also clear that expatriates today can better maintain contacts and keep abreast of political developments through television, mobile phone and the internet, and are more likely to make frequent return visits. Thus, whatever the past, such arguments carry less weight today, at least with respect to first-generation emigrants.

A second argument against votes for emigrants applies to those who have become dual citizens by naturalising in their new country of residence. This is the objection that granting votes in their country of origin will give them *double-voting* powers; but this is not a valid objection, as there is a difference between having two votes in an election for one institution and having votes in elections for two different institutions. Having two votes is objectionable only when it involves having more than one vote in the same electoral context. If it is possible to have connections and a stake in the future in two countries, it may be reasonable to have a political voice in both these contexts. Thus, although there may be no right to vote for external citizens, there are some strong arguments for granting votes at least to first-generation emigrants in ways that do not swamp resident citizens.

Underlying this question is the larger question, who should be citizens? This is a contested topic, and one that each state is considered to have the right to decide itself. However, while policies thus vary, there is an international legal norm that citizenship should be based on some 'genuine connection' with the state (Nottebohm Case, 1955). Given that citizenship affords important protections and may not be easily granted by a new host country, the conditions for extending citizenship by descent abroad should perhaps be more generous than for voting rights, but citizenship should not be indefinitely extensible in the absence of some genuine connection.

External Voting in Practice

A brief comparative analysis gives some idea of the extent to which contemporary practice corresponds to these recommendations. A significant and fast-growing number of countries provide voting rights for citizens abroad. About 115 countries have some kind of external voting, of whom about two-thirds give rights to all external citizens, and one-third to restricted categories of citizens (International IDEA & IFE, 2007).

The comparative context considered here focuses on European countries, drawing examples from both member states and neighbours of the EU.[6] There is a remarkable and recent trend in external voting in European states. Those with a longer history include the UK (1918), Iceland (1949), Finland (1958) and Sweden (1968); in the 1970s and 1980s these were followed by France (1976), Portugal (1976), Switzerland (1977), Denmark (1980), Luxembourg (1984) and Germany (1985). Since 1990 there has been a new wave in which Austria, Bulgaria, Poland, Romania (1990), Croatia, Estonia, Latvia, Lithuania, Slovenia (1992), Moldova (1993), Spain (1995), Belgium (1999), Czech Republic (2002), Italy (2003) and Hungary (2004) have all introduced schemes (International IDEA & IFE, 2007). Of EU member states, in addition to Ireland, only Cyprus, Greece, Malta and Slovakia have no general system of external voting.[7]

This trend reflects not only the extent of emigration, but also a greater consciousness that emigrants maintain ties with their countries of origin. External voting has been introduced in post-conflict situations or in transitions to democracy where there had been a large political emigration. In other countries, recognition of shared national identity and heritage has been decisive. While the introduction of external voting has often depended more pragmatically on perceived political advantage by political elites, in these cases external voting may also be independently justified.

The provisions for external suffrage vary widely, and the scope, weight and accessibility of external voting in no case fully match domestic voting. External voting may be available for all elections or only selected types of election – from legislative and presidential to referendums. The countries that grant votes in legislative and (where relevant) presidential elections and referendums are: Austria, Belgium, Bulgaria, Croatia, Denmark, Finland, France, Iceland, Luxembourg, Netherlands, Norway, Poland, Portugal, Romania, Slovenia, Switzerland, Sweden and the UK. Votes are granted for the legislature in the Czech Republic, Germany, Moldova and Turkey, and for the legislature and in referendums in Estonia, Hungary, Italy and Sweden.

Most European countries include external voting along with other votes in regular territorial constituencies. Votes are counted in reserved constituencies only in Croatia, France, Italy, Portugal and Romania. The weight of these votes is determined principally by the number of reserved seats. In France, Italy and Portugal a fixed number of seats is allocated. In Croatia, the number of seats depends on the proportion of the external to the territorial vote, following criticism of the 1995 elections when the large number of seats allocated to the external constituency gave a disproportionate weight to external citizens' votes. In most countries voting is direct, but in France it is carried out through an indirect election from an emigrant representative council.

Voters are required in most cases to travel to an embassy or consulate in their country of residence. However, a significant number of European countries provide postal voting; some offer a combination of options, including proxy voting or more flexible alternatives, notably electronic voting (Estonia, France and, on an experimental basis, the Netherlands and Switzerland) (International IDEA & IFE, 2007; ACE, 2010).

At least as important as the issues of scope, weight and access is the eligibility to vote – whether this includes all citizens, or only certain categories, and if all citizens, how extensible abroad is citizenship itself.

Extensibility of Citizenship Abroad and Eligibility to Vote

Whether votes for external citizens generally are justified may depend on how liberally citizenship is available to those who live outside the state. The basis on which formal citizenship is acquired and retained abroad varies widely even among

European states; this combines with electoral provision to result in a wide range of voting eligibility for citizens abroad.

Citizenship can be acquired through descent (*ius sanguinis*) in all European states. Citizenship abroad can be extended indefinitely by birth to two citizen parents without restriction or threat of loss in the absence of residence or registration in Bulgaria, Czech Republic, Estonia, France, Greece, Hungary, Italy, Latvia, Lithuania, Luxembourg, Romania, Slovenia and Slovakia. Extension beyond the first generation born abroad requires registration in Belgium, Croatia, Cyprus, Germany, Ireland, Malta, Portugal and the UK. Acquisition of citizenship beyond the first generation born abroad is either restricted or is subject to loss if residence or a substantial connection is not subsequently established in Belgium, Denmark, Finland, Iceland, Netherlands, Norway, Spain, Sweden and Switzerland. In some of these cases, citizenship is lost by those born abroad if another citizenship is acquired by application (Austria, Czech Republic, Denmark, Estonia, Germany, Latvia, Lithuania, Norway, Slovakia and Spain) (De Groot & Vink, 2010b). Thus, the most expansive forms of citizenship by descent abroad are found in Bulgaria, Greece, Hungary, Italy, Luxembourg, Romania, Slovenia and Slovakia. It may be argued that an indefinite extensibility of citizenship abroad beyond the second generation without any residence or connection requirement departs from the principle of genuine connection.

Access to citizenship, however, translates directly into eligibility for voting only in a minority of European countries. The range of those eligible to vote varies from those normally resident but temporarily abroad (Hungary), to those on diplomatic or military service (Ireland) or in expatriate employment (Denmark), to those who have previously been resident (Norway, Sweden) and have been away for not more than a certain number of years (Germany, UK, Denmark), up to Estonia and Italy, where all citizens are eligible to vote, regardless of past residence or length of absence.

Who qualifies as an external voter thus varies widely among countries. Table 1 shows the range of combinations of electoral and citizenship extensibility abroad in a number of European countries. Countries with the most generous system of external voting are not always those with the most generous extension of citizenship, and vice versa. On the one hand Hungary, which allows citizenship to pass by descent abroad without any restriction, provides external votes only for those temporarily abroad. Sweden and Norway offer rather generous systems of external voting, but are moderately restrictive in the extension of citizenship abroad. Estonia and Italy are among the most generous combinations, allowing all citizens to vote and citizenship to be passed down without restriction.

There would be a real danger of swamping where large emigrant populations and extensible citizenship combined with broad eligibility to vote among external citizens. In practice, only a few European countries are estimated to be subject to potential swamping by expatriate electorates, and it has been noted that these have either been slower to introduce external voting, such as Greece and Ireland, or have limited its impact by having reserved constituencies. In most cases restrictions to certain categories of citizen make the number of external citizens eligible to vote considerably

Table 1. Extensibility of external citizenship and external voting

	Restrictive external citizenship No automatic extension of citizenship abroad, and/or citizenship is liable to be lost without residence, or if a second citizenship is gained by application	Moderate external citizenship Extension or retaining of citizenship beyond first generation born abroad requires registration	Generous external citizenship Extension of citizenship abroad is possible indefinitely without requirement of residence or registration
Restrictive external voting Only specified categories of citizen can vote externally	*Denmark* Only those abroad as employees of state or Danish firm, students, for health reasons, away for up to 2 years, and will return in 2 years (Postal)	*Ireland* Only diplomatic and military personnel posted abroad (Postal)	*Hungary* Only for temporary absentees (Personal)
Moderate external voting All external citizens with certain previous residence can vote, but with time limits abroad	*Germany* Limit 25 years abroad (except for those living in Council of Europe member states) (Postal)	*UK* Limit 15 years abroad (Postal/proxy) *Portugal* 'Effective ties' defined by time-limit (Postal – parliamentary; personal – presidential)	

Substantial external voting
All external citizens with certain previous residence/ local registration can vote abroad with no time limit

Sweden
Must register after 10 years (Postal, personal, proxy)

Switzerland
Must register every 4 years. (Postal, personal – e-voting pilot)

France
(Indirect). Registered (Postal, e-voting)

Norway
Must register after 10 years (Postal)

Netherlands
(Postal, proxy, e-voting)

Estonia
(Postal, personal, e-voting)

Austria
No residence requirement, but must register with a municipality every 10 years (Postal)

Italy
Reserved constituencies (Postal)

Generous external voting
All external citizens can vote without any residence, local registration requirement

Spain
Must register after 10 years (Personal and proxy)

Belgium
Compulsory (Postal, personal, proxy)

Finland
On population register (Postal)

Croatia
Reserved constituency (Personal)

Note: This table is drawn from sources cited in the text, Waldrauch (2006) and from individual research. Given the difficulties of establishing exact details in this area, the classification is a preliminary one, pending the extension to electoral rights of the systematic work on access to citizenship in the EUDO Citizenship project (see note 7).

smaller than the total of external citizens, and procedural and access restrictions make the turnout and impact of external votes lower than those of domestic voters. Exceptions to this have, however, give risen to concerns about tipping. In 2006, the first Italian legislative election in which external votes were available, there was a turnout of 38.5 per cent of the 2.7 million registered external electorate (Mascitelli & Battiston, 2008), which appeared to constitute a tipping force. Even after an adjustment of the numbers of seats available to emigrants, in the 2007 Croatian parliamentary elections the votes from external citizens were considered to be decisive (Ragazzi & Štiks, 2010: 14).[8] In both of these cases all citizens are eligible, and citizenship is extensible by descent abroad, if more generously in the case of Italy than of Croatia. Thus, some of the risk of swamping and tipping arises because of the extensibility of citizenship itself.

Although many countries offer votes to their citizens abroad, in cases where these would potentially exert a dominant influence on political life the scope and weight of voting tend to be contained. While an expansion of remote electronic voting would make external voting more accessible, there is no strong trend in this direction, or towards more equal scope or weight for resident and expatriate votes, or equal access for all categories of citizen. Indeed, generally low turnout and cost and security issues are cited as reasons not to introduce or to abolish external voting except in special circumstances.

The Irish Case

From Table 1, it can be seen that Ireland, while relatively generous in its extension of citizenship abroad, is one of the most restrictive in external voting as it includes only those posted abroad on military and diplomatic service. If Ireland were to introduce a broader system of external voting, a range of options would arise with respect to which citizens qualify as external voters, the scope of elections, weight of votes and access to voting.

The question of external voting has increasingly arisen. A 1991 Labour Party Bill proposed votes for those absent for less than 15 years. In the mid-1990s, when President Mary Robinson addressed a specially convened meeting of the Oireachtas on the subject of Ireland's emigrant population, a government proposal for three dedicated Senate seats was outlined. In 2002 the Task Force on Emigrants explicitly set the issue aside, and a report of the Oireachtas All-party Committee on the Constitution concluded that the right to vote in Dáil elections should remain confined to citizens resident in the state, while recommending that the Taoiseach should nominate one or more senators 'with an awareness of emigrant issues', comparable to the treatment of Northern Ireland (Government of Ireland, 2002: 59). The 2009 renegotiated Programme for Government proposed an Electoral Commission to consider the feasibility of votes in presidential elections for the Irish abroad.[9]

The arguments most often advanced to support extending votes to emigrants focus on three main claims. The first is the importance of recognising the Irish diaspora. The second is that, in the past and again today, a significant proportion of emigration is involuntary, representing less a choice than the lack of economic opportunity at home; and the third, the contribution that emigrants have made and are expected to make to Irish society.[10]

It should be noted that most of the concrete proposals advanced have recommended votes only for people who have previously lived in Ireland, and have not been away for more than a certain period. Yet by referring to the 'Irish abroad', broader notions of national identity tend to be invoked in debates on the topic. Indeed, the Constitution itself contributes to this ambiguity, Article 2 stating that 'the Irish nation cherishes its special affinity with people of Irish ancestry living abroad who share its cultural identity and heritage'; but the same article distinguishes this from membership of the nation and both of these from citizenship (Irish Constitution, Article 2).

Thus, there is considerable ambiguity about the appropriate recognition for the wider diaspora. On the arguments above, shared national identity or sense of belonging alone does not warrant the grant of voting rights. Indeed, citizenship itself may be too expansively awarded if transferable indefinitely by descent abroad, without reference to genuine connections with the polity. Irish citizenship abroad is quite expansive in comparative terms in Western Europe, requiring only registration from generation to generation (since 2004 the granting of citizenship on the basis of Irish associations has been given a narrower interpretation). If it is not justifiable to extend citizenship abroad beyond the second generation without real connections, there may be a role for some recognition short of citizenship for those with a sense of Irishness based on descent, even if the 2010 government proposal to award Certificates of Irishness to people who wish to express their Irish identity does not quite fit the bill (Cullen, 2010).

A second recurring argument for voting rights rests on the fact that most emigrants leave out of economic need rather than freely chosen career opportunities or other goals. It has been suggested that it is 'adding insult to injury' for these emigrants to lose their votes when they leave (Farrell, 2010). Yet, as argued above, this kind of involuntary emigration does not in itself constitute a ground for a right to vote comparable to the case of refugees and forced exiles in civil war and democratic transitions.

Finally, it is argued that emigrants have made a significant contribution to Irish society. While traditionally this was highlighted in emigrants' remittances (which merited a separate entry in the national accounts), current claims refer to the call on the diaspora to invest in Ireland or to contribute otherwise to the solution of the economic crisis, as, for example, in the 2009 Farmleigh forum. While such contributions may indeed be admirable, the argument that political rights (and indeed citizenship) are not the appropriate reward for economic contribution prevails here.

Although the arguments advanced for votes for emigrants on national identity, involuntary emigration or contribution do not provide a strong case for external votes in the Irish case, we may still find grounds for granting votes to those with significant continuing ties and future orientated interests. This supports granting votes to the first generation whose biographical subjection and prospect of return make it possible to consider them genuine stakeholders.

This is supported by significant rates of return migration among Irish emigrants. For example, the number of those born in Ireland returning is estimated to have risen continuously from 1987, reaching 27,000 in 2002 and remaining steady at under or around 20,000 per year from 2003 to 2008 (Migration Information System, 2009). These figures provide evidence of a genuine connection among a significant proportion of emigrants. As argued above, if links and the possibility of return are more significant in the first generation, and there is no reason to think Ireland is an exception in this respect, it is reasonable to confine the external vote to this category. It is not so clear that there should be a time limit in years abroad, as many emigrants, retaining their ties, return at retirement.[11]

Arguments for votes for emigrants regularly meet a number of objections, focusing on size, knowledge and subjection. It is argued further that external voters do not have to bear the consequences of legislation and policies. This is sometimes termed the 'no representation without taxation' view. This can be understood in two ways, one of which, focusing on the absence of contribution, carries little weight, but the other, focusing on the absence of subjection, is, as we have seen, a significant consideration and undermines claims to a right to vote by external citizens *per se*, while not ruling out the grant of a political voice to those who have and may again be subject to the country's law and government.

The size and possible swamping impact of such a significant number of potential voters, based on an estimate of 70 million people considering themselves Irish around the world, is often cited. However, there are only about three million Irish passport-holders outside Ireland, of whom it is estimated just under one million were born in Ireland. This still constitutes a significant number relative to the electorate of roughly three million at the general election of 2007. Thus, there could be genuine concerns about swamping; but this can, as already noted, be addressed by counting external votes within a reserved constituency, whether in the Dáil or Senate (as long as it continues in existence).

Finally, the knowledge objection has been advanced – that emigrants are not able to keep up with changing contexts and options in Irish politics, and that this is particularly important in the context of Ireland's proportion representation-single transferable vote system, where preferences far down a ballot paper can contribute to electing a candidate. It has also been argued that emigrants, especially in the USA, have supported unconstitutional parties, reflected in the levels of financial support for Sinn Féin in the USA during the Troubles in Northern Ireland. As argued above, such arguments do not provide definitive arguments against providing external votes.

Conclusion

The demos should consist of those whose lives are interdependent in their subjection to a common authority, and have shared future interests. National identity, contribution and emigration out of economic necessity do not provide strong arguments for granting voting rights to emigrants. The strongest grounds for external voting lie in emigrants' continuing substantial connections with the polity and a reasonable prospect of return.

Neither normative nor comparative analysis can determine the detailed requirements for external voting in any specific case. However, it can be suggested that in Ireland the patterns of connection and rate of return constitute good grounds for extending votes to first-generation emigrants, while their potential numbers warrant containing such votes in a reserved constituency.

Acknowledgements

This paper has benefited from helpful suggestions offered by Rainer Bauböck and other participants at the UCD Citizenship and Voting Rights in Europe, 3 December 2010.

Notes

1. By external citizens I refer to those permanently resident abroad. Citizens temporarily absent at election time present a simpler case, which can be accommodated with improved technology. Here I address only the principled normative grounds for external voting, not practical concerns, including security and cost, which are important in decisions about implementing such provisions. See International IDEA & IFE (2007).
2. Alternatively, Beckmann defines 'affected' as 'affected by law' in a way that comes close to the subjection view (Beckman, 2009).
3. Such 'interests are genuinely political ones and emerge because individuals happen to be permanently dependent on, and jointly subjected to, established institutions of government that they can accept as legitimate if they are adequately represented in these institutions' (Bauböck, 2009: 480).
4. External voting concerns not only global diasporas but also 'kin-minorities', blocs of co-nationals in a neighbouring state. The different considerations involved cannot be addressed in the space available here; it has been argued that, because of their potential impact on both states, full rights in their country of residence are more important (Bauböck, 2007: 2441). The issue of votes in Northern Ireland (with almost half a million Irish passport-holders by 2010) may be considered to fall into this category (MacDonald, 2010), but in view of the acknowledged right of those born in Northern Ireland to Irish citizenship, and the move to engage North and South in the Good Friday Agreement, itself passed on the basis of votes in both parts of the island, there may be a stronger claim for votes of some kind for Irish citizens living in Northern Ireland than in kin-states more generally. Chapter 5 of the 2002 Report of the Oireachtas Committee on the Constitution discusses this at greater length than the issue of votes for emigrants, but concludes that there should not be any extension of voting beyond the state, and notes that the decision on emigrant votes is influenced in part by the desirability that both categories of citizen should be treated similarly.
5. Residents who will be more immediately exposed to the political decisions that they authorise through their vote have a qualitatively stronger claim to self-government than external citizens. This is why it is legitimate to differentiate external voting rights so that they reflect a presumptive strength of citizenship involvement and so that domestic residents cannot be outvoted (Bauböck, 2009: 488).
6. The countries considered are those included in the EUDO Citizenship research project on access to citizenship in Europe, available at: http://www.eudo-citizenship.eu

7. Malta allows external votes for some of those on public service outside the country. Greece has a constitutional provision for external votes, which has yet to be implemented. In Greece and Slovakia, those living abroad but present for the election can vote legally.
8. Although these were mainly in neighbouring Bosnia-Herzegovina.
9. It can be argued that the pressure for votes for emigrants has been weakened by the fact that Irish people in Britain have automatically had a right to vote there and that they have also been politically successful in the USA, thus accounting for two primary emigration destinations. The voting rights in Britain are indeed peculiar to Ireland, but this does not explain why the large numbers of emigrants to the USA have not led to pressure for external votes, as in the case of Italy and Greece, for example.
10. For a sample of current views, see a thread on emigrant voting in the Political Reform.ie blog at http://politicalreform.ie/2010/07/29/votes-for-emigrants/, Global Irish.ie at http://www.globalirish.ie/2010/tracking-the-emigrant-voting-issue/ and the websites Amhran Nua at http://amhrannua.com/ and Charter for a New Ireland at http://tangibleireland.com/tangible-blog/blog/charter-for-new-ireland.html. See also http://ballotbox.ie/ for an emigrant internet poll carried parallel to the 2011 general election.
11. This does not prevent second-generation citizens establishing residence and regaining citizenship.

References

ACE, the Electoral Knowledge Network (2010) Available at: http://aceproject.org/ (accessed 26 October 2010).

Bauböck, R. (2007) Stakeholder citizenship and transnational political participation: a normative evaluation of external voting, *Fordham Law Review*, 75(5), pp. 393–447.

Bauböck, R. (2009) The rights and duties of external citizenship, *Citizenship Studies*, 13(5), pp. 475–499.

Beckman, L. (2009) *The Frontiers of Democracy: The Right to Vote and its Limits* (Basingstoke: Palgrave Macmillan).

Cullen, P. (2010) Certificate of Irishness open to 70 million people worldwide, *Irish Times*, 21 June, available at: http://www.irishtimes.com/newspaper/frontpage/2010/0621/1224272953828.html (accessed 4 October 2011).

De Groot, G.-R. & Vink, M. (2010a) *Birthright Citizenship: Trends and Regulations in Europe*, EUDO Citizenship Observatory, available at: http://eudo-citizenship.eu/docs/birthright_comparativepaper.pdf (accessed 4 October 2011).

De Groot, G.-R. & Vink, M. (2010b) *Loss of Citizenship: Trends and Regulations in Europe*, EUDO Citizenship Observatory, available at: http://eudo-citizenship.eu/docs/loss_paper_updated_14102010.pdf (accessed 4 October 2011).

Farrell, D. (2010) Political reform will not be enough?, *Irish Times*, 1 February, available at: http://www.irishtimes.com/newspaper/opinion/2010/0201/1224263502087.html (accessed 4 October 2011).

Global Development Network/IPPR (2010) *Development on the Move: Measuring and Optimising Migration's Economic and Social Impacts, Report*, available at: http://cloud2.gdnet.org/cms.php?id=global_report_migration (accessed 4 October 2011).

Goodin, R. (2007) Enfranchising all affected interests and its alternatives, *Philosophy and Public Affairs*, 39(1), pp. 40–67.

Government of Ireland (2002) *Seventh Progress Report of the All-party Committee on the Constitution: Parliament* (Dublin: Stationery Office).

Hirschman, C., Kasinitz, P. & DeWind, J. (1999) *The Handbook of International Migration: The American Experience* (New York: Russell Sage Foundation).

Honohan, I. (2002) *Civic Republicanism* (Abingdon: Routledge).

Honohan, I. (2007) Bounded citizenship and the meaning of citizenship laws: Ireland's ius soli citizenship referendum, in: L. Cardinal & N. Brown (Eds) *Managing Diversity: Practices of Citizenship in Australia, Canada and Ireland*, pp. 63–87 (Ottawa: University of Ottawa Press).

International IDEA & IFE (2007) *Voting from Abroad: The IDEA Handbook*, chapters available at: http://www.idea.int/publications/voting_from_abroad/index.cfm (accessed 4 October 2011).

Isin, E. F. (2008) Theorizing acts of citizenship, in: E. F. Isin & G. M. Nielsen (Eds) *Acts of Citizenship* (London: Zed Books).

López-Guerra, C. (2005) Should expatriates vote?, *Journal of Political Philosophy*, 13(2), pp. 216–234.

MacDonald, D. (2010) Voting snub to North's citizens must end, *Irish Times*, 7 October, available at: http://www.irishtimes.com/newspaper/opinion/2010/1006/1224280472332.html (accessed 4 October 2011).

Mascitelli, B. & Battiston, S. (2008) The challenges to democracy and citizenship surrounding the vote to Italians overseas, *Modern Italy*, 13(3), pp. 261–280.

Migration Information System (2009) *Country Report Ireland: From Rapid Immigration to Recession*, available at: http://www.migrationinformation.org/Feature/display.cfm?ID=740 (accessed 4 October 2011).

Nottebohm Case (*Liechtenstein v. Guatemala*) (1955) Second Phase, International Court of Justice (ICJ), 6 April, available at: http://www.unhcr.org/refworld/docid/3ae6b7248.html (accessed 4 October 2011).

Oireachtas All-party Committee on the Constitution, Seventh Report (2002) Available at: http://www. constitution.ie/reports/7th-Report-Parliament.pdf (accessed 4 October 2011).

Owen, D. (2009) Resident aliens, non-resident citizens and voting rights, in: G. Calder, P. Cole & J. Seglow (Eds) *Citizenship Acquisition and National Belonging* (Basingstoke: Palgrave).

Ragazzi, F. & Štiks, I. (2010) *Country Report Croatia*, EUDO Citizenship Renewed Programme for Government, 10 October 2009, available at: http://www.taoiseach.gov.ie/eng/Publications/ Publications_2009/Renewed_Programme_for_Government,_October_2009.pdf (accessed 4 October 2011).

Rubio Marin, R. (2006) Transnational politics and the democratic nation-state: normative challenges of expatriate voting and nationality retention of emigrants, *New York University Law Review*, 81, pp. 117–147.

Waldrauch, H. (2006) Rights of expatriates, multiple citizens and restricted citizenship for certain nationals, in: R. Bauböck, E. Ersbøll, K. Groenendijk & H. Waldrauch (Eds) *Acquisition and Loss of Nationality. Policies and Trends in 15 European States*, pp. 359–384 (Amsterdam: Amsterdam University Press).

Can the Internet Reinvent Democracy?

MARIA LAURA SUDULICH
University of Amsterdam, The Netherlands

ABSTRACT   *The internet has been expected to modify the very nature of the political discourse by delivering a democratic surplus. It has frequently been regarded as the medium though which the right balance between participation and representation can be achieved. The vary nature of the medium has generated great levels of interest and debate on what type of political activity could be performed online. This paper studies the heuristics of online participation in Ireland and, by addressing the issue of who participates online, it investigates the type of scenario that can be expected to develop in the near future. Using survey data from the Irish National Election Study 2007, this article offers an insight on the process of gathering politically relevant information online and on whether such an activity may lead to further political engagement. Evidence of quite limited but possibly escalating forms of online engagement is found.*

Democracy and the Internet: A Natural Pair?

Knowledge about facts, subjects or events is inextricably bound to virtually every aspect of democracy. (Bruce Bimber, 2003: 10)

It is widely recognized how radio and TV changed the face of political communication (Kavanagh, 1996), and both phenomena had a certain political dimension. However, they were never expected to change the face of the democratic process at large. The internet, on the other hand, has been accompanied since the beginning of its broad diffusion by the idea that it would have been able to modify the very nature of the democratic and political discourse. First-generation cyber-enthusiasts (Negroponte, 1995) confronted the concept of representative democracy and envisaged the internet as the instrument capable of challenging the hierarchical structure of political power (Mosco & Foster, 2001; Mosco, 2004). Even without sharing such a faithless vision of the medium's capabilities, it has been argued that the internet is in fact revolutionary in relation to at least three elements: *quantity* of information available, *speed* of information transmission and *direction of information flaws*. The volume of information available online is almost limitless (Norris, 2001). The quantity of data transmitted is diverse (video, audio, text, etc.) and capable of taking different formats depending on users' needs. Shared platforms specializing in particular formats of communication as social networking sites are growing in popularity and levels of usage, as indicated by the latest figures from the Pew Research Centre (Lenhart, 2009) and by data reported by the *Financial Times* (16 March 2010) that show that the social website Facebook has recently become the most used website in the world, overtaking the search engine Google. With regard to speed, the level of innovation brought about by the internet is self-evident: gathering information through search engines takes only a few moments. Moreover, the possibility of uploading information in real time has no precedents. With the continuous development of new technologies and the broad diffusion of smart phones and wireless devices, publishing information on the internet is possible almost from any location with no need for a computer. Finally, in terms of direction of information flaws, anybody can communicate in real time with people geographically located anywhere in the planet and the information published online can be shared or even modified by other users. Wikis are indeed based on the principle of shared knowledge and circulation of information. The information can be published by well-established media as well as by private citizens. There is little limit to the possibilities users are provided with; moreover, contrary to traditional media, editorial control is fully decentralized. In watching television or listening to the radio the individual has a passive role, whereas in using the internet (both for consultation and for publication of information) he or she is being absolutely active. Finally, there is a considerable economic upside embedded in the medium: it is rather cheap. Connections are becoming less expensive, having a free wireless is a common practice of many public spaces such as libraries, parks and cafés, the cost of having a website is also relatively low and social networking sites are completely free.

Given the medium's capabilities, its flexibility and its capacity of both creating and capturing trends, it is understandable how and why expectations had grown high. Coleman points out how 'with the rise of the broadcast media, a style of politics evolved that emphasized the role of voters as spectators upon the deliberation of the Great and the Good' (Coleman, 1999: 196), and with the advent of the internet the spectator may even be able to be become a protagonist of the deliberative process. Indeed, not only have theorists (Negroponte, 1995; Barber, 1998) emphasized their belief in the democratic possibilities brought about by the advent of new technologies, but also private projects (such as the Centre for Democracy and Technology) and publicly financed ones (for instance the Virtual Agora project) are attempting to accomplish real experiences of cyber-democracy. Former US Vice-President Al Gore made no secret of his endless confidence in the democratic and democratizing potential of the internet, and President Obama is very receptive to the inputs coming from technological innovation. Barak Obama, in fact, ran the most successful internet campaign to date, producing a communication revolution, which generated an unprecedented enthusiasm for the internet's political capabilities. Thanks to new technologies, a novel dimension of knowledge, information and communication became available to a large public, with the strong potential to improve the relation between representatives and represented. Moreover, recently there has been a steep rise in the number and success of Voting Advise Applications (VAAs). These platforms 'work according to a comparable logic. Participants answer a series of questions about their political preferences on a special website. The application contains (weighed) information about parties' programmatic stances. Drawing on this information, the VAA calculates which parties' electoral offer comes closest to the participant's preferences' (Walgrave *et al.*, 2008: 51–52). VAAs seek to make parties' policy preferences transparent and accessible to voters, who can compare their own views with parties' stands on a number of key policies.

Literature Review

The above-mentioned successful experiences strengthen theoretical considerations based on the assumption that democracy is an egalitarian collective decision-making process. Central to such a process is access to two dimensions: information and communication. These are indeed core elements to collective decision-making on two interrelated levels: the actual decision-making process and the gathering of policy relevant information.

The democratic potential of the internet has, however, been questioned from a number of perspectives, and even in the cyber-optimists cohort there is a certain degree of disagreement. Indeed, a sort of disjuncture characterizes normative positions on the democratizing potential of the internet: on one hand we have the *optimists*, who argue that the internet will revitalize and reinvent politics by introducing diffuse practice of participation and multiplying arenas of civic engagement. Anstead and Chadwich (2009) point out an important distinction is to be made between different types of optimist, the *representative democracy optimists* and the *direct democracy optimists*, the watershed being their attitude towards representative democracy.

On the one hand, representative democracy optimists argue that the internet's potential to reinvent politics will apply within the frame of representative democracy and it will transform politics within such a frame, altering its *mode* rather than its *frame*. This form of cyber-optimism also sees the internet as capable of bringing about a form of empowerment for resource-poor actors. The internet represents the ideal channel of diffusion of information for those agents that would struggle to circulate their message trough traditional channels. Indeed, given the relatively low-cost nature of making information available on the internet, poorly resourced actors can compete with better resourced actors on a hypothetically equal basis.

On the other hand, direct democracy optimism (Morris, 1999) is more radical and argues that the internet may be able actually to recreate the Greek agora in the form of virtual agora. Theorists of strong democracy envisaged in technology part of the answer for the actual implementation of a more participatory democracy (Barber, 1984). With the internet mass diffusion myths such as the 'open society' and the 'public sphere' (Pateman, 1970; Macphearson, 1977; Habermas, 1987) became illuminated by the new technological development. The internet rapidly turned into a platonic form of democratic advancement to those who see it as being able to 'revitalize citizen-based democracy' (Rheingold, 1993: xxix).

Such a form of enthusiasm for the implementation of deliberative arenas, typical of the early 1990s, started to fade away at the beginning of the new millennium. Indeed, the direct translation of internet characteristics into engines of change has a number of weaknesses. First, in order for the process of global online deliberation to work, *all* barriers to access to the internet would have to be removed. Second, the existence of a *digital divide* has posed major difficulties to this notion, cooling down the initial enthusiasm for the endless capabilities of the medium. The digital divide separates those who have the internet at their disposal, together with the capacity of operating it and adequate technical skills, from those who do not. Levels of digital divide do not appear to decrease with growth of internet usage (Mossberger *et al.*, 2003; Mossberger & McNeal, 2007). The wealthy outnumbered the poor in terms of internet usage. The digital divide consequently results in a democratic divide (Norris, 2001), which makes questionable the very idea of the virtual agora, to say the least. Finally, even if material costs could be removed, there is another fundamental obstacle that prevents the internet from being able to produce a revolution in power's equilibrium in modern society: the sheer quantity of knowledge necessary to take informed decisions for the day-to-day life of a modern state clashes with a logical constraint, namely limitations in citizens' time. The scale and number of decisions and people involved with the implementation of those decisions in a modern state generates an unsolvable problem of time. Even if time and cost constraints could be removed, the concept of representation and mediation between citizens and government it is most certainly unchangeable. Therefore, an investigation of what impact ICT could have on the political process is certainly more constructive than any speculation on the establishment of direct internet democracy.

Finally, some critical voices have even questioned the fact that the internet has a positive impact on institutions at all. It has been argued that forms of e-democracy might be likely to enhance the risk of populism (Kampen & Snijkers, 2003), and some concerns have been raised with regard to the agenda-setting of online deliberation. Who would verify the procedures (Moore, 1999)? And: 'if everybody speaks, who will be listened to?' (Noam, 2005: 10). As such, the direct democracy argument is more than flawed. The debate is now rather vivid between the *representative democracy optimists* and the so-called *normalizers*, who argue that the political scenario online will eventually reflect the political scenario offline, with dominant actors establishing their prominence also in the online world (Margolis & Resnick, 2000).

The above discussion on whether the internet could indeed ameliorate the quality of democracy serves as a basis for the rest of the paper. As such, I shall look at patterns of internet usage for political information under the assumption that if no substantial amount of information is circulated/shared/consumed online, the possibility of the internet playing a key role in reinvigorating democracy becomes much slimmer. Introducing a two-stage least-squared model, I shall then validate this key assumption by researching whether consumption of online news plays a role in affecting the likelihood of going further in online activity by looking at candidates and parties' websites.

Conditio Sine Qua Non

The speculation on what sort of sociopolitical changes can be driven by technology has inevitably to deal with the heuristics of what is actually taking place in the real world. This study will be primarily concerned with the analysis of empirical data, analysing the case of Ireland, for which no previous studies on the subject have been produced. I shall bind the discussion to the empirical analysis of survey data, proceeding to an exploratory as well as explanatory study of the political dimension of the internet in the country. There is an easily identifiable gap in the literature on whether the internet has made an impact on Irish democratic practices, and, if so, to what extent.

Even though the level of internet penetration in the country has been growing dramatically in the past decade and figures on internet diffusion have been systematically collected for a number of years by the Central Statistic Office, research on the political relevance of the internet has been a minor concern in political science. Knowing how many internet connections are active in the country – and their growth rate – does not advance our knowledge of how the internet may be inducing political change. Recently, the inclusion of a few questions on patterns of internet usage for political information in the Irish National Election Study 2007 (INES) has given a much more detailed account of real-world dynamics. Thus, we explore the most original empirical data on the subject by first looking at the raw figures and then by analysing patterns of internet usage. The existence of a large-scale survey as the Irish National Election Study 2007 allows for a snapshot of how the internet is actually used and insights regarding who Irish users actually are.

The previous section mentions the digital divide as one of the major obstacles to optimistic views on the role of the internet in improving the quality of modern democracy. By understanding who is online and who uses the internet to gather news and political information one can assess the extent to which the digital divide can turn into a democratic divide, and how that undermines the internet's potential to reinvigorate democracy. As such, this study contributes to the literature by looking for the first time at patterns of internet use for political information in Ireland. On the basis of what empirically detected, we shall be able to set expectations on how the internet may affect Irish democracy.

In listing the innovative characteristics of the internet, one of its key features lies in the capacity of disseminating information. The volume of information to be gathered online is almost limitless and costless. Even if the informative role is probably not the most revolutionary characteristic of the medium, its informative function is almost a *conditio sine qua non* more interactive activities can take place online. In other words, if the internet is not used for political information, its likelihood of being actively used as an instrument of political participation decreases dramatically. The possibility of citizens using the internet to play an active role (whatever form it may take) in politics without using the internet to gather information is highly unlikely. Therefore, understanding how much citizens actually make use of such a medium for political information is a primary concern. If the internet is not used, at least for political information gathering, its added value to democracy becomes very questionable and theoretical speculations would crash against factual evidence. If the internet cannot change the way citizens inform themselves and communicate, the internet most certainly cannot reinvent democracy. Mossberger & McNeal (2007: 1) claim that 'the internet has the potential of benefit[ing] society as a whole', even though strong evidence of a persistent digital divide shadows such a potential. The empirical analysis will be oriented towards the investigation of whether the internet actually is disclosing such a potential.

Patterns of Use

The INES was first run in 2002; but only the 2007 wave poses questions on internet use to gather political information.[1] Some descriptive tables on patterns of internet usage and figures on levels of trust, in comparison with other media, are shown, representing the departure point for further investigation.

Table 1 shows that almost 69 per cent of Irish citizens do not use the internet for political information. Two out of three Irish citizens never browse the web for political news. If compared with other media usage patterns, such a figure appears even more striking. Three-quarters of the Irish population read a newspaper everyday, a fifth listen to the radio daily and over 40 per cent watch news on television. On the contrary, only 5 per cent of Irish citizens browse the web daily to get political news. The difference between new and old media usage is dramatic. In late 2006, just a few months before Irish data were collected, the US-based Pew Internet Centre collected data on the same issue, reporting that 15 per cent of American citizens used the internet as their main source of political information. The same report indicated that 31 per cent of US citizens gather political news on the internet *at least* three times a week. Only 16 per cent of Irish citizens did so in mid-2007. In 2008, 40

Table 1. Percentage frequencies of consultation of media for political news

	Never							Always
	0	*1*	*2*	*3*	*4*	*5*	*6*	*7*
Newspapers	2	2	3	6	5	9	8	64
TV	7	7	7	11	10	8	7	41
Radio	14	4	5	5	6	10	6	49
Internet	69	7	4	3	3	3	2	**5**

Note: The question: About how often do you consult each of the following for news on political events in any given week?

Table 2. Levels of trust in media among Irish citizens

	Never trust				Always trust	Do not know
	0	*1*	*2*	*3*	*4*	
Newspaper	12	10	40	27	9	2
TV	5	6	30	39	19	1
Radio	9	7	28	37	17	2
Internet	*43*	4	15	9	3	*26*

Note: The question: On a scale of 0–4 where '0' means 'Never trust' and '4' means 'Always trust' how much do you trust political information from these different media?

per cent of Americans gathered information on the electoral campaign online. The internet seems far from being a mainstream medium in Ireland; however, there has been a slight increment in online political news consumption since 2004. Data gathered after the 2004 European election indicated that only 6 per cent of Irish citizens had browsed the web for political news on the election.

The interpretation of the data obviously depends on the reference category selected. If we look at it in comparison with the USA's figures, it appears that Irish citizens are not interested in the internet as a source of news. However, if we look at the European scenario, the 6 per cent reported by the Eurobarometer 2004 is representative of the rather low European average (Lusoli, 2005). As such, the indication given by Table 1 that 27 per cent of Irish citizens gather news online is not *per se* pointing towards any major lack of impact of the medium itself. However, it is self-evident that the internet is still the least popular medium for political information.

Data on the level of trust that citizens place on different media in Table 2 offer a further snapshot of Irish attitudes. By and large, the internet is the least trusted medium, with 43 per cent believing that the internet is never trustable. It also remarkable that a quarter of Irish citizens do not have an opinion on the subject. This lies in contrast to other media where a small minority of never more than 2 per cent had no opinion. This suggests that the internet still represents to many something rather difficult to understand.

The descriptive tables shown here do not answer many of the questions on the impact of the internet on politics. Compared with newspapers, TV and radio, the internet is the least frequently used and the least trusted medium; it is also the newest one, and this study seeks to clarify whether it is in use by an identifiable subgroup (or a number of subgroups). Therefore, the next section investigates the characteristics of internet users.

What Divide?

This study seeks to explain what makes individuals more likely to use the internet for political information. Therefore, building on previous research I test whether the common knowledge about internet users – young, well-educated males – holds in the Irish context. I also control for whether use of other sources of political information (newspapers and TV) makes a difference in determining online news consumption. Finally, I include controls for political knowledge (determined on the basis of a set of questions contained in the survey), confidence and interest in politics. As such, I base expectations on what is found in other national contexts and I hypothesize that socio-economic status may possibly explain not only internet usage but also patterns of internet use for political information. Finally, I expect interest in politics and political knowledge to be positively related to the dependent variable, which is measured as a dichotomy ('1' indicates having used the internet for political information at least once a week and '0' corresponds to no use at all). Formally, I test the following model:

$$pj = \frac{1}{1 + e - z}$$

where:

$$z = \beta_0 + \beta X_1 + \beta X_2 + \beta X_3 + \beta X_4 + \beta X_5 + \beta X_6 + \beta X_7 + \beta X_8 + \beta X_9$$
$$+ \beta X_{10} + \beta X_{11} \tag{1}$$

pj = Probability of gathering political news online;
X_1 = Other sources of information (TV);
X_2 = Other sources of information (newspapers);
X_3 = Gender;
X_4 = Age;
X_5 = Education;
X_6 = Level of political knowledge;
X_7 = Income;
X_8 = Interest in the election, socially discussed;
X_9 = Interest in the campaign;
X_{10} = Urban/rural household;
X_{11} = Political trust.

Table 3 reports findings of our logistic model explaining online news consumption.[2] Gender, age, level of education and urban location of the household are significant predictors of online news consumption. Young, well-educated males are, as expected, more likely to gather political news online. Being based in a city, as opposed to a rural area, is also a significant predictor of online political news consumption. Surprisingly enough, the level of income does not significantly modify chances of using the internet for political news. Social status seems to be a good predictor, whereas the economic one is not. Of the non socio-economic variables, only

Table 3. Determinants of online news consumption

	Coefficient	Robust SE
Watch TV news	0.026	(0.51)
Read a newspaper	−0.039	(1.06)
Gender of respondent	−0.382	(2.25)*
Date of birth-year	0.033	(5.10)**
Highest level of education	0.242	(3.60)**
Political knowledge	0.146	(1.72)
General level of household income	0.067	(0.88)
Having discussed the election with family/friend/acquaintance	0.175	(0.80)
Interest in the campaign	0.025	(0.22)
Urban−rural household	0.618	(3.63)**
Political trust	−0.056	(1.05)
Constant	−67.761	(5.34)**
Nagelkerke pseudo R^2	0.18	
Observations	879	

*Significant at 5%; **significant at 1% level.

political knowledge is significantly related to the dependent variable; level of interest on the 2007 campaign does not affect the likelihood of gathering news online, nor does level of trust in politics. Getting political news from alternative sources such as the newspaper and TV do not affect the likelihood of also using the internet as a source.

As logistic coefficients are not immediately meaningful, the probability of a positive outcome given a series of possibilities is calculated, and relative probabilities and estimated change are presented in Table 4 by making use of the clarify package in Stata 10.[3]

Table 4. Predicted probabilities of positive outcome

	Probability positive outcome	Change
Every predictor at its mean	25%	
Highly knowledgeable about politics, everything else at the mean	32%	+7%
Not knowledgeable about politics, everything else at the mean	21%	−4%
Young, well-educated male in urban environment	50%	+25%
Young, well-educated female in urban environment	27%	+2%

Table 4 shows that the probability of a positive outcome (that being: looking at online news at least once a week) is about a quarter when all the predictors are kept at their mean values. The extent of change in the probability is also calculated when the stereotypical young, well-educated male in an urban environment is taken as predictor. The probability goes up by 25 per cent, indicating that common knowledge (or, perhaps, common sense) about internet users is indeed backed up by empirical analysis. Gender seems to be playing an important role here: when the same probability is computed for young, well-educated women in an urban environment, the increment is only 2 per cent from the average value. Clearly, males are more prone to making use of the internet as a source of political information. Finally, I try to clarify the extent to which political knowledge is an important element in determining a positive outcome. I do so by keeping every other variable at the mean and assigning to political knowledge first the highest possible value and then the lowest one. In the first case, the likelihood of online news consumption goes up by 7 per cent; in the second case (lowest level of political knowledge), there is a decrease of 4 per cent from the average level of online consumption. As such, citizens who are highly knowledgeable about politics are 11 per cent more prone to make use of the internet for political information than those with little knowledge about Irish politics.

Overall, one finds strong evidence that being a 'typical internet user' is a good predictor of gathering political information online. That is, perhaps, not a surprising finding. However, the findings suggest cogent evidence of a serious 'gender divide', with women being significantly less likely to use the internet for political information. Political knowledge also proved to be a strong predictor of interest in online political news.

As such, this first analysis of the Irish online public suggests a rather pessimistic scenario, where the extent to which the internet can re-engage citizens is limited to a very specific part of the Irish population. The online audience seems to be well defined by social characteristics and empirical evidence points towards a specific type of online news consumer. As I described 'using the internet for gathering political news' as a *conditio sine qua non* that political activity online can take place, the next step of this research focuses on actual levels of political activity online.

A Step Further

As discussed above, if people do not look for political news online they probably will not go any further with political engagement on the internet. Therefore, 'looking for political news online' is a precondition for any other form of political engagement online. Such an assumption is tested here by running a two-stage model that instruments the variable 'looking up political news online'; the dependent variable of such a model is a more specific form of online political activity: 'looking up candidates and parties' websites'. We know from previous research in other states (Gibson & McAllister, 2008) that a small percentage of the population visits parties/politicians' websites. However, there are no previous data to estimate such a phenomenon in the

Republic of Ireland. The estimated model is a two-step model, whose dependent variable is 'looking up candidates and parties websites', and the independent variables are socio-economic status, political knowledge, interest in the forthcoming election, party voted and the instrument 'looking up political news online', which served as a dependent variable for our previous model. Such a model has the advantage of controlling for endogeneity (Rho test) and provides a strong empirical validation of the above-mentioned assumption. Table 5 reports its outcomes.

As in the case of the previous logistic regression, although the coefficients are also not immediately meaningful, the table offers some basic indications. First, the significance of the Rho test tells us that the instrumented variable is indeed endogenous. Thus, the model in use is the correct one and it accounts for such endogeneity by providing a correction in its estimations. Second, the table clarifies that the initial assumption was also correct: surfing the web in search of political news is a good way of approaching the study of online engagement. It is very strongly correlated to the dependent variable, so that it can safely be assumed that looking up political news online is indeed a *conditio sine qua non* that more engaging levels of online political activity may take place. Third, the level of interest in the campaign, which was not a significant predictor in the model shown in Table 3, is now a significant predictor of our dependent variable. It is positively related to it, so that higher levels of interest in the campaign are a good predictor of visiting candidates and

Table 5. Predictors of visiting parties/candidates' websites

	Coefficient	Absolute value of z
Internet	2.41	0.207**
General level of household income	−0.125	0.050*
Sex of respondent	0.108	0.115
Date of birth-year	−0.002	0.004
Highest level of education	0.137	0.055*
Political knowledge	−0.011	0.059
Interest in the campaign	−0.249	0.077*
Fine Gael	−0.246	0.144
Green Party	−0.069	0.202
Labour Party	−0.570	0.405
Progressive Democrats	−0.413	243
Sinn Féin	0.017	0.195
Independents	−0.282	0.179
Constant	30.73	
Athrho	−0.998	0.298*
Observations	891	
Test of Rho, exogeneity	0.005	

*Significant at 5%; **significant at 1%.

parties' websites. This is a key point for the literature on the efficacy of online campaigns. Indeed, the literature (D'Alessio, 1997; Gibson & McAllister, 2006, 2008; Sudulich & Wall, 2010) has suggested that campaigning online is positively correlated to electoral gains, but the mechanism through which such a gain takes place remains unobserved. Here, we have some evidence supporting the fact that on the demand side there is a certain correspondence between online news consumption and interest in parties/candidates' websites. Far from explaining which mechanism brings marginally more votes to cyber-active candidates, the outcomes suggest that some attention should be devoted to the demand side in trying to clarify such a mechanism. A further interesting finding is that some of the significant socio-economic predictors of model 1 are not significant predictors of model 2. Gender and age do not make a difference anymore; once a subject is interested in online news consumption his or her social characteristics do not matter in determining whether or not he or she will move to a more specific type on online activity, namely visiting parties or candidates' websites. Such an effect would possibly take place despite gender and socio-economic differences. Education still plays a role here, with highly educated people being marginally more inclined to visit campaign websites. Finally, I performed a control for party preference, measured by party chosen in the ballot at the 2007 election. There seems to be no major difference determined by such a variable, which only points to a significant difference between Fianna Fáil and Fine Gael's voters, with the former being marginally more inclined to consult parties/candidates' websites.

Overall, this paper has shown that consuming online political news is positively associated with and is a significant predictor of visiting candidates and parties' websites. Controlling for endogeneity, I have shown how online news-gathering may lead to higher level of political engagement in cyberspace. Unfortunately, the structure of the available data is not suitable for examining the process any further, but further research would attempt to establish clearly that such a mechanism is an important step in understanding to what extent the internet can intervene in the political realm.

Conclusions

After having presented a theoretical discussion of the extent to which the internet can contribute to revitalizing democracy, this paper explored some empirical evidence from Ireland. The paper aimed to understand better how and whether the internet could possibly intervene in the political process by looking at the voter side. Most studies discussing the potential of the internet focus on the supply-side (Gibson & Ward, 1998, 2000; Gibson et al., 2003; Rommele, 2003; Ward & Gibson, 2003; Ward et al., 2003; Schweitzer, 2005; Vaccari, 2008; Gibson & Rommele, 2009) by looking at political actors online, their strategies and their effectiveness. The demand-side seems to be much less of a concern in the literature and its results are under-investigated. This study approached the problem by looking at citizens and how they use the internet for political information. It was found that making a little step, such as gathering news online, is strongly correlated with taking a more focused form of online political action such as looking up parties and candidates' websites. As such, the paper has shown that there is room for the web to drive some changes, but from the data at our disposal we cannot estimate how large the potential change could be. A further novelty of this research is that it is a first attempt to report on online political engagement in Ireland, and it has shown that the internet has a certain mobilizing potential, even though the internet seems to be used by a relatively small group of citizens. The findings of this study confirm that an individual's socio-economic status have a strong impact on the likelihood of using the internet to gather political information, where higher educated, male urban citizens are more prone to do so. However, those who are somehow using the internet for political purposes may find it easy to experience an escalation in political engagement; consulting online news could bring citizens to a higher level of consciousness and political engagement.

Overall, this research has found that there is not much room for excessive cyber-enthusiasm, where the impact of the internet is rather small. The process that leads from gathering general political news online to visiting candidates and parties' websites is part of a larger form of online engagement and the mechanism behind it needs to be disentangled by further research. Evidence of positive correlation between online gathering and more sophisticated forms of political participation online has been identified here. Yet, the small size and stereotypical profile of internet surfers do not suggest that the internet is currently playing a major role in implementing a better quality of democracy in the Republic of Ireland.

Notes

1. Some limited data on Ireland are available from the Flash Eurobarometer 2004, which included a question on political information on the web.
2. A detailed description of the variables in use is available at www.tcd.ie/ines, where a codebook and data set can be downloaded.
3. The clarify package allows for translation of logistic regression coefficients into probabilities, making the process of interpretation of regression outputs rather intuitive (http://gking.harvard.edu/clarify/docs/clarify.html).

References

Anstead, N. & Chadwick, A. (2008) Parties, election compaigning and the internet: toward a comparative institutional approach, in: A. Chadwick & P. Howard (Eds) *Handbook of Internet Politics* (New York: Routledge).

Barber, B. (1984) *Strong Democracy: Participatory Politics for a New Age* (Berkeley, CA: University of California Press).

Barber, B. R. (1998) Three scenarios for the future of technology and strong democracy, *Political Science Quarterly*, 113(4), pp. 573–589.

Bimber, B. A. (2003) *Information and American Democracy: Technology in the Evolution of Political Power* (Cambridge: Cambridge University Press).

Coleman, S. (1999) Cutting out the middle man. From virtual representation to direct deliberation, in: B. Hague & B. Loader (Eds) *Digital Democracy. Discourse and Decision Making in the Information Age* (London and New York: Routledge).

D'Alessio, D. (1997) Use of the World Wide Web in the 1996 US election, *Electoral Studies*, 16(4), pp. 489–500.

Gibson, R. K. & McAllister, I. (2006) Does cyber-campaigning win votes? Online communication in the 2004 Australian election, *Journal of Elections, Public Opinion & Parties*, 16(3), pp. 243–263.

Gibson, R. K. & McAllister, I. (2008) Do online election campaigns win votes? The 2007 Australian 'You Tube' election, *Political Communication*, 28(2), pp. 227–244.

Gibson, R. K. & Rommele, A. (2009) Measuring the professionalization of political campaigning, *Party Politics*, 15(3), pp. 265–295.

Gibson, R. K. & Ward, S. J. (1998) UK political parties and the internet: 'politics as usual' in the new media?, *The Harvard International Journal of Press/politics*, 3(3), pp. 14–38.

Gibson, R. K. & Ward, S. (2000) *Reinvigorating Democracy? British Politics and the Internet* (Aldershot: Ashgate).

Gibson, R. K., Nixon, P. & Ward, S. (2003) *Political Parties and the Internet: Net Gain?* (Abingdon: Routledge).

Habermas, J. (1987) *The Theory of Communicative Action* (Boston: Action Beacon Press).

Kampen, J. K. & Snijkers, K. (2003) E-democracy: a critical evaluation of the ultimate e-dream, *Social Science Computer Review*, 21(4), pp. 491–496.

Kavanagh, D. (1996) New campaign communications: consequences for British political parties, *The Harvard International Journal of Press/Politics*, 1(3), pp. 60–76.

Lenhart, A. (2009) Adults and social network sites, Pew Internet Project, 14 January.

Lusoli, W. (2005) The Internet and the European Parliament elections: theoretical perspectives, empirical investigations and proposals for research, *Information Polity*, 10(3), pp. 153–163.

Macpherson, C. B. (1977) *The Life and Times of Liberal Democracy* (New York: Oxford University Press).

Margolis, M. & Resnick, D. (2000) *Politics as Usual: The Cyberspace 'Revolution'* (Thousand Oaks, CA: Sage Publications).

Moore, R. K. (1999) 3 Democracy and cyberspace, in: B. Hague & B. Loader (Eds) *Digital Democracy: Discourse and Decision Making in the Information Age* (London: Routledge).

Morris, D. (1999) *Vote.com* (Los Angeles: Renaissance Books).

Mosco, V. (2004) *The Digital Sublime: Myth, Power, and Cyberspace* (Cambridge, MA: The MIT Press).

Mosco, V. & Foster, D. (2001) Cyberspace and the end of politics, *Journal of Communication Inquiry*, 25(3), pp. 218–236.

Mossberger, K. & McNeal, R. S. (2007) *Digital Citizenship: The Internet, Society, and Participation* (Cambridge, MA: The MIT Press).

Mossberger, K., Tolbert, C. & Stansbury, M. (2003) *Virtual Inequality: Beyond the Digital Divide* (Washington, DC: Georgetown University Press).

Negroponte, N. (1995) *Total Digital* (Munchen: Bertelsmann).

Noam, E. M. (2005) Why the internet is bad for democracy, *Communications of the ACM*, 48(10), pp. 57–58.

Norris, P. (2001) *Digital Divide: Civic Engagement, Information Poverty, and the Internet Worldwide* (Cambridge: Cambridge University Press).

Nuttall, C. & Gelles, D. (2010) Facebook becomes bigger hit than Google, *Financial Times*, 16 March, available at: http://www.ft.com/cms/s/2/67e89ae8-30f7-11df-b057-00144feabdc0.html

Pateman, C. (1970) *Participation and Democratic Theory* (Cambridge: Cambridge University Press).

Rheingold, H. (1993) *The Virtual Community: Finding Connection in a Computerized World* (Boston, MA: Addison-Wesley Longman).

Rommele, A. (2003) Political parties, party communication and new information and communication technologies, *Party Politics*, 9(1), pp. 7–20.

Schweitzer, E. J. (2005) Election campaigning online: German party websites in the 2002 national elections, *European Journal of Communication*, 20(3), pp. 327–351.

Sudulich, M. L. & Wall, M. (2010) 'Every little helps'. Cyber-campaigning in the 2007 Irish general election, *Journal of Information Technology & Politics*, 7(4), pp. 340–355.

Vaccari, C. (2008) Surfing to the Elysee: the internet in the 2007 French elections, *French Politics*, 6(1), pp. 1–22.

Walgrave, S., van Aelst, P. & Nuytemans, M. (2008) 'Do the vote test': the electoral effects of a popular vote advice application at the 2004 Belgian elections, *Acta Politica*, 43, pp. 50–70.

Ward, S. & Gibson, R. (2003) On-line and on message? Candidate websites in the 2001 general election 1, *The British Journal of Politics & International Relations*, 5(2), pp. 188–205.

Ward, S., Gibson, R. & Nixon, P. (2003) Parties and the internet: an overview, in: *Political Parties and the Internet: Net Gain* (London: Routledge).

Are the Citizens of a Democracy a Just Target for Terrorists?

COLM McKEOGH

University of Waikato, New Zealand

ABSTRACT   *This article investigates how issues of political responsibility connect to the combatant/civilian distinction in armed conflict. It does so by looking at an attempted moral justification of terrorism in a democracy by a just war theorist. The attempt was by Igor Primoratz, who claims that civilians who actively support injustice do not merit immunity from targeting. Primoratz suggests amending the principle of civilian immunity to permit targeting of civilians who are culpable for an unjust war. This article argues that culpability plays no role in the justification of targeting combatants and cannot be used to justify the targeting of civilians. Combatants may be targeted in war because of a convention-dependent permission that they may be treated as instruments. Civilians may not be targeted in war because no such convention-dependent permission exists (and there are no benefits to creating such a convention). Nor can the justification of self-defence be used to justify the targeting of civilians in armed conflict because there is a threshold of culpability to be met before self-defence is permitted, and the citizens of a democracy do not meet that minimum standard.*

Introduction

Igor Primoratz proposes that the principle of civilian immunity in war be amended on the grounds that not all civilians deserve immunity from targeting in war. Some, he claims, are culpable for the unjust cause of their country and for that reason may be targeted in war, should it be useful for (and proportionate to) the achievement of the *ad bellum* goal of the war:

> In a perfect democracy, where all citizens are well informed about state policies and fully and effectively participate in political life, the responsibility for an unjust war would fall on those who voted for it ...
> If she actively supports the government and the war – if she votes for the ruling party, gives allegiance to the government that is pursuing the war, expresses her

support for the war effort on appropriate occasions – then [the citizen of a democratic state] is fully responsible for the war. She is therefore a legitimate target of deliberate military attack. The fact that she takes no part in the fighting or in the debates within the government and the decisions it takes concerning the fighting makes no difference. For both the government and the armed forces are but the executors of her will and the will of others like her. (Primoratz, 2002: 232, 236)[1]

Primoratz suggests that the practical implications of his proposal are minimal as current technological limitations mean that bombs, shells and missiles cannot discriminate between those who support and those who oppose an unjust war and so the principle of civilian immunity must continue in practice. This may be so in interstate war but it is not the case in intrastate war. Detailed knowledge of fellow citizens' political involvement, and the precise targeting offered by small arms and car bombs, would permit discrimination between 'culpable' and innocent civilians on the streets of a community in strife. For this reason, Primoratz's proposal will be investigated with regard to terrorism and with references to Northern Ireland. Terrorism is defined here as the targeting of civilians in armed conflict.

The Northern Ireland Conflict

Primoratz makes his suggestion with regard to perfect democracies in which all citizens are well informed about state policies and fully and effectively participate in political life. He points out that before 1789 the armed forces were agents of the monarch; since then they have became the agents of the people. What was once done in the ruler's name, and on his or her behalf, is now done in the people's name and on their behalf. It is the case that Northern Ireland has not been a democracy but a province of a larger sovereign entity whose political system was parliamentary. Political authority in Northern Ireland rests with the Crown and not, as in the Republic of Ireland, with the people. This difference may, however, be of little relevance as both the crown and the people are notional entities; in both Northern Ireland and the Irish Republic the responsibility of the people for state policies is indirect and dilute. None the less, there were in Northern Ireland civilians who were well informed about state policies and who sought to participate fully and effectively in the province's political life.

The conflict in Northern Ireland caused 3,285 violent deaths between July 1969 and 31 December 1993 (Sutton, 1994). The armed forces and police services of the UK and the Republic of Ireland were responsible for 360 of these killings and republican and loyalist paramilitary groups were responsible for 2,837. The killings by paramilitary groups in Northern Ireland included the indiscriminate killing of civilians, the targeted killing of civilians, the killing of politicians and state employees, the killing of police and the killing of military personnel. An example of the indiscriminate killing of civilians is the bombing of the Remembrance Day parade in Enniskillen, Co. Fermanagh, by the Irish Republican Army (IRA) on the 8 November 1987. The bomb killed 12 people, 11 civilians and one police officer, all of whom were

Protestant. The bombing was part of the IRA's ongoing campaign to show British rule of Northern Ireland to be ineffective and untenable. The attack was indiscriminate in that the civilians were not targeted as individuals even though, given the nature of the parade, it was to be expected that the civilian casualties would be from the Protestant not the Catholic community. Such indiscriminate targeting of civilians is not the strongest example by which to assess Primoratz's proposal.

Discriminate killings of civilians in Northern Ireland included individuals targeted for their political activism. Malcolm Sutton lists 133 sectarian killings of Protestant civilians by the IRA and another 18 by the Irish National Liberation Army (INLA), and 713 sectarian killings of Catholic civilians by loyalist groups. In addition, four members of the Ulster Unionist Party were killed by the IRA and one member of the Ulster Democratic Party. Five members of the Social Democratic and Labour Party (SDLP) were killed by loyalist paramilitary groups and two members of the Irish Independence Party (updated affiliations taken from CAIN, 2009). It is killings of this latter type that are relevant to Primoratz's proposal: those Catholic civilians targeted because of their active support for the political causes of their community and those Protestant civilians targeted because of their active support for Northern Ireland as a province of the UK. A stronger case for Primoratz's proposal can be made by focusing on such civilian targeting.

Primoratz's Proposal

Broadly, Primoratz's proposal is based on three claims:

1. that civilians may be culpable for the unjust cause of their country or party;
2. that the deaths of such civilians may at times be militarily efficacious in combating that unjust cause;
3. that preventing or undoing that injustice is a just cause for war.

The second and third claims will not be disputed, that is, it will be accepted that the targeting of civilians may be efficacious towards the attainment of a just end. It will be accepted too that non-state and paramilitary organisations may be fighting for a just end; but Primoratz's proposal will be rejected on the grounds that civilians will rarely be sufficiently culpable.

In order to clarify the role of culpability in the justification of killing in war, a typology of four types of killing will be briefly outlined: consensual killing, killing as punishment, killing in self-preservation and killing in self-defence (developed from McKeogh, 2002). The killing that is typical of war will then be distinguished from these four and presented as a distinct type.

Consensual Killing

Consensual killing occurs when the victim agrees to it or to the significant risk of it. Killing is not unjust if an informed adult, *compos mentis*, consents to death, or to the risk of death. Examples of consensual killing include duels, violent sports, voluntary euthanasia and assisted suicide. In such cases, certain conditions are required for death or the risk of death to be just; these include that the person be adult, of sound mind and free from duress at the moment that they consent to death, or to the risk of death. The justice of consensual killing does not rely on claims of either fault or good consequences.

Punitive Killing

Punitive killing (PK) is killing as punishment for a wrong done. In capital punishment, the fault of the person executed is the defining characteristic of the killing. The act must be one of great wrongness and the culpability of the accused for that act must be established at an appropriate level of confidence (the process often involves a fair trial, impartial judges, a right of defence, and the investigation and assessment of relevant information). Though consequentialist arguments may be used to support the practice of execution (e.g. deterrence of others from commission of such crimes), the primary justification for capital punishment may be non-consequentialist. The justice of PK can be based solely on the fault of the person killed: they are guilty and they deserve death as a punishment.

Killing in Self-preservation

In contrast to punitive killing, killing in self-preservation (SP) is characterised by the fact that no claim is made of the fault of the person killed. The justification of SP is purely consequentialist: the death of the person is the necessary means to the survival of another. No claim is made about the person deserving of death, only about their death's instrumentality towards a desired end. A classic example of SP was the subject of the *Stevens* case, in which two starving seamen, Stevens and Dudley, were convicted of killing and eating a boy with whom they were shipwrecked (Kemp, 1996: 338). The boy had done nothing to merit such treatment; thus to kill him was wrong even though it was the only means of survival available to the two sailors. As a purely consequentialist justification of killing, SP is widely held to fail to meet the standard of a justified taking of human life.

Killing in Self-defence

By killing in self-defence (SD) we mean the taking of the life of the person defended against (PDA) in order to prevent them acting in a way that would result in the loss of human life.[2] It is assumed here that taking their life is the only available means to prevent their act and to avert its consequences. Self-defence is characterised by two components, a likelihood of good consequences eventuating and a claim of fault: first, taking the life of the PDA is the means to avert a certain consequence; second, the PDA is held to have in some way become a permissible target of such violence. Self-defence then has features in common with both PK and SP. First, with SP it shares a concern with consequences. Self-preservation and SD are both instrumental to the achievement of a certain end. Indeed, both SD and SP are motivated wholly by the achievement of a certain consequence (survival). This instrumentality is the sole justification of SP; it is a necessary but insufficient condition of SD.

Second, with PK, SD shares a concern with the status of the person targeted. This is the second necessary condition of SD. Whereas SP pays no attention to the status of the person killed (they are treated simply as a means to an end, an instrument for survival), SD does look at the status of the person targeted. In SP, the person killed is innocent and uninvolved; in SD, some claim is made about the PDA's culpability, responsibility, involvement, engagement or agency in the commission of a lethal act. What distinguishes SD from SP is precisely this claim of some degree of involvement and/or non-innocence on the part of the person killed.

Of the two conditions of SD (first, it is the only means to save the life of the person who would otherwise be killed, and, second, the lethal violence is directed against one from whom, or via whom, the threat is emanating) it is this second, non-consequentialist condition of SD that warrants further investigation here. The person killed in SD is claimed to be different in a crucial way from the person killed in SP. It is this different status of the person killed that distinguishes SD from SP and that, of the two types of killing, makes SD alone morally permissible. But what precisely is it that distinguishes SD from SP?

The Judgment of Fault in the Justification of Self-defence

Very broadly, we can discern three positions that are taken on the level of fault required for SD. One requires a fault on the part of the PDA in SD and requires that fault to be of the same type and magnitude as the fault of the person executed in PK. The second position requires no fault on the part of the PDA for legitimate SD to take place. The third position is an intermediate one: it requires there to be some degree of fault on the part of the PDA for legitimate SD to take place but it need not be a fault of the same type or magnitude as the fault in PK.

Judgment of fault: one extreme. At the former extreme is the eighteenth century English jurist Sir William Blackstone. He required the same degree of fault in SD and PK when he declared: 'No act may be prevented by death unless the same if committed would also be punished by death' (Rodin, 2002: 96–97). To Blackstone, then, the wrong that may be averted through SD must be the wrong of murder. Self-defence requires the same degree of wrong as PK. It is a wrong so great that 'guilt' is the appropriate term. As the degree of guilt is the same in SD and PK, all that distinguishes the two is the element of time: in SD, the killing of the guilty one takes place before he can perform his wrongful act; in PK, it occurs after the act. Thus, to the question 'Does this person deserve to be killed?' Blackstone can answer that the person does deserve to be killed. The PDA deserves to be killed because of his intent to commit a great wrong (and it is fortunate that the killing can take place before the harmful consequence of their criminal intent can occur).

Judgment of fault: the other extreme. At the other extreme is the justification of SD given by Hugo Grotius who justifies killing in self-defence with no reference to the culpability of the PDA. This seventeenth century Dutch jurist based the right of self-defence in natural law and on the natural orientation towards self-preservation that we share with every living thing:

> ... when our bodies are violently attacked with danger to our lives, and there is no other way of escape, it is lawful to fight the aggressor, and even to kill him ... We must note that this right of self-defence derives its origin primarily from the instinct of self-preservation, which nature has given to every creature, and not from the injustice or misconduct of the aggressor. Wherefore, *even though my assailant may be guiltless*, as for instance a soldier fighting in good faith, or one who mistakes me for someone else, or a man frantic with insanity or sleeplessness, as we read sometimes happens, in none of these cases am I deprived of my right of self-defence ... (Grotius, 1949: 73, italics added)

Grotius here accepts that natural law permits killing in self-defence in any case where the threat to one's life comes via the PDA. The PDA may be the unwilling or even unwitting agent or vehicle of the threat to one's life but he may nevertheless be killed.

Judgment of fault: the central case. In between the extremes represented by Blackstone and Grotius is a justification of SD that requires some degree of non-innocence on the part of the PDA, though not one so great that it equates to the guilt required for PK. Such an approach is taken by David Rodin, who is clear that there is a judgment of moral fault made against the PDA in SD, at least in what he calls the 'central case' of SD. The central case of SD is distinguished by four characteristics. Anyone who believes killing in SD ever to be acceptable, Rodin writes, will believe it to be acceptable when these four characteristics are all present. The four characteristics are as follows:

1. an aggressor makes an *intentional* attack on the victim's life, which will succeed unless the victim uses lethal force against the aggressor;
2. the attack is objectively *unjust* in the sense that the attacker has no legitimate right to make the attack, for example, he is not a law enforcement officer acting within his duty;
3. the aggressor is fully *culpable* in making the attack;
4. the victim is wholly *innocent* with respect to the attack (for example, he has not provoked the aggressor in any faultworthy way) (Rodin, 2002: 29, italics in original).

To Rodin, the judgment of fault is a key element of SD: the PDA ('aggressor' to Rodin) is *doing something wrong* and that is a crucial part of the reason why the PDA may be killed. In Rodin's central case of SD, although the PDA is guilty of a wrong, it need not be a wrong of similar type or magnitude to that of the criminal in PK. The fault in SD, which makes the PDA liable to lethal force (should such force be the only way to save the life of his victim), may not be a fault of sufficient severity as to make the PDA subject to capital punishment should he succeed in killing his victim. In short, Rodin claims that the killing of the PDA is justifiable, but he does not claim that the PDA deserves to be killed.

Rodin believes, however, that SD must, and in the 'central case' does, meet an important standard in the treatment of people. To describe that standard, he quotes Nagel:

> whatever one does to another person intentionally must be aimed at him as a subject, with the intention that he receive it as a subject. It should manifest an attitude to *him* rather than just to the situation. (Nagel, 1979: 66, italics in original)

Yet in all cases of SD, including Rodin's central case, what makes the PDA a legitimate target for lethal violence is not only factors to do with him as a person but also circumstances. Factors to do with him as a person, such as his intent and the action in which he is deliberately engaged, are insufficient alone to justify the killing of him. What makes the PDA a legitimate target for lethal violence are also factors that are not to do with him as a person, namely, the circumstances (which are such that there exists an opportunity to prevent the killing of the victim by taking the life of the PDA).

Does SD manifest an attitude to the PDA as a person and not just to the situation? The answer is that SD is a response to *both* the person and the situation (whereas PK may be a response to the person, and SP is a response to only the situation). But *to what extent* is SD a response to the person? And to what extent is it a response to the situation? Implied in Nagel's standard is that killing in self-defence is a response to the PDA as a person in some *non-negligible, non-trivial* way. The answer to this question about the extent to which SD is a response to the PDA as a person lies in the non-consequentialist component of SD. Two questions can be asked about this non-consequentialist component. First, how great must the 'fault' on the part of the PDA be in order to warrant the use of lethal force to stop him? Second, how confident must one be about the existence of fault at such a level before lethal force is employed preventively?

How Great Must the Fault Be?

How great must the fault be on the part of the PDA for lethal force to be justifiably used to stop him? The degree of fault required by Blackstone seems unusually high for proponents of SD. That of Grotius is too low.[3] Rodin is more typical in settling for a lesser degree of wrongness on the part of the PDA. Indeed, he does not use the term 'guilt', but, rather, 'appropriate normative connection':

> ... if one is to be justified in inflicting harm in an act of defence, then there must be an appropriate normative connection between the wrongfulness of the threat one is seeking to avert and the person one harms; the threat must derive from him as a moral subject, not just as a physical entity. (Rodin, 2002: 88)

He continues that this normative connection must be 'sufficiently substantive'. The right of SD, Rodin wrote,

> is grounded, not simply in the fact that the defensive action is a necessary pro-
> portionate response to an unjustified threat to life, but also in the fact that there
> is a sufficiently substantive normative connection between the unjustified threat
> and the person against whom one uses defensive force. (Rodin, 2002: 89)

The existence of this sufficiently substantive normative connection between the wrongfulness of the threat one is seeking to avert and the person one harms generates what Rodin terms the 'moral asymmetry' between the victim and the PDA. To Rodin this moral asymmetry is a crucial feature of SD. Self-defence differs from SP in this moral asymmetry; the wrongness of SP lies in the lack of any such moral asymmetry.[4] What degree of moral asymmetry must exist between the victim and the PDA for the former to be justified in killing the latter to save his own life? If the degree of wrong for SD can be less than for PK, then why is this so? Why kill to prevent the commission of a non-capital offence? Why is it permissible to kill a person in SD when that person's wrong is less than sufficient to merit death as a punishment? The only answer is consequences, that is, there exists the chance to avert the consequences of his act by killing him before he commits it.

How Confident Must One Be about the Fault of the PDA?

The 'normative connection' must be sufficiently substantive, but it must also be established at an appropriate level of confidence. It is not simply to be inferred from the fact of the PDA's role in the threat to the victim's life. There must be other grounds for judging such a 'normative connection' to be present. That degree of confidence need not be certainty. This means that, on the one hand, the victim need not have unequivocal knowledge that the PDA has a sufficient degree of fault before defending himself with lethal force. On the other hand, it must mean too that the victim need not have unequivocal knowledge that the PDA is without a suffi-cient degree of fault before allowing himself to be killed. In SD, it is the case that the judgment of fault must often be made by the victim. Yet the victim is hardly well placed to make a proper and impartial assessment of fault. The victim is operating under acute time pressure and lacks the required knowledge of the circumstances of the PDA's action, the PDA's motivation, and the rights and wrongs of the case. The victim also has a personal interest in the case that makes his assessment of fault on the part of the PDA biased.

The Duty of Non-self-defence

That the normative connection must be sufficiently substantive for SD to be justified implies that there may be cases where the normative connection is insufficiently sub-stantive or where one is not sufficiently confident of one's assessment of such a connection. In such cases SD is unjustified and is not to occur. There are circumstances in which the victim is not justified in using lethal force, even though it is the only means to save his life. Rodin explicitly accepts this implication: 'there may sometimes be situations in which there is a duty to abstain from SD, a duty ... of martyrdom' (Rodin, 2002: 67). He holds it to be no more justifiable to save oneself by killing an 'innocent aggressor' or an 'innocent threat' than by killing an innocent bystander (Rodin, 2002: 81). However, it is not only 'innocent aggressors' who may not justly be killed, but also insufficiently guilty ones. The duty of non-SD ('martyrdom' to Rodin) may cover far more cases than Rodin allows if it is not only 'innocent aggressors' who may not justly be killed, but also insufficiently guilty ones and ones whose guilt cannot be established to a sufficient degree of confidence.

The key role played by fault in the justification of SD limits the cases to which SD may be applied. People may be culpable for and instrumental in an unjust lethal attack but not sufficiently culpable or instrumental to permit lethal force to be used to defend against the attack. In short, we may be innocent victims of attack, yet we may not be justly able to self-defend violently. There may be no one we can justly use violence to self-defend against. I now wish to argue that the justification of SD, limited as it is by the requirement of fault, cannot be used to justify the killing of many combatants in war and therefore does not offer a basis for a justification of killing civilians.

Killing in War

In a just war, people are killed because their deaths are useful towards the attainment of the goal of the war, which is the undoing of an injustice. They are killed for reasons of political, not personal, justice. They are killed because there are no other means of attaining the political justice that is the *ad bellum* aim of the war. The killing that is typical of war cannot be justified as consensual, punitive, self-preservative or self-defence.

Killing in war is not consensual. Consensual killing can justify the killing in war only of those who consent to the role of combatant. Unwilling conscripts and child-soldiers cannot be deemed to have consented to be targeted even when they pose no immediate threat. Yet they may be killed in war.

Killing in war is not punitive: if the end could be achieved without killing, we ought not to kill (killing in war, then, occurs because of political, technological or circumstantial limitations; at the time, the end cannot be achieved by other means). That the killing of combatants in war is not akin to punishment for wrongdoing is also evident from the principle of belligerent equality, which gives to soldiers on both sides an equal freedom to kill the enemy regardless of the justice of their side's cause.

Killing in war is not akin to self-preservative killing as the principle of civilian immunity prohibits the targeting of civilians even when it is the most (or only) effective means to a justified end. Not all whose deaths may contribute towards the end of the war may be killed. Some people ought not to be killed however much their deaths might contribute to victory. These are civilians, the targeting of whom is prohibited by the principle of civilian immunity.

The killing of combatants in war is not akin to self-defence. The justification of SD and the justification of killing combatants in war are similar in that in both cases there are two conditions of targeting, functionality and legitimacy, but the functionality and legitimacy are different in the two cases. First, in both cases an end must be served by killing the person. In SD there must be an immediate threat that is averted by violence; the end is survival. In war there need not be an immediate threat posed by the person killed; the end sought is a longer-term goal of promotion of the chances of military success in the war, thereby preventing or overturning an injustice. The current legal position permits the targeting in war of all combatants at any time. Combatants need not be engaged in combatant acts at the moment that they are targeted. They can be legitimately targeted when they pose no immediate threat. Military personnel far from the frontline may be targeted in war. Second, in both SD and the justification of killing in war, the person must be a legitimate target of violence. In SD the person defended against must be sufficiently culpable for the act defended against (they must not be an 'innocent aggressor'). In war fault plays no role in the justification of killing. Combatants on both sides may be killed in war regardless of which side has a just cause.

Why then is it permissible to kill combatants in a just war? What makes combatants a legitimate target? The answer is convention. The killing that is typical of war, that is, the direct and intentional killing of combatants for instrumental purposes, is just because it is based on a convention, on a widespread acceptance that it is permissible to do so. The killing of combatants in war is thus justified as a convention-dependent permission (i.e. it is permissible to do so only because of an acceptance in custom and/or law that it may be done). The person in the role of combatant is acknowledged as a legitimate target of military violence by law and custom. The laws and customs of war, as they currently stand, are founded on this acceptance that those in the role of combatant may, in war, be treated as instruments. They may be killed with no claim that they as individuals deserve it and they may themselves kill without incurring blame. No distinction is made between willing combatants and unwilling conscripts. The legality of killing combatants in war is thus dependent on the laws and customs of international society; if such laws and customs did not exist, then the killing of combatants in war would not be permissible in war in all the circumstances it is now. That combatants may be killed in war, even when the justifications of self-defence, punishment and consent do not apply, is one of the 'rules of the game' of war, similar in nature to the rules of the road.[5] Attacks on such combatants cannot be justified except on the basis of existing law and custom. Without this customary and legal acceptance, fewer people could be targeted in war than is currently the case.

For this reason, the attacks by the IRA on personnel of the armed forces are in a different category from IRA attacks on police, politicians and civilians. This applies even to the Regent's Park and Deal barracks attacks. On 20 July 1982 an IRA bomb hidden underneath the bandstand in Regent's Park exploded during a performance by the Royal Green Jackets band, killing seven soldiers, all bandsmen. On 22 September 1989 the IRA again targeted musicians with a bomb attack on the

Royal Marines School of Music at the Royal Marines barracks in Deal, Kent, killing 11 Marines, all of whom were training to be bandsmen and battlefield medics (Sutton, 1994). These attacks, though they provoked widespread revulsion, are not to be categorised with attacks on civilians, either indiscriminate or targeted attacks. They were attacks on personnel in military uniform.

This discussion of killing in war suggests that the killing of combatants in war is not, and cannot be, justified as SD. The culpability of combatants in war is insufficient (in degree and in certainty) for the killing of combatants in war to be justified as SD. Indeed, in a just war, one party is engaged not in injustice but in justice, yet combatants on both sides may legitimately be killed. In war then combatants are not killed in SD. They are killed because their deaths are useful towards the attainment of the goal of the war, which is the undoing of an injustice. They are killed for reasons of political, not personal, justice. They are killed because there are no other means to attain the political justice that is the *ad bellum* aim of the war. Fault plays a more minor role in the justification of killing in war than in SD and that fault is political, not personal.

Civilians in War

Primoratz holds that civilians are granted a special status in war and he questions whether they deserve it in all circumstances – but he is wrong. Civilians have no special status in war and there can therefore be no issue of their losing this status. Democratic participation cannot be grounds for removing from civilians something they do not possess. It is not civilians who are given a special status in war, but combatants. Combatants are ascribed a special status in war, one that permits them to be targeted with lethal violence when they have done nothing to deserve death. It is not civilians who are granted immunity from targeting in war – all people have such immunity from lethal attack unless they give it up or lose it. In war, combatants lose this immunity.

The justice of targeting combatants in war is based on a convention-dependent permission, but the obligation not to target civilians in war is not a convention-dependent obligation. It is justice that requires that civilians not be killed in war. The targeting of civilians, as Primoratz proposes, cannot be justified as SD. For the targeting of civilians in war to be justifiable as SD, a sufficiently substantive normative connection must be established at a sufficient degree of confidence. Primoratz's claim is that a sufficiently substantive normative connection can be found in civilians' involvement in the threat even though their involvement falls short of combatancy. Civilians, he asserts, can be part of the causal chain of threat. In a democracy, he claims, many civilians may comprise part of the chain of threat, in a place behind the political leadership, as the ultimate wielders of sovereignty in a democracy. However, the culpability of such civilians is too weak to meet the minimum level required for SD.

Conclusion

Primoratz's proposal has been investigated here in the context of the inter-communal strife in Northern Ireland. Though Northern Ireland was far from the 'perfect democracy' hypothesised by Primoratz, it was a conflict in which participants could know the political loyalties and activities of individuals. Even so, targeted killings of politically active civilians were a fraction of the deaths in the Troubles: of the 3,285 killings in Northern Ireland from 1969 to 1993, at most 876 were of civilians targeted for their political affiliations or activities. Such killings were not just. First, the conventional acceptance that combatants may be treated as instruments does not cover civilians. Second, the targeting of civilians in war cannot be justified as SD. Quite how much political involvement or culpability qualifies one for politically efficacious killing will always be problematic: political involvement and culpability are scalar concepts whereas life and death are sortal ones (Hyland, 1995: 49–50). No precise delineation is possible. However, to put it in Rodin's words, a sufficiently substantive normative connection must be established at a sufficient degree of confidence. The finding here is that even civilians who participate in the democratic politics of their country are insufficiently culpable to be killed in self-defence. The culpability of a citizen in a democracy is simply too weak to permit the just targeting of them in war as violent aggressors. They are so weakly responsible for the injustice that their culpability in this regard is negligible. They cannot be targeted in SD as they are akin to, if not innocent aggressors, then insufficiently guilty ones. A duty of non-SD applies. As civilians, even in a democracy, are insufficiently culpable to be targeted as SD, the terrorist targeting of civilians is akin to SP rather than SD. The republican and loyalist paramilitaries were like Stevens and Dudley and the politically involved civilians of Northern Ireland were like the boy with the misfortune to share their boat. The terrorists sought a (possibly good) end at the expense of the lives of those who had not done enough to merit such treatment.

Afternote: How could Primoratz's Proposal be Just?

How could terrorism be just? Self-defence cannot justify the targeting of civilians in war (as a sufficiently substantive normative connection cannot be established) and so Primoratz's proposal would require a change in our customary delineation of legitimate killing in war. There is a customary and legal acceptance that in armed conflict some people (those in the role of combatant) may be treated as instruments rather than persons in order to create the possibility for a political injustice to be violently overturned. Without this customary and legal acceptance of their treatment, much (but not all) killing of combatants in war would be unjust. The benefits of the current delineation of legitimate targets in war are its practicality, its widespread acceptance, its limitation of war and its instrumentality towards political justice. Primoratz's proposal would require a broad acceptance of new rules of the game that permit civilians to be targeted, an extension (to cover civilians who are citizens of a democracy) of the legal and customary convention that those in uniform may be killed in war when justifications based on consent or SD do not apply. Without customary acceptance, the change would be unjust. Such a customary and legal change is promoted by Primoratz in his article. He seeks an amendment to the current legal and customary acceptance of who may be targeted in war at any time. Whether or not it would be a good idea depends on issues of practicality, efficacy and the balance of political justice and personal injustices. Should the rules be changed? Should the targeted killing of politically responsible civilians be made just through the widespread acceptance of a convention that permits it?

The aim of Primoratz's proposal is greater justice. Permitting the targeting of certain categories of civilian when this would be militarily effective can produce greater justice either by increasing the chances of the attainment of the *ad bellum* end of war or by lowering its costs. It is unlikely that it would achieve either. First, it is unlikely that Primoratz's proposal would reduce the killing in war. It is more likely that both parties to the conflict would target the civilians of the other when it becomes legal to do so, claiming enemy civilians to be culpable and targeting them when they believe it to be militarily advantageous. Primoratz's proposal thus opens the door to total war. Second, there is no likelihood that the proposed change would make the side with just cause any more likely to prevail. The military advantage of targeting civilians cannot be limited to the side with just cause (just cause is the very issue in dispute in the conflict). The current moral and legal situation represents one particular balance of *ad bellum* justice and *in bello* injustices. It is a situation in which many personal injustices on the *in bello* level are tolerated because of the possibility of undoing a political injustice on the *ad bellum* level. Under Primoratz's proposal political justice is no more likely to be achieved and greater personal harm will certainly be committed. If *ad bellum* justice is no more likely to be achieved and greater *in bello* injustices will be committed, then nothing is gained under Primoratz's proposals and much is lost. There are no persuasive reasons for the change Primoratz proposes.

Notes

1. The position Primoratz put forward in 2007 with respect to Iraq hinges on the same practical considerations: 'Enemy civilians who could be considered eligible for attack … would virtually always live thoroughly intermingled with other enemy civilians who would not be eligible … There is no way of making sure that in an attack on a civilian target, only the former are hit, while the latter emerge unscathed' (Primoratz, 2007: 35).
2. To describe the person as 'attacker' or 'aggressor', as occurs in discussion of this issue, may seem to imply wrongdoing on their part, the very issue being investigated here.
3. The position outlined – but not recommended – by Grotius removes questions of justice and morality from the issue of SD. An unlimited right to self-defend negates attempts to limit violence, which was the Dutch jurist's greatest concern. He thus urges us *not* to avail of this natural law right.
4. Rodin's phrase 'moral asymmetry' may seem to suggest that even the slightest modicum of responsibility for a fault (however small) will suffice to generate a significant difference between the victim and the PDA; but for him it is not the case, in a situation in which either the attacker or the attacked is to die, that even the slightest difference in moral standing between the two can be allowed to decide the issue. Moral asymmetry is not enough for Rodin; the 'normative connection' must be 'sufficiently substantive' (Rodin, 2002: 89).
5. These rules can be found in legal form in the Hague Regulations on Land Warfare of 1907 as updated in the Geneva Conventions of 1949, as applied to irregular war by the Additional Protocols of 1977.

References

CAIN (Conflict Archive on the Internet) (2009) Available at: http://www.cain.ulst.ac.uk/ (accessed 2 December 2009).

Grotius, H. (1949) *The Law of War and Peace (De Jure Belli ac Pacis)*, translated by L. R. Loomis with an introduction by P. E. Corbett (Roslyn, NY: Walter J. Black).

Hyland, J. L. (1995) *Democratic Theory: The Philosophic Foundations* (Manchester: Manchester University Press).

Kemp, K. W. (1996) Punishment as a just cause for war, *Public Affairs Quarterly*, 10, pp. 335–353.

McKeogh, C. (2002) *Innocent Civilians: The Morality of Killing in War* (Basingstoke: Palgrave).

Nagel, T. (1979) War and massacre, in: *Mortal Questions*, pp. 53–74 (Cambridge: Cambridge University Press).

Primoratz, I. (2002) Michael Walzer's just war theory: some issues of responsibility, *Ethical Theory and Moral Practice*, 5, pp. 221–243.

Primoratz, I. (2007) Civilian immunity in war; its grounds, scope, and weight, in: I. Primoratz (Ed.) *Civilian Immunity in War* (Oxford: Oxford University Press).

Rodin, D. (2002) *War and Self-defense* (Oxford: Oxford University Press).

Sutton, M. (1994) *Bear in Mind these Dead: An Index of Deaths from the Conflict in Ireland 1969–1993* (Belfast: Beyond the Pale Publications).

Bombings to Ballots: The Evolution of the Irish Republican Movement's Conceptualisation of Democracy

GARRETT O'BOYLE

Trinity College Dublin, Ireland

ABSTRACT   *People do political violence for a reason. That is, the tactic of violence is resorted to in order to achieve a purpose. So what might lead the perpetrators of political violence to abandon its use and embrace peaceful democratic political activity? From the perspective of the perpetrator, the answer will lie in the nature of the ends/means relationship and the re-evaluation of the usefulness of particular means to achieve a given end. This paper explores the Irish Republican Movement's 'transition to democracy' and its apparent adoption of a different interpretation of democracy that no longer prioritises simple majoritarianism.*

Introduction

In August 2010, Sinn Féin President Gerry Adams succinctly stated the current position of the Irish Republican Movement: 'The attempt by Sinn Féin to initiate dialogue with the political groups linked to some armed republican factions is a genuine attempt by us to put very directly to these groupings that ongoing armed actions have no place in the struggle for Irish unity ... There is a peaceful and democratic path available to a united Ireland ... This engagement is about pointing out to these groups the futility of ongoing armed actions and the political space that is there for them to move into' (Irish Republican Publicity Bureau, 2010).

This echoes and amplifies the July 2005 IRA statement that formally ordered an end to their armed campaign. The statement included an order to all members to 'assist the development of purely political and democratic programmes through exclusively peaceful means', going on to say that 'our decisions have been taken to advance our republican and democratic objectives, including our goal of a

169

united Ireland. We believe there is now an alternative way to achieve this and to end British rule in our country' (Irish Republican Publicity Bureau, 2005).

Contrast these statements with earlier, more militaristic Republican rhetoric – for example, that contained in a 1980 interview with former IRA chief of staff Seán Mac Stiofáin: 'The position of the IRA [is] that the Dublin government is illegal, the Stormont government is illegal, and the Westminster presence in Ireland is also illegal and that involvement in any of those parliaments would be tantamount to recognition of them. And this would be in effect denying the right of the IRA to exist. And we saw it not to be merely a fine point of revolutionary theory – these were illegal parliaments and therefore we couldn't be involved in them – we knew that sooner or later the people playing a parliamentary role would abandon the armed struggle' (Mac Stiofáin, 1980: 10).

What might account for this transition? How do groups that have used political violence as part of a sub-state insurgent campaign to force political change in a particular society evolve into willing participants in the democratic process? Standard interpretations of the Northern peace process would point to the journey beginning with the Republican Movement's 'discovery' of electoral politics in the aftermath of the H-Block protests, the dropping of the policy of abstentionism in 1986, and continuing with the Sinn Féin/SDLP (Social Democratic and Labour Party) talks that began in 1988.

There is, however, more to it: a democratic alternative can only be an attractive option for those with a basically functional – indeed, an essentially liberal – conception of democracy. To put it another way, not all politically violent groups might be tempted by the possibilities of a non-violent democratic alternative. If there is to be a negotiating table to which the British government must be brought, then there must be something capable of being negotiated.

This brings us to the issue of the nature and character of a particular politically violent group, both in terms of (a) their general ideology and (b) how the members of that group conceptualise the relationship between ends and means. With regard to (a), what is the political nature of the society that the group envisages establishing once they have driven their enemies into the sea? A group that envisages the establishment of a liberal democracy in the event of their victory is surely, *a priori*, more likely to be amenable to democratic alternatives and persuasion than groups that desire the establishment of, say, a totalitarian theocracy.

With regard to (b), the conceptualisation of the relationship between ends and means, the issue can be put in these terms: Are their political demands maximalist and absolutist or is there the possibility of negotiation? Or, put another way, does the group justify its use of violence in broadly consequentialist or non-consequentialist (deontological) terms (O'Boyle, 2002)?

Consequentialist or Not?

Even the most reviled of politically violent groups use some sort of ethical justification for their actions: at the very least, they need to justify such actions to themselves and to their supporters before they ever take the decision to use violent tactics. Differences can be seen between groups in terms of the ethical bases of their justifications, differences that are significant in terms of assessing how they see the world: some groups exemplify a *consequentialist* basis, others a *non-consequentialist* (or deontological) basis. In broad terms, *deontology* can be considered to mean the belief that an action is right if it conforms to a particular moral code. The fundamental issue is the *non*-consequentialist nature of the judgement: that is, that the criterion of goodness or right action is the adherence to the moral rule, and that consideration of the consequences of an action is, at best, of secondary importance. Similarly, *consequentialism* can be taken broadly to refer to any code of ethics or guide to action that prioritises the actual outcomes and consequences of those actions rather than adherence to *a priori* principles alone. Consequentialism is thus the doctrine that says that the right act in any given situation is the one that will produce the best overall outcome in terms of the identified end. However, in practice it is more complex than a reformulation of the adage that the ends justify the means.

Consequentialists may find that their decisions on the means to be used and the actions to be taken are side-constrained by the recognition that there are certain egregious forms of action that hardly anyone would want to attempt to justify their engagement in. So, while the ends might justify some means, they do not necessarily justify *all* means. Even the most committed consequentialist is not debarred from holding certain types of action to be unjustified in the pursuit of his or her ends. That is, a thoroughgoing consequentialist might have a pre-categorisation of permissible actions – actions that are side-constrained by certain other principles. This idea of principled consequentialism might also feed into the suggestion that groups that base their justifications on consequentialism might be more moderate in their demands as well as their means when faced with a persuasive argument that *those* means will not attain *those* ends. A consequentialist will, by definition and inclination, be open to taking into account the complexity of the potential consequences of his or her actions – and not just in terms of those actions' likelihood of achieving the ultimately desired end, but also in terms of considering the short-term consequences, such as, for example, continued death and destruction. In terms of a simple example, what is the point of establishing, say, an egalitarian society wherein all can flourish and develop their distinctive human potentialities, if the only way of getting to that point is to annihilate 95 per cent of the human population by way of nuclear weapons? So consequentialists, because they are consequentialists, may tend to take into account the complex consequences of their actions – or the balance of consequences – and might realise that the achievement of their overall ultimate end goal may not justify all the consequences of the actions undertaken in pursuit of that end.

A crucial point in a nuanced understanding of consequentialist justifications for political violence is the idea that even an overwhelmingly consequentialist justification for violence need not accept *all* means as neutral and equal. A consequentialist could, for example, take seriously Rawls's idea of the 'plurality and distinctiveness of individuals' (Rawls, 1972: 29) and accept that – even in terms of what is posited as the ultimately desired consequence or end goal – the use of means that inflict harm on individuals is, other things being equal, undesirable (or even 'wrong'). It is precisely this feature of violent means that leads politically violent groups to feel that they need to explain or justify their actions in the first place: certain means tend to be seen by ordinary people, in real-life situations, as wrong, morally questionable or unjustifiable. To cope with this apparent contradiction between the desired ultimate benefits of the ends and the costs of the means employed at present, two main strategies seem to be employed. First, there is the attempt to mitigate the 'wrongness' of the violent act by implying the guilt or complicity of the victims. Second is the claim that violence is the last resort, that it is the only possible means available for the achievement of the desired end. However, with regard to the Republican Movement, it may well have been the realisation that there are possibly other, more efficacious, means available – or a change in the calculation as to the effectiveness of violence, given the circumstances – that was behind the ultimate transition from the use of violence to engagement in conventional politics. The question is to what extent does the Republican Movement exemplify this type of consequentialism?

Analysing the Rhetoric

An analysis of the justificatory statements made by the Republican Movement over the years seems to indicate clearly a broadly consequentialist tenor, of the crude form 'we reluctantly do *x* as a last resort in order to achieve *y*'. That said, there have always been calls for a parallel political strategy. Even though the split in the Republican Movement in 1969/70 was characterised as a split between those who wished to orient the movement towards Marxist political activity in a broad-front type scenario and those who were seen as traditional old-school 'physical force' republicans, the latter – who formed the Provisional IRA – developed their own left-wing political ideas within a couple of years, perhaps as a result of an influx of rapidly politicised young recruits. By the mid-1970s, there was a clear tension between what has been described as 'the "Young Turks" who supported [Gerry] Adams' and 'the old guard' (Dillon, 1990: 84). The former ultimately prevailed and the Republican Movement increasingly began to develop a parallel political strategy.

   The traditional belief that the unity and self-determination of Ireland, which 'were the essential conditions for the freedom and development of Ireland', 'could never be fully realised while Britain retained a presence in the country' and that 'physical force offered the only avenue by which this situation might be changed' (quoted in Cronin, 1980: 335), remained the bedrock of the republican position up to and including the stage of more radical politicisation in the 1970s. Indeed, part of the tensions between the so-called Adams faction and the older Provisional IRA leadership in the mid-1970s was related to the fact that the younger faction began to see the current leadership as 'the type of men who stand up with every generation and say that at least they fought but lost and left it to another generation' (quoted in Dillon, 1990: 83).

In 1980, a major analytical exposition of Irish Republican political philosophy was published in *An Phoblacht/Republican News* (*AP/RN*) (Flynn, 1980: 6–7). Interestingly, the article argued that:

> Only a fool, or the politically naive, would suggest that imperialism can be defeated by the armed struggle alone, however successful it is, or even by action in the six counties alone ... Republicans must act as the mass organiser of the people, to lead them in agitationary activities on issues such as land, for better working, living and social conditions; showing them in all these fights that their enemies are their landlords and their gombeen exploiters banded together into the establishment.

In essence, the writer is arguing that (or explaining why) the Republican Movement should involve itself in a more diverse set of activities and political engagements than simple and traditional armed struggle; but he is not arguing that there is no place for armed struggle – indeed, he argues that it is the very continuation of armed struggle that gives the movement the legitimacy to engage in these other diverse areas of activity, as the leading exponent of Irish anti-imperialism.

First Electoral Steps

Although Sinn Féin would eventually capitalise on the first electoral success represented by the election of hunger striker Bobby Sands, there was still in those early days an apparently high level of distrust of the usefulness of the democratic process. After Sands' election, the IRA's annual Easter statement (*AP/RN*, 25 April 1981) said:

> The electorate of Fermanagh and South Tyrone were asked to act by proxy on behalf of the Irish people. They have given a lead to the rest of us and an answer to the British government who showed, yet again as they did after the general election of 1918 and the setting up of Dáil Éireann, that they are not prepared to recognise the will of the people even when that will is expressed peacefully and democratically. That clearly leaves armed struggle as the only other option, an option tried and trusted in Ireland and by other peoples throughout the world. Only through armed struggle will we be listened to, only through the struggle waged by the Irish Republican Army can we win national freedom and end division and sectarianism in Ireland.

To dismiss as a failure, a mere couple of weeks later, the election of Sands on 9 April, although Sands was to die on 5 May, seems to show – at the very least – a certain impatience with the pace of electoral politics. Nevertheless, the statement reiterates the idea that only violence will work and incorporates again that 'last resort' element, in that electoral politics have been tried, have failed owing to British intransigence, hence armed struggle is the only means left if the goals are to be attained. It

seems not to matter that the purpose for engaging in that particular instance of electoral politics was the short-term goal of concessions on prisoners' political status
rather than the long-term overall goals of the Republican Movement, so the statement
seems to imply a rejection of electoralism – but ends with the ambitious and somewhat politically ambiguous statement that 'the Republican Movement commits itself
to securing the political leadership of the whole people of Ireland ... we are determined to secure conditions in which all the people of the country will unite in a 32
county democratic socialist republic' (Irish Republican Army, 1981b: 13). How
they were to attempt this was ultimately shown to be through the twin tracks of political violence and electoral politics.

The Twin-track Approach: Early Days

The decision to engage more fully in electoral politics, alongside continuing political
violence, clearly represents a consequentialist calculation regarding the relationship
of means to ends and the efficacy of those means. The acceptability of the possibilities
of a parallel electoral strategy is shown in an interview with an IRA spokesman in the
5 September 1981 issue of *AP/RN*, and it is instructive to compare Mac Stiofáin's
statements from the previous year's *Hands Off Ireland!* (quoted above) with regard
to the issue of contesting elections. By September 1981, the position had evolved
somewhat, perhaps because the possibilities of real successes on the electoral front
had been seen. The IRA (1981a) said that 'there is room for republicans to
examine if the struggle for independence can be improved by an intervention in
the electoral process in order to show clearly that people support radical republicanism and resistance to the British presence more than they support any other collabora-
tionist tendency' (an apparent reference to the SDLP). In an analysis that contradicts
Mac Stiofáin's 1980 interview, the IRA spokesman said:

> Generally speaking, what was wrong with the 'Sticks' [Official Sinn Féin and
> the Official IRA] was not that they contested elections but that they had a totally
> incorrect analysis of the nature of British imperialism. They believed that the
> six-county state could be 'democratised' from within and that the so-called
> democratic process was one method by which this reformation could be
> made. There was also, at the time of the split, a simplistic republican attitude,
> heightened by the 1969 pogroms, to the Stickies' position. Therefore, there was
> a reaction within the Republican Movement against taking political control
> within the nationalist community or examining methods, even electoral, for
> doing this. (Irish Republican Army, 1981a)

The statement goes on to remind readers of past republican involvement in the electoral process, albeit with the caveat that 'the republican attitude towards elections
cannot be divorced from our total rejection of the six-county state, our struggle for
the last 12 years of unbroken resistance to the British government and its crown
forces, and our refusal to compromise with loyalism' (Irish Republican Army,

1981a). For those who might be concerned that the emerging electoral strategy 'is a new tendency or departure, they can be assured that the military struggle will go on with all the energy at our disposal, and, in fact, would actually be hastened with the development of a complementary radical political offensive' (Irish Republican Army, 1981a). Although the development of this radical political offensive should be a matter of debate within the Republican Movement, 'what should not be the basis for discussion is whether this intervention means a run-down of the armed struggle. It patently does not' (Irish Republican Army, 1981a). Moreover, the statement ends with: 'We must fight on many fronts and the armed struggle has been historically and contemporarily shown to be the most important. It must be coupled, of course, with political and economic resistance' (Irish Republican Army, 1981a).

It has become common in recent years to talk of the difficulty of the Republican Movement's leadership in bringing along with them, in the process of electoral politicisation and the wider peace process, those more grass-roots traditional or simply physical-force nationalists. From this statement, it looks as if the leadership's awareness of this difficulty stretches back further than many had thought.

The message is backed up by an article in *AP/RN* in July 1982 (Dowling, 1982: 6–7). In it, the writer says that 'the effective show of military might by the British in the South Atlantic should finally lay to rest any simplistic notions of the IRA physically driving the British out of the six counties ... the idea of getting rid of the British by purely military means is totally unrealistic' (Dowling, 1982: 6):

> No guerrilla war of national liberation anywhere has ever been, nor ever will be, won on the basis of military success alone. It is a question of favourably changing the balance of *political forces*, not just in Ireland, North and South, but also in Britain. The IRA can never hope to militarily defeat the British army. What it must eventually do is break the will of the British – their army, people and government – to remain in Ireland. A necessary part of this process will, of course, be *military successes*, but that is far from being sufficient. (Dowling, 1982: 6, emphasis in original)

By 28 April 1983, *AP/RN* was speaking of a 'struggle for national liberation [that] is dynamic and developing, finding new levels' and 'the nationalist revolution in the North [that] has seen the Republican Movement develop its political potential through Sinn Féin, just as on the military front the IRA gives the crown forces the only answer they are prepared to heed' (*AP/RN*, 28 April 1983, p. 1). Significantly, in the same issue Sinn Féin's publicity director, Danny Morrison, is quoted as saying the party should be prepared to enter into talks with the SDLP 'on a principled basis' and that 'there is nothing to be lost for us at least having been seen to have attempted to secure maximum nationalist successes' in the forthcoming Westminster elections (*AP/RN*, 28 April 1983, p. 3).

By the IRA's 1984 Easter statement, the refrain is familiar – 'armed struggle linked to political action will end the British connection' – but with a twist. The statement also welcomes Sinn Féin's 'continuing political successes ... in the electoral field' and says that 'the IRA's use of revolutionary force results from the inescapable fact that we are left with no peaceful or democratic alternative by which to achieve the national rights of our people ... It is a reluctant course of action for any oppressed people to take ...' (Irish Republican Army, 1984: 2). This, of course, seems to open the door to the idea that, if such peaceful and democratic alternatives *were* available, then the use of political violence would no longer be necessary and/or justifiable.

'A Scenario for Peace'

The usual justifications for IRA political violence and traditional nationalist analyses continued right up to the mid-1990s. However, in the late 1980s there were some significant developments. They were significant because they represented the beginning of a process whereby a movement that had traditionally seen the use of violence as the primary means of attaining its political objectives was ultimately persuaded that violence had outlived its usefulness in terms of achieving those desired goals.

One of these developments was the beginning of talks between Sinn Féin and the SDLP in 1988. Another was the publication of the Sinn Féin discussion paper *A Scenario for Peace* in 1987. Both of these seem to be linked to the internal debates on political alternatives that took place in the mid-1980s, exemplified by the speech Gerry Adams gave to what is described as an 'internal conference' in 1986. In an interesting extended metaphor, which is worth quoting in full, Adams compared the Republican Movement's political journey with a planned trip to a 'destination which we want to travel to'. He said:

> ... let us say for some unimaginable reason, somebody persuaded us that if a hundred of us were to get to Cork City by next week we could use our combined skills there to secure a much better way of life and that this was conditional only on a hundred of us getting there. Of course, there would be obstacles on our route which would have to be overcome, but these would be merely logistical difficulties which could be overcome by handpicking out contingent. Now, if a hundred of us were persuaded to set off for Cork merely because of rhetoric, we wouldn't have travelled very far outside this hall before doubts would set in. After walking for a while, some of us would be tired and drop out. They only went along for the crack. They hadn't really thought it out ... Somewhere else along the route somebody else might decide, for example, that Cashel is as nice a place as Cork and, anyway, they never really intended to go any further from the start. In the course of the journey, recriminations would start – it's better going this way or that – it's better doing it like this – so eventually if any of us ever got to Cork, our original one hundred would have diminished, and those remaining would be disunited and divided. However, if first of all we got agreement on going to Cork, an agreement on what that meant, we could more easily get agreement on how to get there. *We could deploy ourselves accordingly, developing a policy from this basis and planning our strategy and tactics to suit our*

resources and the prevailing conditions. We could agree to take a bus or a train or even to walk. *We could know that not everybody wanted to go the whole way, but if we planned accordingly on short-term objectives we could pick up new recruits on route.* We could even agree to go from bus stop to bus stop, from short-term objective to short-term objective, taking the maximum number with us each time. *The important thing, of course, is that those really committed to getting to Cork would be in charge and that they would proceed with the maximum support from the maximum number involved.* That way, we would arrive united and intact. (Adams, 1986, emphasis added)

The destination, Adams continued, was 'the reconquest of Ireland by the Irish people', meaning 'the expulsion of imperialism in all its forms, political, economic, military, social and cultural'. On the issue of the appropriate means to that end, he said: 'What will make a movement like ours revolutionary is not whether it is committed to any particular means of achieving revolution, for example, street agitation or physical force, but whether all the means it uses – political work, propaganda and mass education, armed struggle, projects of economic resistance – are conducive to achieving the revolutionary end' (Adams, 1986). This is a clear consequentialist statement that the means used must be assessed – and continually assessed – in the light of whether they are conducive to the attainment of the desired ends.

Sinn Féin credits *A Scenario for Peace* for directly leading to the 1988 talks with the SDLP. In the 1988 Sinn Féin document on those talks, the use of political violence is demoted from the level of necessary tactic to the level of 'a political option'. In another classically consequentialist consideration of the efficacy of means, the use of violence is described as being 'considered in terms of achieving national political aims and the efficacy of other forms of struggle' (Sinn Féin, 1988). The clear implication of this is that, if other forms of political struggle were seen to be effective, then political violence would be redundant as a tactic. However, at that stage, Sinn Féin still stated that it was opposed to a 'power-sharing Stormont assembly' and said that there 'cannot be a partitionist solution', rejecting what it termed the SDLP's 'gradualist solution' (Sinn Féin, 1988).

The traditional republican rhetoric and justification for violence remained apparent in the 1992 discussion document, *Towards a Lasting Peace in Ireland*. However, it contains interesting references to the tactic of political violence: it has historically been seen as 'a legitimate part of a people's resistance to foreign oppression', it is an 'option of last resort', 'there is no constitutional strategy to pursue national independence', and, 'in the circumstances, the onus is on those who condemn the option of armed struggle to advance a credible alternative' (Sinn Féin, 1992: 4).

Tactical Use of Armed Struggle?

In a document apparently circulated for discussion in the Republican Movement before the 1994 IRA cessation, a 'TUAS option' was referred to. Known as *The 'TUAS' Document*, it has been speculated that the acronym refers either to totally unarmed strategy or to tactical use of armed struggle. In it, the traditional aims are restated, including no internal settlement, but it also says that 'a straightforward logic' indicates that 'republicans at this time and on their own do not have the strength to achieve the end goal' (Republican Movement, 1994). The strategy is thus to build 'an Irish nationalist consensus with international support', involving the Irish government, the SDLP, the EU and the USA. The document concludes:

> Tuas has been part of every other struggle in the world this century. It is vital that activists realise the struggle is not over. Another front has opened up and we should have the confidence and put in the effort to succeed on that front. We have the ability to carry on indefinitely. (Republican Movement, 1994)

This statement clearly illustrates the movement's intention at least to explore alternative means towards the achievement of their stated goals; and the subsequent cease-fires and the on-again/off-again engagement in the decommissioning process indicate that the movement as a whole finally took the plunge to abandon the use of violence.

The Road to the Ending of the Armed Campaign

Statements throughout the 1990s and into the early years of the new century revisited much well-travelled ground about the IRA's commitment to the peace process, its historic and unprecedented initiatives, the British government's bad faith, crises in the peace process, the nature of the decommissioning process, the need to fulfil the potential of and commitments made in the Good Friday Agreement, and to remove the causes of conflict so as to allow both communities to pursue their political goals peacefully, alongside a smattering (and much less than even 10 years before) of the traditional republican historical and justificatory analysis.

During those years, however, there were some interesting elements to some of the statements. An example is contained in the private statement given to both governments on 13 April 2003. In it, the IRA said: 'We are resolved to see the *complete and final closure of this conflict* ... Furthermore, the full and irreversible implementation of the agreement and other commitments will provide a context in which the IRA can proceed to *definitively set aside arms to further our political objectives*' (Irish Republican Army, 2003, emphasis added). Here, the language use seems to indicate that the IRA has adopted the (non-violent) peace process as the necessary consequentialist means to its end, and to have abandoned the use of political violence as a means.

In a speech by Gerry Adams in October 2003, he referred to the previous 10 years as 'a political and emotional rollercoaster ride for republicans and unionists, nationalists and loyalists' (Adams, 2003). The speech is interesting for a number of reasons, not least the argument that political ideologies should be capable of evolution and not simply be set in stone. He said that the struggle – and he refers to the 1986 'journey analogy' discussed above – means that republicans should engage in 'the battle of ideas', take initiatives and put their case to their opponents. In a probable criticism of dissident republicans, he said: 'Being an Irish republican means more than paying lip-service to the 1916 Proclamation or to the ideal of the "The Republic". It means refusing to stand still. It means taking risks. It means reaching out to others. It means moving forward'. Later in the speech, he spoke of 'seeking to change minds and attitudes', 'trying to build new and better relationships between the people of this island, and between us and the people of Britain' (Adams, 2003).

Perhaps more importantly, he said that 'republicans have worked to have the Good Friday Agreement implemented, not only because that is our obligation, not only because that is the right thing, but because *it fits into a strategy to create an alternative to conflict. It is a peaceful means of bringing about change* and of sustaining and anchoring the peace process' (Adams, 2003, emphasis added). This is a classically consequentialist statement that newer and potentially more effective means are now available towards the achievement of the desired ends, and those means have the advantage of being peaceful.

So, in the balance of consequentialist calculation about the efficacy of means to ends, it seems obvious that the means that will cause less harm to (perhaps) achieve the given ends should be preferred to those that will cause greater harm in the pursuit of a similarly uncertain achievement of the given ends. In short, the Republican Movement seems to have worked out, decided or been persuaded that mainstream politics might be as efficacious – or more so, especially given the post-2001 'war on terror' – for the achievement of their goals as the use of political violence.

Be that as it may, Adams's position in 2003 was:

> ... to reiterate my total commitment to playing a leadership role to bring an end to conflict on our island, including physical force republicanism. Our strategy to do this is based on creating a purely peaceful and alternative way to achieve democratic and republican objectives ... The Good Friday Agreement, with its vision of a fair and just society operating exclusively democratically and peacefully, was democratically endorsed by the vast majority of the people of both states on the island of Ireland. Sinn Féin is committed to the full implementation of the agreement. The IRA leadership wants the full and irreversible implementation of the Good Friday Agreement in all its aspects and they are determined that their strategies and actions will be consistent with this objective. (Adams, 2003)

There was certainly significant evolution between this speech and the IRA's position in a statement on 30 April 1998 that the agreement was unsatisfactory as a basis for a lasting peace and that simultaneous North/South joint referendums would not represent a democratically valid exercise in national self-determination (Irish Republican Publicity Bureau, 1998).

The speech (Adams, 2003) contains more examples of interesting and largely (in the traditional republican lexicon) atypical phraseology: 'total and absolute commitment to exclusively democratic and peaceful means of resolving differences';

'opposed to any use or threat of force for any political purpose'; 'collectively building a new future based on justice and peace'; 'things have changed. Our success in bringing this about was not a matter of chance, it was a matter of choice'; 'totally committed to establishing an entirely new, democratic and harmonious future with our unionist neighbours'; 'like it or not, we're all in this together'. He concluded by saying that 'we can build a future of equals on this island', a peaceful future that 'empowers, and enriches and cherishes all the children of the nation equally' (Adams, 2003).

Consequentialism in Action

The overall tone of the justifications employed by the Republican Movement seem straightforwardly consequentialist, and to a large extent this is borne out by the fact that the IRA voluntarily adapted or abandoned their use of violence when faced with a changing political context that either allowed them to recognise that their chosen means would be ineffective in the pursuit of their desired ends or to realise that alternative peaceful political means were a realistic and preferable alternative. Of course, the nature of the desired end goals may also have radically changed, and this may have facilitated this recognition.

With regard to the Republican Movement, there have been clear adaptations of the means used to advance the desired goals – ceasefires, cessations of violent activity, engagement in electoral politics, negotiations and ultimate voluntary disbandment – and this seems to clearly indicate that there is a consequentialist calculation at work concerning the relationship between ends and means. At the very least, it seems to indicate that the ends are more important than the means. The reasons for such an adaptation may lie in the realisation that:

1. violence will not lead to the achievement of their desired real-world objectives, and/or
2. current political conditions render the continued use of violence less effective than non-violent political action, and/or
3. violence has got the group as far along the road towards their ultimate demands as is possible, and/or
4. the continued use of violence cannot be justified in conditions where non-violent political action seems capable of further advancing those demands.

If any of these reasons for an adaptation of means are verifiable, it would mean that there was a consequentialist calculation concerning the relationship between ends and means at work.

An analysis of the changing nature of the Republican Movement's justificatory literature bears out the conclusion it recognised that the initially chosen means were ultimately unable to achieve the consequences sought. This is clearly indicative of consequentialism in action. It involves the recognition that if the means are ineffective, the means should be discarded.

The Republican Movement accepted the possibilities of a parallel electoral strategy. Ultimately, this was to become, first, their dominant strategy, and then their only strategy. This was a process whereby a movement that had traditionally seen the use of violence as the primary means of attaining its political objectives ultimately realised (or was persuaded) that violence had outlived its usefulness in terms of achieving those desired goals. This is classically consequentialist: the means used must be assessed, and continually assessed, in the light of whether they are conducive to the attainment of the desired ends – if other forms of political activity are seen to be effective, then political violence would be redundant as a tactic.

There is an interesting element to the IRA abandonment of violence that relates to the importance of the secondary ideology. Apart from a 32-county socialist republic, which had not been mentioned as a policy item for at least 10 years, the point of Irish national liberation for the Republican Movement was the creation of an independent and *democratic* 32-county republic. The interesting element relates to the issue of majoritarianism and consent. If democracy is thought of by the Republican Movement primarily in purely majoritarian terms – that is, as not necessarily inclusive – then unionist consent would not be necessary, either in terms of them being a 'national minority' (as the traditional nationalist one-nation approach would have it) or in terms of them being ultimately outvoted in a demographic sectarian headcount.

There is, however, evidence from the (more recent) statements analysed that some level of unionist consent is seen as either pragmatically necessary for a 'just and lasting peace', or even democratically required. In the conclusion to 1997's *Peace in Ireland – Freedom, Justice, Democracy, Equality* (Sinn Féin's submission to strands one and two of the peace talks), it said: 'Being marginalised, abandoned and disempowered is wrong for nationalists. It would also be wrong for unionists' (Sinn Féin, 1997: 5). This has important implications for justifications of violence. If in either or both of these perceptions (pragmatic necessity or democratic legitimacy) violence comes to be seen as an ineffective and/or illegitimate means, and, in the latter case, comes to be seen as illegitimate insofar as it contradicts the desired consequence that is the basis of the justificatory argument in the first place, then a change in the conception of what the desired consequences are can result in a re-evaluation of the means. Perhaps this is what we have seen with regard to the Republican Movement.

References

Adams, G. (1986) *A Bus Ride to Independence and Socialism*, available at: http://cain.ulst.ac.uk/issues/politics/docs/sf/adams88 (accessed 21 September 2006).

Adams, G. (2003) Text of speech delivered on 21 October 2003 at the Balmoral Hotel, Belfast, available at: http://cain.ulst.ac.uk/issues/politics/docs/sf/ga211003.htm (accessed 12 September 2010).

Cronin, S. (1980) *Irish Nationalism: A History of Its Roots and Ideology* (Dublin: The Academy Press).

Dillon, M. (1990) *The Dirty War* (London: Arrow).

Dowling, P. (1982) Lessons of Malvinas, *An Phoblacht/Republican News*, 8 July, pp. 6–7.

Flynn, P. (1980) What is republicanism? *An Phoblacht/Republican News*, 11 October, pp. 6–7.

Irish Republican Army (1981a) Interview with spokesman, *An Phoblacht/Republican News*, 5 September.

Irish Republican Army (1981b) Annual Easter statement, *An Phoblacht/Republican News*, April, p. 25.

Irish Republican Army (1984) Annual Easter statement, *An Phoblacht/Republican News*, 26 April, p. 2.

Irish Republican Army (2003) (Private) statement on recent developments, 13 April, available at: http://cain.ulst.ac.uk/othelem/organ/ira/ira130403a.htm (accessed 12 September 2010).

Irish Republican Publicity Bureau (1998) IRA statement on decommissioning, 30 April, available at: http://cain.ulst.ac.uk/events/peace/docs/ira30498.htm (accessed 12 September 2010).

Irish Republican Publicity Bureau (2005) IRA statement on the ending of the armed campaign, 28 July, available at: http://cain.ulst.ac.uk/othelem/organ/ira/ira280705.htm (accessed 12 September 2010).

Irish Republican Publicity Bureau (2010) Adams – dialogue with armed groups, available at: www.sinnfein.ie/contents/19031 (accessed 12 September 2010).

Mac Stiofáin, S. (1980) Interview with Sean Mac Stiofáin, *Hands Off Ireland!* (Revolutionary Communist Group's publication), 10 April, pp. 10–15.

O'Boyle, G. (2002) Theories of justification and political violence: examples from four groups, *Terrorism and Political Violence*, 14(2), pp. 23–46.

Rawls, J. (1972) *A Theory of Justice* (Oxford: Oxford University Press).

Republican Movement (1994) *The 'TUAS' Document*, available at: http://cain.ulst.ac.uk/othelem/organ/ira/tuas94.htm (accessed 12 September 2010).

Sinn Féin (1987) *A Scenario for Peace*, available at: www.sinnfein.ie/files/AScenarioforPeace.pdf (accessed 12 September 2010).

Sinn Féin (1988) *The Sinn Fein/SDLP Talks*, available at: www.sinnfein.ie/files/SF_SDLP_talks.pdf (accessed 12 September 2010).

Sinn Féin (1992) *Towards a Lasting Peace in Ireland*, available at: www.sinnfein.ie/files/TowardsLastingPeace.pdf (accessed 12 September 2010).

Sinn Féin (1997) *Peace in Ireland – Freedom, Justice, Democracy, Equality*, available at: www.sinnfein.ie/files/MultiParty_7.pdf (accessed 12 September 2010).

Index

Page numbers in *Italics* represent tables.
Page numbers in **Bold** represent figures.
Page numbers followed by n represent endnotes.

Related titles from Routledge

Defending Democracy and Securing Diversity

Edited by Christian Leuprecht

The chapters in this volume strive to enlighten the debate on democracy by laying out the concepts, clarifying theoretical issues, and providing empirical evidence. The case studies draw on Canada, Guyana, the Netherlands, South Africa, and the United Kingdom. They examine ethno-cultural, gender, and sexual-minority diversity in a variety of missions, including Bosnia-Herzegovina and Afghanistan. Although scholarly in nature, the book is readily accessible to professionals and practitioners alike.

This book was published as a special issue of *Commonwealth and Comparative Politics*.

Christian Leuprecht is associate professor of political science at the Royal Military College of Canada and cross-appointed to the School of Policy Studies and Department of Political Studies at Queen's University.

July 2010: 216 x 138mm, 256pp
Hb: 978-0-415-57649-9
£85 / $133

Available from all good bookshops

Related titles from Routledge

Democracy, Equality, and Justice

Edited by Matt Matravers and Lukas H. Meyer

In addressing democracy, equality, and justice together, the book stimulates discussions that go beyond the sometimes increasingly technical and increasingly discrete literatures that now dominate the study of each concept. The chapters fall into four categories: on justice and democracy; justice and equality; justice and community; and justice and the future. Concerns of justice unite all the chapters in this volume. However, these concerns now manifest themselves in interesting and new directions. Politically, the book confronts urgent problems of democracy, equality, community, and of how to respond to potentially catastrophic climate change.

This book was previously published as a special issue of the *Critical Review of Social and Political Philosophy*.

Matt Matravers is Professor of Political Philosophy at the University of York.

Lukas H. Meyer is Professor of Practical Philosophy, University of Berne.

December 2010: 234 x 156: 272pp
Hb: 978-0-415-59292-5
£90 / $133

For Product Safety Concerns and Information please contact our EU
representative GPSR@taylorandfrancis.com
Taylor & Francis Verlag GmbH, Kaufingerstraße 24, 80331 München, Germany